KU-737-735

CONTENTS

INTRODUCTION

This book and its supporting resources have been produced to build on prior knowledge from Level 1 and to guide apprentices and students through their academic studies, while working towards completion of the Level 2 Diploma in Bench Joinery.

Each of the seven chapters is specifically designed to focus entirely on the units contained within the Occupational Standards set by the Awarding Body (City and Guilds), but is not exclusive to people studying in this area. Hundreds of fully coloured illustrations, current regulations and good working practices are demonstrated throughout this book, with editorial input from a senior examiner to ensure factual accuracy and theoretical rigour.

Frequently asked questions occur in appropriate places throughout each chapter to clarify terminology and expand on specific detail in direct and clear language that readers can understand. At the end of each topic, activities are used to re-enforce students' understanding and also as a source of revision before completion of the unit. Multiple-choice questions at the end of each chapter will also enhance students' prior understanding in preparation for their final assessment of the core and occupational units. Trade secrets are introduced to this book to develop students' knowledge from the perspective of experienced craftsmen working in the industry. Information contained within these segments will also help to bridge the transition between the knowledge and simulated assessments completed at their training organisation, through to employment within the construction industry.

A supporting website for this book – www.hodderplus.co.uk/carpentry – contains sample video footage of technical skills and electronic versions of the multiple-choice questions.

Website username: carpentry2
Website password: construction

Swindon College

Learning Resource Centre
Tel: 01793 498381

Swindon College

54050000339705

Please return this book on or before the last date stamped below:

NOT TO BE
TAKEN AWAY

SWINDON COLLEGE

LEARNING RESOURCE CENTRE

SERIES EDITOR: MARTIN BURDFIELD

HODDER
EDUCATION
PART OF HACHETTE UK

SWINDON COLLEGE

2nd February 2010

LEARNING RESOURCE CENTRE

54050000339705

Orders: please contact Bookpoint Ltd, 130 Milton Park, Abingdon, Oxon OX14 4SB. Telephone: +44 (0)1235 827720. Fax: +44 (0)1235 400454. Lines are open from 9.00am to 5.00pm, Monday to Saturday, with a 24-hour message-answering service. You can also order through our website www.hoddereducation.co.uk

If you have any comments to make about this, or any of our other titles, please send them to educationenquiries@hodder.co.uk

British Library Cataloguing in Publication Data
A catalogue record for this title is available from the British Library

ISBN: 978 0 340 98333 1

First Edition Published 2009
Impression number   10 9 8 7 6 5 4 3 2 1
Year   2012, 2011, 2010, 2009

Copyright © 2009 Stephen Jones

All rights reserved. No part of this publication may be reproduced or transmitted in any form or by any means, electronic or mechanical, including photocopy, recording, or any information storage and retrieval system, without permission in writing from the publisher or under licence from the Copyright Licensing Agency Limited. Further details of such licences (for reprographic reproduction) may be obtained from the Copyright Licensing Agency Limited, of Saffron House, 6–10 Kirby Street, London EC1N 8TS.

Hachette UK's policy is to use papers that are natural, renewable and recyclable products and made from wood grown in sustainable forests. The logging and manufacturing processes are expected to conform to the environmental regulations of the country of origin.

Cover photo © Jean Miele / CORBIS
Typeset by Pantek Arts Ltd
Printed in Italy for Hodder Education, an Hachette UK Company, 338 Euston Road, London NW1 3BH

ACKNOWLEDGEMENTS

I would like to thank Stephen Halder and the team at Hodder Education for the opportunity to write this book, and for their continued support. Thank you to Martin Burdfield for his expertise and guidance while devoting his time to work with me on this project.

Most of all, special thanks and love to my wife Rebecca for believing in me, and my beautiful family: Daniel, Rachel and Jessica for sparing me the time to complete this book.

The authors and publishers would like to thank the following for use of photographs in this volume:

Figure 1.1 Reproduced under the terms of the Click-Use Licence; Figure 1.3 © RichVintage/istockphoto.com; Figure 1.11 with kind permission of CSCS Ltd; Figure 1.12 © Paul Gibbings – fotolia.com; Figure 1.19 © Stas Perov/istockphoto.com; Figure 1.27 © Dan Wilton/istockphoto.com; Figure 1.31 © Andrew Howe/Getty Images; Figure 1.32 © Image Source/Construction Photography; Figure 1.34 © Rob Fox/istockphoto.com; Figure 2.7 © -Vladamir-/istockphoto.com; Figure 2.8 © Branko Miokovic/istockphoto.com; Figure 2.20 © George Peters/istockphoto.com; Figure 2.21 © Nicholas Bailey/Rex Features; Figure 2.22 © Roger Milley/istockphoto.com; Figure 2.30 © Ryan McVay/Getty Images; Figure 5.6 © Selahattin BAYRAM/iStockphoto.com; Figure 5.7 © David Freund/istockphoto.com; Figure 5.8 © istockphoto.com; Figure 5.9 © istockphoto.com; Figure 5.10 © Brian Adducci/istockphoto.com; Figure 5.12 © Nicholas Belton/istockphoto.com; Figure 5.13 © Leszek Maziarz/iStockphoto.com; Figure 5.14 © Dave White/iStockphoto.com; Figure 5.15 © Nicholas Belton/iStockphoto.com; Figure 5.16 © Arnold Laver Timberworld; Figure 5.17 © Nancy Nehring/iStockphoto.com; Figure 5.18 © Nancy Nehring/iStockphoto.com; Figure 5.19 © Arnold Laver Timberworld; Figure 5.20 © iStockphoto.com; Figure 5.21 © Selahattin BAYRAM/iStockphoto.com; Figure 5.22 © Alessandro Oliva/iStockphoto.com; Figure 5.23 © Pawel Klisiewicz/iStockphoto.com; Figure 5.24 © Gillian Mowbray/iStockphoto.com; Figure 5.25 © BRANDT Kantentechnik GmbH; Figre 5.30 © damn designs - Fotolia.com; Figure 5.32 © Ales Veluscek/iStockphoto.com; Figure 5.33 © Emrah Turudu/istockphoto.com; Figure 5.34 © Bill Noll/istockphoto.com; Figure 5.35 © jack thomas/Alamy; Figure 5.48 © Mandy Hartfree-Bright/iStockphoto.com; Figure 5.51 © svlumagraphica - Fotolia.com; Figure 5.53 © mipan – Fotolia.com; Figure 5.54 © keith morris/Alamy; Figure 5.55 © Chris Pollack/iStockphoto.com; Figure 5.57 © Rotring; Figure 6.3 © Power Adhesives Ltd; Figure 6.67 © Steven Miric/istockphoto.com; Figure 6.77 © thumb/istockphoto.com; Figure 6.84 © M. Eric Honeycutt/istockphoto.com; Figure 7.38 © Construction Photography/Corbis; Figure 7.39 © NICHOLAS BAILEY/Rex Features; Figure 7.52 Jon Woodfine; Figure 7.57 © Ryan McVay/Getty Images; Figure 7.67 © marc fischer/istockphoto.com; Figure 7.68 © digitalskillet/istockphoto.com; Figure 7.70 © Jim Jurica/istockphoto.com

All illustrations in this volume by Oxford Designers & Illustrators

Every effort has been made to trace and acknowledge ownership of copyright. The publishers will be glad to make suitable arrangements with any copyright holders whom it has not been possible to contact.

SAFE WORKING PRACTICES

LEARNING OUTCOMES

By the end of this chapter you should have developed a knowledge and understanding of:

- health and safety regulations;
- accident, first aid, emergency procedures and reporting;
- identifying hazards on construction sites;
- health and hygiene;
- safe handling of materials and equipment;
- basic working platforms;
- working with electricity;
- using appropriate personal protective equipment (PPE);
- fire and emergency procedures.

INTRODUCTION

The aim of this chapter is for learners to be able to recognise situations that may put themselves and others at risk through work activities. It also highlights the duty holders' responsibilities to conform to current health, safety and welfare law in the United Kingdom. In addition, this chapter explains the relevant health and safety legislation and good working codes of practice recommended by the Health and Safety Executive (HSE).

HEALTH AND SAFETY LEGISLATION

Pre-1974, the construction industry suffered an exceptionally high number of accidents and deaths occurring in the workplace. During that period there were various legislations loosely controlling activities in places of work. Following the Robens Report the government passed a primary piece of law known as the Health and Safety at Work Act (HASAWA) 1974. The Act is an umbrella piece of legislation that facilitates a number of other laws and regulations underneath it. Its aim is to promote and encourage high standards of health and safety in all places of work. When the HASAWA was introduced it superimposed many older laws and legislations with others being phased out or replaced with new regulations and supporting 'codes of practice'.

The text below gives an overview of the Health and Safety at Work Act and some of the regulations under its enabling umbrella.

HEALTH AND SAFETY AT WORK ACT 1974 (HASAWA)

GENERAL DUTIES OF EMPLOYERS TO THEIR EMPLOYEES:

1. to ensure the health, safety and welfare at work of all his/her employees;
2. to provide and maintain equipment and systems of work that are safe and without risks to health;
3. to make arrangements for ensuring safety and absence of risks to health in connection with the use, handling, storage and transport of articles and substances;
4. to provide information, instruction, training and supervision as is necessary to ensure the health and safety at work of their employees;
5. to provide safe access and exit for employees to their place of work;
6. to provide a safe working environment with adequate welfare facilities;
7. to prepare and revise a written statement of his/her health and safety policy.

GENERAL DUTIES OF EMPLOYEES AT WORK

It shall be the duty of every employee while at work:

1. to take reasonable care for the health and safety of themselves and of other persons who may be affected by his/her acts at work;
2. to comply with their employer or any other person under any of the relevant statutory legislations, to cooperate with them so far as is necessary to enable that duty or requirement to be performed or complied with;
3. not to interfere with or misuse things provided for health, safety or welfare.

GENERAL DUTIES OF MANUFACTURERS, DESIGNERS AND SUPPLIERS:

1. to ensure that the article/substance provided will be safe without risks to health and safety at all times when it is being used, handled, processed, stored and transported;
2. to provide information about the use for which the article/substance is designed, tested, dismantled or disposed of, to ensure health and safety;
3. to make sure that the article/substance is designed and constructed so that it will be safe without risks to health and safety.

HEALTH AND SAFETY EXECUTIVE (HSE)

The Health and Safety Executive was appointed as part of the Health and Safety at Work Act 1974. Its role is to control the risks and exposure to hazards in the workplace by providing health and safety legislation, information and enforcement of the law.

Health and safety inspectors may visit workplaces to investigate reported occurrences, either from the local authority or directly for the HSE. Health and safety inspectors have many powers, including the following:

- they may enter any premises at any reasonable time;
- if necessary, use the police to prevent an obstruction of their duties;
- examine and investigate;
- take photographs, measurements, samples and recordings;
- destroy or dismantle dangerous items of equipment or machinery;
- seize equipment and render it harmless if it poses an imminent danger to health and safety;
- retain documentation to carry out their investigations;
- take possession of materials;
- take written statements and declarations from employers and employees;
- issue improvement or prohibition notices.

FREQUENTLY ASKED QUESTIONS

▶ What are prohibition and improvement notices?

A 'prohibition notice' is a ban imposed by the health and safety inspector. A prohibition notice may be issued on a particular item of equipment if it is considered to pose a risk of serious personal injury. The equipment will not be permitted to be used until the fault has been rectified.

An 'improvement notice' requires the duty holder to put right an item of equipment or method of work within a specified period of time.

Failure to comply with the Health and Safety Executive and the law may initiate the prosecution of the duty holder. In a court of law, those found to be guilty of compromising the health and safety of others may have heavy fines imposed upon them, a jail sentence or even both.

REPORTING INJURIES, DISEASES AND DANGEROUS OCCURRENCE REGULATIONS 1995 (RIDDOR)

It is a legal requirement to report injuries, diseases and dangerous occurrences in the workplace to the Health and Safety Executive. This allows them to investigate the report, advise the employer and reduce the likelihood of it happening again. The HSE will need to be informed immediately of the following events, known as 'reportable incidents':

- dangerous occurrences or near misses;
- injuries resulting in employees being absent from work for three days or more;
- injuries to members of the general public;
- major injuries;
- work-related deaths;
- work-related diseases.

FREQUENTLY ASKED QUESTIONS

▶ **How can you inform the Health and Safety Executive of an incident at work?**

There are several methods that can be used to contact the HSE. The quickest methods are as follows.

1. Complete and submit an 'F2508 incident report form' online. A copy of the report will be sent from the HSE for your records, to comply with RIDDOR requirements.

2. Telephone the incident contact centre (ICC). The operator will ask you questions in order to complete the report form before sending a copy for your records.

Alternatively, the HSE can be informed via email or post. In the event of a fatality or serious injury out of working hours, the duty officer will need to be informed.

The Reporting Injuries, Diseases and Dangerous Occurrence Regulations apply to all work activities, but not all incidents are reportable. Employers and people in control of premises have a duty under the regulations to report incidents to the HSE as soon as possible after the event (certain incidents up to ten days). Employees also have a responsibility to inform their employers if they have witnessed a dangerous occurrence, had an accident at work or been certified by a doctor as having a reportable work-related disease. This will then allow the employer to complete a report and pass the information provided to the Health and Safety Executive. Duty holders have a responsibility to keep records of any reportable incidents at work for a minimum of three years after the event.

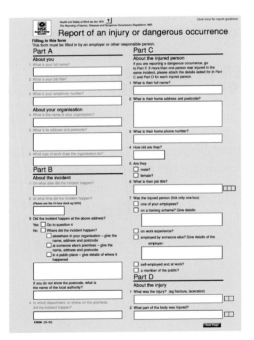
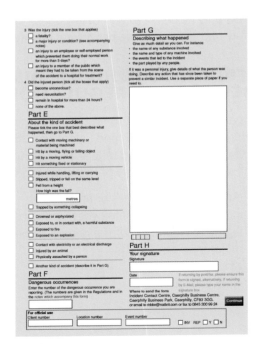

FIGURE 1.1 HSE Report of an injury or dangerous occurence form

CONSTRUCTION (DESIGN AND MANAGEMENT) REGULATIONS 2007 (CDM)

The new CDM Regulations have been revised in recent years and therefore supersede the CDM Regulations 1994 and the Construction (Health, Safety and Welfare) Regulations 1996, to combine the two laws into one single regulation. The aim of the CDM Regulations is to:

- reduce accidents and raise awareness of health and safety in the industry;
- coordinate the correct people at the correct time to manage health and safety on site;
- centre on effective planning and managing health and safety risks in the industry.

The CDM Regulations place legal responsibilities on almost everybody involved in the construction process, including:

- CDM coordinators – the client is responsible for appointing a competent person to manage the process of health and safety on sites that last for more than 500 person days or lasting more than 30 days; this person is known as the 'Construction (Design and Management) Coordinator';
- clients – the source of funding for a concept and project;
- subcontractors – are usually employed by the principal contractor to complete portions of the contract;
- designers – this is a broad term used for architects, engineers and quantity surveyors, or anybody else involved in the preparation of drawings, schedules and specifications, etc.;
- principal contractors – the main contractor appointed by the client to complete a project;
- workers – this term is used for anyone that is involved in the maintenance, alteration, construction or demolition of a building or structure.

The CDM Regulations 2007 are divided into five parts:

- Part 1 deals with the application of the Regulations and definitions;
- Part 2 covers general duties that apply to *all* construction projects;
- Part 3 contains additional duties that apply *only* to notifiable construction projects, i.e. those lasting more than 30 days or involving more than 500 person days of construction work;
- Part 4 contains practical requirements that apply to *all* construction sites;
- Part 5 contains the transitional arrangements and revocations.

PROVISION AND USE OF WORK EQUIPMENT REGULATIONS 1998 (PUWER)

In general, these regulations require any equipment and machinery provided at work to be safe for its intended use. Employers also have duties to ensure that adequate training, instruction, and supervision in the use and maintenance of the equipment is given to employees. The Provision and Use of Work Equipment Regulations is covered in further detail in Chapter 4, Circular Saws.

ACTIVITIES

Activity 1 – Health and safety regulations

Read through the following questions and answer them as fully as you can to help you develop your underpinning knowledge of this subject area.

1. What do the initials HASAWA stand for?
2. What organisation enforces health and safety legislation in the construction industry?
3. List three powers of the Health and Safety Executive.
4. List three reportable incidents under the RIDDOR.
5. List the key responsibilities of employers under the Construction (Design and Management) Regulations (CDM).

MANUAL HANDLING OPERATIONS REGULATIONS 2002 (MHO)

Manual handling injuries occurring in the workplace account for an alarming proportion of reportable occurrences. The Health and Safety Executive (HSE) has reported that, between 2007 and 2008, 29 per cent of reported injuries were caused by handling, moving or lifting objects.

The majority of handling accidents and injuries are caused as a result of the following:

- people using awkward postures to move or lift items;
- heavy manual labour;
- manually handling materials.

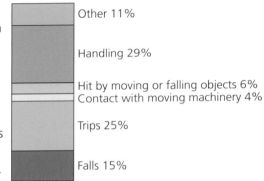

FIGURE 1.2 Injuries reported to the HSE during 2001/2 resulting in a minimum of three days' absence from work

The Manual Handling Operations Regulations 2002 place the following duties on employers and employees.

EMPLOYERS' DUTIES:

1. if possible avoid their employees having to undertake any manual handling operations which pose a potential risk to their health and safety;
2. carry out assessments to record significant risks;
3. as much as reasonably possible, take steps to remove or reduce the risk of injury;

FIGURE 1.3

4. provide employees with adequate information to carry out manual handling operations. Employees are normally informed of the risks posed through manually moving or lifting objects in a 'risk assessment'.

The assessment should be reviewed if there is reason to suspect that it is no longer valid or there have been significant changes in the MHO.

FREQUENTLY ASKED QUESTIONS

▶ **What is a 'method statement'?**

A 'method statement' is a written document, normally completed by a competent person appointed by an employer. They are used to detail safe methods of work to reduce or eliminate the risks highlighted in risk assessments.

EMPLOYEES' DUTIES:

1. employees are responsible for complying with the safe systems of work enforced by their employer;
2. use the equipment provided by the employer;
3. report hazards encountered;
4. make sure that their activities do not endanger others.

RISK ASSESSMENTS

SAFETY METHOD STATEMENT	
Description of work	Re-manufacture of MDF panel products
Risks	• Irritation to the skin, eyes, nose ot throat • Possible explosion
Company training and safety method statements to be observed	• Housekeeping • Manual handling • Using power tools • Using wood-working machines
Requirements to be observed	• Always wear gloves when handling MDF • Eye protection and dust masks should be worn • Wash and brush down at the end of your shift and before eating drinking or going to the toilet, to ensure all dust has been removed • Use barrier cream • Do not smoke
First aid procedures	• In the event of skin irritation or discomfort, please seek treatment from your first aider or consult a doctor

FIGURE 1.4 Sample method statement

Manual handling of items should always be a last resort, after every other possible method has been discounted. While carrying out a manual handling 'risk assessment' you should consider the following questions.

1. Will the operation involve twisting repetitively?
2. Can you avoid having to move the object?
3. Could a 'lifting aid' be used?
4. Will the lifting operation require more than one person?
5. Is the load harmful, bulky, heavy, stable, etc.?
6. Can the load be divided into smaller parts to reduce the weight?
7. Are there risks imposed by the environment, e.g. weather conditions, lighting, floor surface (uneven, slippery, etc.)?
8. What personal protective equipment (PPE) will be required to undertake the task safely?
9. How far will employees be expected to carry the load?
10. How long will employees be expected to repeat the manual handling operation?

MANUAL HANDLING OPERATIONS

The Health and Safety Executive (HSE) has recommended maximum lifting weights for manual handling stable objects with both hands.

RDJ contractors

RISK ASSESSMENT

Activity: __manually handling plasterboard__

Participants: __site operatives__

Does the activity involve any potential risk?

Yes / ~~No~~ (delete as appropriate)

Please indicate the level of risk?

~~Low~~ / Medium / ~~High~~ (delete as appropriate)

Please provide details of action taken to protect against potential risks:

1 __Wear safety boots__

2 __Wear gloves__

3 __Use panel carrier (lifting aid)__

4 __No more than two sheets to be carried at one time – between two operatives__

5 __Ensure correct lifting techniques are used__

Signature of risk assessor: __D Smith__

Date of assessment: __8 January 2009__

Action to be taken by: __21 March 2009__

Date of reassessment: __3 April 2009__

FIGURE 1.5 Sample risk assessment

Stage 1 – think before lifting

Stage 2 – adapt a strong, stable position

Stage 3 – place feet slightly apart, straight back, squat over the object with knees slightly bent and feet slightly apart

Stage 4 – keep the load close to the waist

Stage 5 – avoid twisting or leaning sideways

Stage 6 – look ahead

Stage 7 – move object and place down, adjust to the desired position

FIGURE 1.6 Correct lifting technique

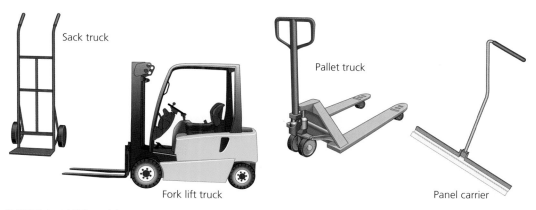

FIGURE 1.7 Lifting aids

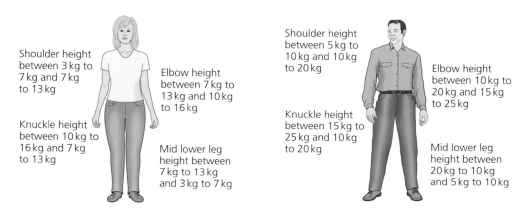

FIGURE 1.8 Recommended maximum lifting weights for a female

FIGURE 1.9 Recommended maximum lifting weights for a male

A SUMMARY OF EMPLOYERS' AND EMPLOYEES' DUTIES

It would be impractical to expect employees to be able to remember all the current health and safety workplace law in the UK, but they should have at least a good general understanding of their responsibilities. Employers also have legal obligations to protect every employee's health, safety and welfare while they are at work. In general employers *must* inform and protect employees at work, while employees have a legal duty to report issues of health and safety to their employer or safety representative.

The following lists give a brief overview of the current responsibilities employers and employees have to comply with workplace legislation.

EMPLOYERS' RESPONSIBILITIES TO INFORM EMPLOYEES OR SAFETY REPRESENTATIVES OF THE FOLLOWING:

1. arrangements to appoint competent people to satisfy health and safety law;
2. changes to health and safety at work;
3. provide information about health and safety planning;
4. provide information on the risks and dangers at work, and the measures in place to reduce or eliminate them.

EMPLOYERS' DUTIES/OBLIGATIONS:

1. appoint a suitably qualified person to deal with matters of health and safety;
2. carry out risk assessments, record significant findings, and arrange health and safety measures;
3. draw up a 'health and safety policy' to bring issues of health and safety to the attention of employees for companies with five or more personnel;
4. eliminate or control the use of substances hazardous to health;
5. ensure machinery, plant and equipment is safe to use;
6. ensure materials and substances are transported, stored and used properly;
7. ensure safe methods/systems of work;
8. ensure suitable safety measures are in place to protect against electrical equipment, flammable and explosive substances, noise and radiation;
9. ensure that the health, safety and welfare arrangements are satisfied in the workplace;
10. inform the Health and Safety Executive of all reportable accidents, diseases and dangerous occurrences;
11. make sure that the equipment provided for work activities is suitable for its intended use, correctly used, and regularly serviced and maintained;
12. provide adequate emergency procedures;
13. provide adequate information, training, instruction and suitable supervision in matters of health and safety;
14. provide adequate lifting aids to avoid unsafe manual handling;
15. provide and maintain adequate safety signs and notices;
16. provide first aid facilities;
17. provide personal protective equipment and clothing free of charge to employees;
18. provide welfare facilities for employees, e.g. toilets, drying rooms, washing facilities;
19. provide a safe working environment without risks.

EMPLOYEES' DUTIES/OBLIGATIONS:

1. act responsibly and take care for their own health and safety in the workplace;
2. cooperate with supervisors, managers and employers in matters of health and safety;
3. not to interfere, damage or misuse any items provided for their health, safety and welfare;
4. take reasonable measures to ensure the health and safety of others affected by their activities;
5. use items of work equipment, plant and PPE in accordance with information, training and instruction.

ACTIVITIES

Activity 2 – Safe handling of materials and equipment

Read through the following questions and answer them as fully as you can to help you develop your underpinning knowledge of this subject area.

1. What is the maximum weight a male and female can lift manually?
2. List the duties of employees under the Manual Handling Operations Regulations 2002.
3. Explain the safe process of manually lifting an object from the floor.
4. List four lifting aids.
5. What are the main causes of manual handling accidents and injuries?

SOURCES OF HEALTH AND SAFETY INFORMATION

CONSTRUCTIONSKILLS

ConstructionSkills was formally known as the Construction Industry Training Board (CITB). It is an employer-led organisation that works with partners in the government responsible for improving the skills and productivity in the sector. In recent years ConstructionSkills has reported a shortage of skilled operatives in the industry and a shortfall of new recruits for degree-level management courses. ConstructionSkills covers all areas of the construction industry from 'professionals', such as architects, to 'craft' workers, such as carpenters and joiners. Its aim is to attract people into the industry to fill significant skill gaps, provide training and help them to achieve their qualifications.

FREQUENTLY ASKED QUESTIONS

▶ What does the term 'professional' mean?

Although, technically, any person that is paid for their services would be considered to be a professional, in the construction industry 'professionals' are people that have completed a university-level degree – for example, architects, structural engineers, civil engineers.

ConstructionSkills supports work-based learning construction apprenticeship frameworks, generally referred to as 'apprenticeships'. All trainees wishing to complete an apprenticeship must have a 'training provider' to support them through their programme. Some training establishments or colleges may provide their own 'work-based learning training provider' to fund trainees through their apprenticeships.

Qualifying construction companies are liable to pay the Sector Skills Council annually sums of money that reflect their turnover and the size of their firm; this is known as a 'levy'. The levy contributes to the funding needed to support apprentices while they are training. Companies that employ apprentices are entitled to several 'grants' in return for the experience and on-site training they provide to trainees.

APPRENTICESHIPS

An apprenticeship qualification is made up of a framework of different components to provide the apprentice with a rounded period of training to prepare them to meet the needs of the industry.

National Vocational Qualification
(NVQ 1 & 2)

On-site training and assessment

Technical Certificate
(Construction Awards/Diplomas)

Simulated training/college based

Modern
Apprenticeship
Framework

Level 1 Key Skills
(Application of number
and Communication)

Employment Responsibilities
and Rights (ERR)

FIGURE 1.10 National Vocational Qualification flowchart

? FREQUENTLY ASKED QUESTIONS

▶ What is ERR?

The Secretary of State requires all apprenticeship frameworks to include 'Employment Responsibilities and Rights'. ERR is a compulsory short course of training that covers nine target areas:

1. employer and employee statutory rights under employment law and other legislation;
2. procedures and documentation;
3. sources of information on employment rights and responsibilities;
4. occupational roles within the industry;
5. occupational and career pathways;
6. roles and responsibilities of representative bodies;
7. sources of information and advice on the industry, occupation, training and career;
8. codes of practice and National Occupational Standards;
9. recognising and forming views of public concern that affect the industry.

CONSTRUCTIONSKILLS CERTIFICATION SCHEME (CSCS)

The ConstructionSkills Certification Scheme was introduced to the construction industry to improve health and safety awareness and standards on site, improve quality and help drive 'cowboys' out. Most construction site managers, employers and clients demand to see evidence that personnel have proven their understanding of and competence in basic health and safety in the industry before being allowed on a site. Enforcement of a card scheme helps employers to comply with current health and safety legislation.

Compliant employers require all persons entering or working on their building sites to have undertaken a theoretical CSCS health and safety test, and produce a certified card as evidence that they have successfully met the minimum requirement. The tests have to be booked through the CSCS card scheme and sat at a local testing centre. The test must be completed within 45 minutes and consists of 40 multiple-choice questions covering a range of various aspects of health and safety in the industry. Candidates must answer a minimum of 34 questions correctly to complete the test successfully, although no feedback is given other than 'pass' or 'fail'.

If candidates are unsuccessful in reaching the required standard, they are able to retake the test on another occasion. The test is selected at random from a bank of questions available from ConstructionSkills; these can be purchased either as a book or on CD-ROM.

TYPES OF CSCS SKILL CARD

There are various types of CSCS card available; each one is awarded to suit each individual and their level of qualifications in the industry:

- Red card – Trainee;
- Green card – Construction site operatives;
- Blue card – Experienced worker/craft;
- Gold card – Advanced craft/supervisory;
- Platinum card – Management;
- Black card – Senior management;
- White/yellow card – Professionally qualified person;
- Yellow card – Visitor with no construction skills;
- White card – Construction-related occupation.

FIGURE 1.11 CSCS Skill cards

THE ROYAL SOCIETY FOR THE PREVENTION OF ACCIDENTS (ROSPA)

The RoSPA is a charity organisation that has been established for over 90 years. Its purpose is to provide sources of information and guidance to help reduce all types of domestic and industrial accidents, and help save lives. The RoSPA has reported the following astonishing statistics, occurring every year in the United Kingdom:

- approximately 350 fatalities to workers and members of the public due to reportable accidents at *work*;
- approximately 1000 deaths in *work*-related road crashes;
- approximately 12,000 early deaths due to past exposure to hazardous agents – for example, asbestos;
- over 36 million working days lost due to *work*-related accidents and ill health.

The RoSPA provides various sources of practical and technical information, guidance and support including:

- advice;
- conferences and events;
- links to further guidance and support;
- press releases;
- resources;
- safety groups;
- training courses;
- videos.

HEALTH AND SAFETY EXECUTIVE (HSE) AND HEALTH AND SAFETY COMMISSION (HSC)

As mentioned previously, part of the HSE and HSC role is to provide information and guidance to allow the duty holders, including employers, to comply with the law. The HSE produces many documents known as 'codes of safe practice'; these give practical advice to follow to comply with current legislation. Further guidance is published on 'information sheets'. These sheets provide specific requirements and details for the safe use of equipment and machinery, and can easily be obtained via the internet.

TOOLBOX TALKS

Developments and changes made on building sites require health and safety arrangements to be reviewed periodically. Consideration of the relevance of previous safety measures in the workplace, and new dangerous situations and risks arising as building work develops, should be highlighted to site personnel. This information is normally communicated to the workers through short verbal discussions known as 'toolbox talks'. Toolbox talks are commonly conducted by the site manager or safety officer during lunch breaks, or as personnel first enter the site at the beginning of the day.

ACCIDENT, FIRST AID, EMERGENCY PROCEDURES AND REPORTING

THE ACCIDENT BOOK (BI 510)

The accident book is a document used to record serious and minor injuries at work. Under the Reporting of Injuries, Diseases and Dangerous Occurrence Regulations (RIDDOR), any notifiable injuries should be reported to the HSE as soon as possible after the event. The accident book is used to meet the requirements of the management of health and safety law by recording the details shown in Figure 1.13.

? FREQUENTLY ASKED QUESTIONS

▶ Who should complete the accident book?

An accident should be recorded as soon as practically possible after the event by the injured person. If that is not possible, then a witness or someone present at the time should complete the details.

Changes in legislation have prevented the information contained in the accident book from being disclosed to third parties without the injured person's consent. This prevents older accident books being used after December 2003. Details of accidents should be stored securely and separately from the accident book to prevent an infringement of personal information under the Data Protection Act (DPA) and confidentiality law.

If an accident has occurred at work, the area should be made safe to prevent further injuries, or fenced off in the event of a serious injury to allow an investigation to take place.

Employers and senior managers should review accident books regularly to investigate all recorded incidents, regardless of whether they were reportable under RIDDOR. This will allow improvements to be made in health and safety in the workplace, by preventing recurrences.

THE FIRST AID BOX

It is a known fact that failure to administer first aid during the early stages of an accident could result in minor injuries becoming major ones or even leading to death. All employers must provide suitable first aid equipment and competent first aiders for all workplaces and the

FIGURE 1.12 First aid box

ACCIDENT REPORT

Person affected/injured

Name:
Address:

Postcode:
Occupation:

Person reporting the incident

Name:
Address:

Postcode:
Occupation:

Details of accident

Date: Time:
Description of incident:

First aid administered:

Notifiable accident

Complete this box if the accident is reportable under the Reporting of Injuries, Diseases and Dangerous Occurrences Regulations 1995 (RIDDOR)

How was it reported?

Date reported: Signature:

Date form was completed:
Signature of injured person to disclose personal information to safety representatives:

FIGURE 1.13 Accident report form

self-employed, regardless of their size. The Health and Safety (First Aid) Regulations 1981 require employers to assess the needs for this provision to provide adequate and appropriate equipment, facilities and personnel to administer first aid to the injured or ill. The exact contents of a first aid box will depend on the number of people it is intended to serve and the type of work undertaken. In general, medication and tablets should not be kept in the first aid box or administered by a first aider. The box should be checked regularly to ensure that it is well stocked and the contents are not out of date. There is no definitive content list for first aid boxes, but the following items would normally be included in a place of work with no special requirements:

- disposable gloves;
- individually wrapped triangular bandages;
- information sheets on administering basic first aid;
- safety pins;
- sterile eye pads;
- various sizes of individually wrapped sterile wound dressings.

The HSE recommends that adequate notices are displayed in the workplace with the names of the nominated first aiders and the location of the first aid rooms and boxes.

Further details can be obtained from the relevant code of practice: The Health and Safety (First Aid) Regulations 1981 L74.

 ACTIVITIES

Activity 3 – Accident, first aid, emergency procedures and reporting

Read through the following questions and answer them as fully as you can to help you develop your underpinning knowledge of this subject area.

1. Name two items that should not be included in a first aid box.
2. Who has the authorisation to complete the details in an accident book?
3. Where should an accident book be stored?
4. List five important details that should be recorded in an accident book after an accident on site.
5. What do the initials RIDDOR stand for?

 ACTIVITIES

Activity 4 – Identifying hazards on construction sites

Read through the following questions and answer them as fully as you can to help you develop your underpinning knowledge of this subject area.

1. Who has a duty to carry out 'risk assessments' in the construction industry?
2. List five methods of good housekeeping on site.
3. What is a method statement?
4. Who should be informed of a 'near miss' on site?
5. If a hazard is identified on a construction site, what action should be taken?

HEALTH AND HYGIENE

WELFARE FACILITIES

All fixed construction sites must have adequate welfare facilities for site personnel, to meet the minimum requirements of the Construction (Design and Management) Regulations 2007. Employers must make suitable arrangements to provide welfare facilities for employees before any construction work starts. Larger sites may require more than one welfare facility to meet the demand of the increased number of workers on site, and to allow convenient access. Employers have a legal duty to provide the following facilities as a minimum requirement:

- hot and cold running water wash facilities, with soap and clean towels or driers;
- drinking water;
- toilets (*note* – men and women can share the same facility provided they are partitioned off from the urinals);
- drying rooms;
- canteen facilities with tables, chairs, a means of boiling water and heating food;
- secure storerooms for work clothing, with separate lockers.

Employers must also ensure that the facilities are clean and tidy (good housekeeping), and adequately lit and heated, with a good source of ventilation. All welfare arrangements should be clearly identified in the site 'Health and Safety Plan' as part of the Construction (Design and Management) Regulations (CDM).

NOISE AT WORK

Exposure to loud noise for long or short periods of time can cause temporary deafness or permanent hearing loss. The Control of Noise at Work Regulations 2005 requires employers to take the following measures to ensure the health and safety of their employees:

- assess the risks in the workplace (risk assessment);
- monitor noise levels in the workplace (these must not exceed the safe legal noise limits);
- provide adequate hearing protection (PPE);
- provide information, instruction and training (signage, safe use of safety devices, etc.);
- reduce noise exposure (length of time exposed to damaging noise levels, etc.);
- reduce the risks as far as practically possible.

Working in an area that requires you to raise your voice to be heard by a person approximately 2 metres away suggests that the noise levels in that area may be too high. Although you may consider the exposure to noise to be only a minor risk, the damage to the inner ear may increase gradually until it becomes noticeable. An early sign of damage to the nerve endings in the inner ear may be the inability to hear normal levels of conversation with background noise. In most cases this type of damage to the inner ear and nerve endings is irreversible and may result in 'tinnitus', permanent ringing in the ear.

FIGURE 1.14 Noise levels are measured and recorded in decibles (dB) with a sound meter

EXAMPLES OF SOUND LEVELS:

- television 20 dB;
- primary classroom 70 dB;
- power drill 90 dB;
- a busy bar or nightclub 100 dB;
- circular saw bench 102 dB.

Employers have a responsibility to make employees aware of the hazards and risks in their place of work by carrying out thorough
risk assessments and providing method statements. They should also display the correct warning signs and create zones where hearing protection should be worn at all times in areas of high risk. The HSE recommend the following safe guidelines:

- 80 dB – employers should assess the risk to health;
- 85 dB – hearing protection zones, personal protective equipment (PPE) should be worn (mandatory);
- 87 dB – maximum exposure limit, taking into account the reduction provided by PPE.

Hearing protection must be worn

FIGURE 1.15 Mandatory sign

FIGURE 1.16 Hearing protection PPE

 TRADE SECRETS

Hearing protection should be worn as recommended on the manufacturer's instructions. Failure to wear the equipment correctly may fail to provide adequate levels of protection or may even damage your hearing; for example, ear plugs inserted too deep into the ear canal may injure the inner ear. Disposable PPE should be worn only once by each user and correctly disposed of at the end of each use. Hearing protection that fits into the ear canal should never be shared with others, as this may cause possible infection to be passed from one person to another.

Hearing protection should reduce noise to a safe level but not eliminate it all together, as this could pose a potential risk if a person is operating machinery or equipment, or if an evacuation alarm is sounded.

ACTIVITIES

Activity 5 – Health and hygiene

Read through the following questions and answer them as fully as you can to help you develop your underpinning knowledge of this subject area.

1. List five essential welfare facilities that should be available on all construction sites.

2. How can you identify a dangerous noise level on site?

3. What measures can be taken to reduce the risk of potentially damaging noises at work?

4. Why is personal hygiene important on construction sites?

5. Men and women are permitted by law to share toilet facilities on site: true or false?

BASIC WORKING PLATFORMS

DANGERS OF WORKING AT HEIGHT

Several thousand major injuries are reported to the Health and Safety Executive every year as a result of falls or falling objects from height causing harm. The Working at Height Regulations 2005 (WaHR) place legal duties on everybody responsible for the welfare of personnel, including employers, the self-employed and managers. In general, duty holders are responsible for ensuring, as far as practically possible, that falls from height are prevented using the following measures:

- all work at height is properly planned and organised;
- all work at height takes account of weather conditions that could endanger personnel;
- assess the risks as a result of working at height;
- consider alternative methods of completing the work;
- ensure equipment for work at height is appropriately inspected;
- health and safety;
- produce method statements for the safe use of the access equipment;
- ensure the place where work at height is done is safe;
- the risks from falling objects are properly controlled;
- those involved in work at height are trained and competent.

Employees also have responsibilities to follow the training and instruction provided by their employers or safety representatives. In addition, they should also use the equipment and safety devices provided properly, and report any safety hazards encountered while carrying out their duties.

SELECTING EQUIPMENT FOR USE

Careful consideration should be given to the type of access equipment used for a particular task, to ensure the minimum amount of risk to the user and anyone in the immediate area. There are several other factors to consider that enable work to take place without personal risk of injury; these include:

- length of time required for use;
- maximum height to be accessed;
- frequency of use;
- static or mobile;
- type of work being carried out;
- amount of people required to use the equipment;
- ground conditions (level or uneven?/firm or soft?/slippery?)
- weather conditions and lighting;
- consider the position of the access equipment; will it pose a threat to the general public or people working underneath?

TYPES OF ACCESS EQUIPMENT AND BASIC WORKING PLATFORMS

Access equipment is interpreted as any item of equipment that allows personnel, tools and materials to gain safe entry or exit to one or more different levels. There are various types of access equipment available for use; these include:

- hop-ups;
- leaning ladders;
- stepladders;
- trestle platforms;
- mobile tower scaffolds;
- independent scaffolds (Figure 1.17).

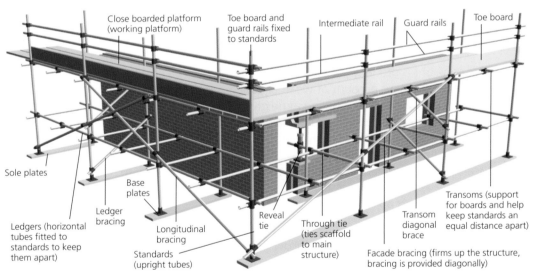

FIGURE 1.17 An independent scaffold

Each item of access equipment requires the user to be suitably trained and informed about its safe use, maintenance and inspection. However, independent scaffolds should only be erected and inspected by fully trained scaffolders, known as 'card holders'.

HOP-UPS

Hop-ups are the smallest items of access equipment, with a maximum of two to three steps giving access to lower levels. This type of equipment should be used only for short periods of time because of its lack of handrail and platform space.

LADDERS

The term 'ladders' refers to several different types of access equipment. These include:

1. leaning ladders;
2. stepladders.

Leaning ladders

Single, double and triple extension ladders are all styles of 'leaning ladders'. Once fully erected they should be positioned at a safe working angle of 75°, or a ratio of 1:4 (one in four units). Wherever possible, leaning ladders should be securely tied at the top and secured to a temporary stake in the ground at the lower level. Alternatively, if the ladder is going to be used only for short periods of time it should be

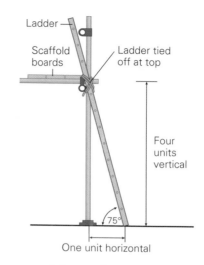

FIGURE 1.18 Safe use of a leaning ladder

supported by an additional person 'footing' the bottom rungs. Ladders used to access a working platform should extend above the stepping-off point by 1 metre; this allows the top rungs to be used as handrails and reduces the risk of the ladder slipping off the platform.

It is good practice to use a single leaning ladder to access a working platform, especially if it is required for a long period of time. Wooden or steel 'pole' ladders are normally used for this purpose, because they do not require overlapping mid-span and therefore have no weak spot. Pole ladders commonly range in size from 3 metres up to 10 metres.

Ladders should be thoroughly inspected at the beginning of the working day by the person intending to use the equipment. The following areas should be considered as part of these daily inspections:

- wooden components should be checked for splits, cracks and significant signs of damage;
- avoid using and report any painted items of access equipment as this may be concealing defects;
- check the rungs are in good condition, not loose, bent, split or missing;
- check the stiles are not bent as this may lead to the ladder collapsing;
- check the non-slip feet of the stiles are not missing or excessively worn.

Stepladders

Traditionally, wooden stepladders were used in the construction industry, although they are rarely used nowadays because of their ability to become unstable through continued use and wear. These types of stepladder are also considerably heavier than their modern aluminium and fibreglass equivalents. Fibreglass ladders are commonly used by electricians because they are safer, due to their inability to conduct electricity in the event of an emergency.

The following inspections should be carried out on stepladders before use:

FIGURE 1.19 A stepladder

- check the locking bars are not bent or missing;
- ensure the stepladder is set up on firm, level ground;
- ensure the stepladder is fully open, with the locking bars fully engaged;
- check the feet of the stiles are not missing and they are in good condition;
- check the platform is not buckled or split;
- check the steps are free of mud and dirt, to avoid slipping;
- check the steps are secure;
- check the stiles are not bent or damaged;
- check the ropes are in good condition and taut when the steps are erected (if applicable).

TRESTLE PLATFORMS

Adjustable steel trestles are normally used used by bricklayers, and suitably heightened as the building work progresses. Alternatively, 'A' frames can be positioned, at either end of trestle boards to create and support a stronger working platform. Trestle platforms (or scaffolds) should be fitted with handrails in positions where the risk assessment has highlighted the need for edge protection. In some cases it is not always practical to fit handrails on both sides of the platform because the type of work would be restricted. The distance and consequences of falling from trestle scaffolds should always be minimised with 'fall arrest equipment' or restricting the maximum height. The duration of work on trestle scaffolds should always be keep to a minimum to reduce the risk of falls from height; alternative methods should be sourced for longer periods.

Trestle scaffolds should always be set up on firm, level ground, with a minimum platform width of 450 mm. The overhang of the working platform on either end of the trestles should be a minimum of 50 mm and maximum of four times the thickness of the boards. These guidelines prevent the boards slipping off the edge of the trestles and flipping up in the event of somebody stepping on their end. Working platforms should also never be positioned higher than two-thirds the overall height of the trestles.

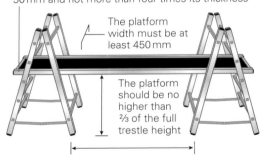

The overhang of the platform must be at least 50 mm and not more than four times its thickness

The platform width must be at least 450 mm

The platform should be no higher than ⅔ of the full trestle height

Up to 3 m span over this additional support required

FIGURE 1.20 Safe use of a trestle platform

Safety nets

Harness and lanyard

Safety air bags

Guard rails

FIGURE 1.21 Safety devices used at height

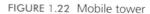

MOBILE TOWER SCAFFOLDS

Mobile tower scaffolds are used for a variety of maintenance, inspection and building work. The loose component parts of the tower allow them to be adjusted to several different heights, with working platforms at intermediate positions in between. Mobile towers should be erected only by trained and competent people authorised to do so, following the manufacturer's instructions.

In general, mobile tower scaffolds should comply with the following recommendations for safe use:

- use only suitable component parts;
- never assemble the tower with damaged or broken parts;
- ensure all handrails are fitted at a minimum height of 950 mm;
- ensure all intermediate rails are fitted below the handrails, leaving a maximum gap of 470 mm between;
- never overload mobile towers with tools, equipment or personnel;
- never move towers with people on board;
- never use in high winds or adverse weather conditions;
- never climb the outside of towers (mountaineering);
- tower should not exceed 4 metres when it is being moved;
- ensure the brakes are engaged before use;
- consider overhead wires, electricity cables and obstructions;
- ensure the ground conditions are suitable for use (e.g. flat, level, firm);
- always move towers manually and never by mechanical means (e.g. vehicles);
- isolate the working areas around mobile towers and use suitable signage to inform people of the hazards.

INSPECTION

The Working at Height Regulations 2005 (WaHR) state that any item of access equipment or working platform where there is a risk of falling 2 metres and over (except mobile towers) should be inspected no more than seven days before use. Further inspections should be carried out at regular intervals to be determined by the person carrying out the method statement. In general, the period of time between re-inspections should not compromise the health and safety of the users or people affected by its use. Static scaffolds are normally inspected by a competent

TRADE SECRETS

While working at height, materials may have to be removed to a lower level. These items should never be thrown or 'bombed' over the edge of the access equipment, or from any height, because of the risks of personal injury to people below. Alternatively, they could be sent safely down a 'rubbish chute' into a covered skip below.

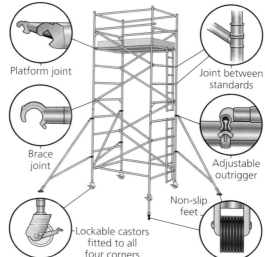

Platform joint

Joint between standards

Brace joint

Adjustable outrigger

Non-slip feet

Lockable castors fitted to all four corners

FIGURE 1.22 Mobile tower

person once they have been erected, and at least every seven days thereafter. During adverse weather conditions, such as frost, snow, high winds and heavy rainfall, further inspections should take place. All inspections carried out should be recorded within 24 hours and kept on the site with the health and safety file. Once the project has been completed, the inspection reports should be stored for a further three months at the company's head office.

 ACTIVITIES

Activity 6 – Basic working platforms

Read through the following questions and answer them as fully as you can to help you develop your underpinning knowledge of this subject area.

1. List three precautions that could be used to prevent falls from height.
2. What is the difference between a 'rung' and a 'step'?
3. At what height should handrails be used on trestle scaffolds?
4. What is the maximum height a mobile tower scaffold should not exceed when it is to be moved?
5. How often should scaffolding be inspected?

WORKING WITH ELECTRICITY

The HSE has reported that approximately 30 deaths a year in the construction industry are a result of electric shock, with many more accidents resulting in severe or permanent injury. Many of these accidents were caused by the casualty coming into contact with the live parts of electricity cables, or burnt as a result of fire caused by electrical faults. Employers have a duty under the Electricity at Work Regulations 1989 to assess the risks and hazards in the workplace, and eliminate or reduce them as much as practically possible.

 FREQUENTLY ASKED QUESTIONS

▶ **What is the difference between a 'risk' and a 'hazard'?**

The term 'risk' means that there is a chance of injury.

The term 'hazard' means that something *will* cause harm or personal injury.

Domestic mains supply electricity is 230 volts; this level is powerful enough to kill anyone who comes into direct contact with it. To reduce the risk of death on site as a result of electrocution, it is recommended that the supply is reduced to a safe level. Most construction sites now use 110 volts by reducing the mains supply with a 'transformer'; 110 volts electricity cables and transformers are easily identified by their yellow casing and round three-pin plugs and sockets.

The risk of serious electric shock from mains supplies can be prevented by plugging a residual current device (RCD) into the power source. RCDs are small, sensitive devices that have the ability to rapidly cut the supply of electricity, making it safe. If an RCD does 'trip out' it is probably because of an electrical fault and should be investigated further before continued use.

FIGURE 1.23 Transformers and 110 volt power tools

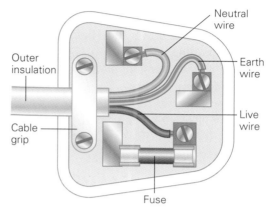

Neutral wire
Outer insulation
Earth wire
Cable grip
Live wire
Fuse

FIGURE 1.24 Wiring a domestic three-pin plug

 FREQUENTLY ASKED QUESTIONS

▶ **If I use 110-volt power tools or an RCD with mains power, does this mean the risk of electric shock is reduced?**

No, these methods will not reduce the risk of being electrocuted. They will only reduce the risk of death as a result of electric shock.

In addition to 110 volts and 230 volts, 415 volts (three phase) must be used to operate large items of equipment and machinery. Sockets, plugs and leads with this power supply are easily recognisable by their blue casing and sheaths.

SAFETY PRECAUTIONS TO BE TAKEN WHEN WORKING WITH ELECTRICITY

The possible risks of electrocution on site apply not only to electricians working directly with wires, cables, etc., they potentially affect everyone on site. The following guidelines should be followed by all personnel.

- If possible, avoid using 230 volts on construction sites.
- Check that plugs and cords on power tools and extension leads are not cracked, split or damaged.
- Check wires are not exposed around plugs and sockets.
- Use another source of power in wet or damp conditions, such as 'compressed air' or 'battery' powered tools.

230 volt plug
110 volt plug
415 volt plug

FIGURE 1.25 Colour coding of different voltages

- Avoid overloading plug sockets.
- Keep leads and power cables above head height if possible to avoid trip hazards, etc.
- Never use damaged items of electrical equipment.
- Follow the site rules and the employer's method statements.
- Always isolate power tools before leaving them on site.
- Keep walkways free of electric power tools and electrical cables.
- Use only double-insulated power tools.
- Ensure all electrical items have a current PAT testing certificate, and that they are regularly maintained.

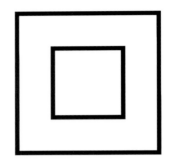

FIGURE 1.26 Double insulation symbol

 FREQUENTLY ASKED QUESTIONS

▶ **What is 'PAT' testing?**

'PAT' is an abbreviation for 'portable appliance testing'. The Electricity at Work Regulations require all portable electrical appliances to be tested regularly to ensure they are safe for use. There are no recommended guidelines stating the period of time between inspections; this generally depends on the frequency of use.

EFFECTS OF ELECTRIC SHOCK

If high levels of electricity run through the human body the current normally heats up the tissue and results in deep burns that are likely to require surgery. The victim may also suffer muscular spasms, cardiac arrest and may stop breathing. All these injuries are potentially life threatening, although the amount of electricity and length of time the victim came into contact with it will have a bearing.

DEALING WITH AN INCIDENT INVOLVING ELECTRIC SHOCK

1. Raise the alarm, without leaving the victim.
2. Do not touch the casualty, as they may still be in contact with the electricity supply.
3. Isolate the power at the source. If this is not possible and the victim is still in contact with the supply, use a non-conductible item, such as a wooden broom, to move the hazard away.
4. Check for signs of a pulse and breathing. If none is found, start mouth-to-mouth resuscitation and chest compressions (consult a trained first aider before attempting).
5. Check for signs of shock.
6. Treat the victim's burns with sterile dressings.

Note: these steps should only be used as a guide. Professional medical advice and training should be sought before treating burn victims.

ACTIVITIES

Activity 7 – Working with electricity

Read through the following questions and answer them as fully as you can to help you develop your underpinning knowledge of this subject area.

1. What colour extension cables should be used with 110-volt portable power tools?

2. What is a transformer?

3. In a 240-volt three-pin plug, what colour sheathing should be used on the neutral wire?

4. What do the initials RCD stand for?

5. What is the purpose of 'PAT' testing?

PERSONAL PROTECTIVE EQUIPMENT (PPE)

Personal protective equipment (PPE) should be worn only as a last resort, after eliminating or reducing all other possible risks and hazards from the working area. Some items of PPE are compulsory on construction sites due to the nature of the project; these items may include:

- safety footwear (boots/shoes/riggers);
- high-visibility clothing (commonly referred to as a 'hi-vis');
- safety helmets;
- builders' gloves.

The minimum requirements for PPE on a construction site will be displayed on information notices and posters on the boundary fence at the entrance to the site. Site personnel will also be informed of the site manager's requirements during their induction onto the site. In addition to these requirements other items of PPE should worn if there is a risk of personal injury.

FIGURE 1.27 A construction site notice

The Personal Protective Equipment at Work Regulations 1992 requires all employers to provide employees and agency workers with all necessary PPE free of charge to allow them to carry out their job safely. PPE is considered to be any item of protective equipment, including weatherproof clothing.

EXAMPLES OF PPE TO PROTECT VARIOUS PARTS OF THE BODY

EYE PROTECTION

Safety glasses/safety goggles/face shields/visors. *Safeguards against* – chemical splashes, dust and dirt, flying objects, gas and vapour, ultraviolet radiation (sun rays).

HEAD PROTECTION

Hard helmets/bump caps. *Safeguards against* – risk of bumping head, impact from falling or flying objects.

? FREQUENTLY ASKED QUESTIONS

▶ What is a 'bump cap'?

A bump cap looks very similar to a baseball cap with built-in head protection. Bump caps are usually lighter and more comfortable to wear than hard hats, and are usually used in areas where the risks of head injury are reduced.

FIGURE 1.28 Eye protection

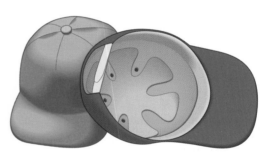

FIGURE 1.29 Bump caps

RESPIRATORY PROTECTION

Disposable moulded dust masks/dust mask with replaceable filters/half- or full-face respirators/air-fed helmets. *Safeguards against* – dust, dangerous gases and vapour.

FIGURE 1.30 Dust mask

BODY PROTECTION

Boiler suits/disposable overalls/aprons/high-visibility vests and coats. *Safeguards against* – entanglement of own clothing, adverse weather, chemical splashes, spray from pressure leaks or spray guns, contaminated dust.

HAND/ARM PROTECTION

Gloves/gauntlets/armlets/wrist cuffs. *Safeguards against* – abrasions, cuts, extreme temperatures, chemicals, skin infection.

FIGURE 1.31 High-visibility jacket

FIGURE 1.32 Gauntlets

FIGURE 1.33 Safety boots

FOOT/LEG PROTECTION

Safety boots, shoes and riggers with steel toe caps/leggings/gaiters. *Safeguards against* – slipping, cuts, falling objects, chemical spills, abrasion, wet conditions.

In some cases, several items of PPE may need to be worn at the same time, causing them to become incompatible with each other. This can be overcome by using specially designed equipment; for example, mounted ear defenders and visors can be added to hard hats.

Employees have a duty to request PPE from their employer and wear it correctly. Any damaged items should be replaced immediately to ensure that the equipment functions properly. Employees should also look after the equipment they have been provided with by storing it correctly and taking reasonable measures to make sure that it is not damaged through neglect.

FIGURE 1.34 Hard hat with ear defenders and visor

ACTIVITIES

Activity 8 – Using appropriate personal protective equipment (PPE)

Read through the following questions and answer them as fully as you can to help you develop your underpinning knowledge of this subject area.

1. List three mandatory items of PPE to be worn on all sites.
2. Employees should provide their own safety boots in the construction industry: true or false?
3. On what part of the body are gauntlets worn?
4. How often should PPE be replaced?
5. If ear defenders are supplied by your employer and you are wearing a hard hat, you are permitted to remove it for a short period of time on site: true or false?

FIRE AND EMERGENCY PROCEDURES

THE FIRE TRIANGLE

Fuel, heat and oxygen are the three elements needed to allow fire to ignite and burn; collectively these are known as the 'fire triangle'. If one of these elements was to be removed the fire will cease to continue burning. These principles are applied to tackle and extinguish fires in the event of an emergency, although the exact method needed will depend on the type of fire. For example, a wood or paper fire could be extinguished with water; however, if the same method was used for an electrical fire there would be a risk of electric shock.

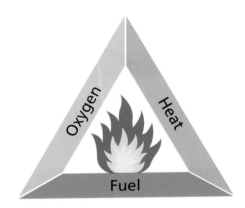

FIGURE 1.35 The fire triangle

There are many different types of fire-fighting equipment and fire extinguishers to deal with various fires. In the past the contents of a fire extinguisher were identified by the colour of its container. Changes in legislation now require all types of fire-fighting equipment and fire extinguishers to be coloured red, and identified by their coloured label and the information contained on it.

CLASSIFICATIONS OF FIRE

British Standards BS EN:2 1992 has categorised fires into five different classes so that the type of equipment can quickly be identified and selected for use.

1. Class A – fires involving solid materials, usually of an organic nature;
2. Class B – fires involving liquids or liquefiable solids;

3. Class C – fires involving gases;
4. Class D – fires involving metals;
5. Class E – fires involving electrical equipment.

TYPES OF FIRE-FIGHTING EQUIPMENT

Type of Extinguisher		Class of fire to be treated
Water extinguisher		A
Foam extinguisher		A, B
Carbon dioxide extinguisher		B, C, E
Dry powder extinguisher		A, B, C, D, E
Fire blanket		A, B, C, D, E (Will smother all fires. Particularly useful for when clothing is alight as there is no risk to skin or breathing. Other extinguishers may be harmful.)

FIGURE 1.36 Fire-fighting equipment

METHODS OF FIRE PREVENTION

Employers should conduct a thorough risk assessment of their place of work to establish the equipment and materials needed in the event of an emergency. They should also provide information and training to employees to eliminate or reduce the risks at their establishment.

During routine risk assessments, employers and people responsible for the health and safety of others should consider the following hazards:

● storage of waste materials on site and good housekeeping;
● storage and quantity of dangerous substances used on site, including petrol, liquid petroleum gas (LPG), paints and varnishes, solvents and dust;
● dust, vapour, gas and mist pose a high risk of fire or explosion if mixed with air.

Employers also have a duty to provide suitable warning and safe conditions signs as well as visual and audible alarm systems. All personnel should be made aware of the escape routes to the nearest assembly points on site, so that they can be accounted for in the event of an emergency evacuation. In preparation for such an event, regular practice drills should be conducted by employers to eliminate any confusion and reduce the length of time taken between raising the alarm and assembly.

FREQUENTLY ASKED QUESTIONS

▶ **Should I return to a burning building to use the equipment provided to fight the fire if I have received training?**

No, even if you have received training in the use of the equipment supplied. These items are provided to gain a safe route from a burning building in the event of a fire. Remember to follow your employer's evacuation plan in the event of an emergency and remain at the assembly point until instructed to do otherwise.

ACTIVITIES

Activity 9 – Fire and emergency procedures

Read through the following questions and answer them as fully as you can to help you develop your underpinning knowledge of this subject area.

1. What element is missing from the following fire triangle: heat, fuel and … ?
2. What class of fire involves electrical equipment?
3. Other than fire extinguishers, name an item of fire-fighting equipment.
4. Extinguishers with black labels contain what substance?
5. What type of extinguisher should be used on gas fires?

MULTIPLE-CHOICE QUESTIONS

1   Which **one** of the following would the Provision and Use of Work Equipment Regulations (PUWER) legislate on?
    a   Abrasives
    b   Adhesives
    c   Machinery
    d   Preservatives

2   Under the Health and Safety at Work Act, which **one** of the following is a responsibility of an employer?
    a   To provide safe transport to work
    b   To provide PPE for use by employees
    c   To report all absences to the HSE
    d   To report the lateness of workers

3   Which **one** of the following acts would legislate on the control of dust in a joinery workshop?
    a   MASK
    b   COSHH
    c   RIDDOR
    d   H&SAWA

4   What colour CSCS card denotes 'trainee' status?
    a   Red
    b   Blue
    c   Black
    d   Yellow

5   Which **one** of the following meetings must be attended when starting work on a new site?
    a   Induction
    b   Timesheet
    c   Cold calling
    d   Ice breaking

6   In relation to manual handling, 'kinetic lifting' means lifting
    a   using a forklift truck
    b   with additional assistance
    c   with mechanical assistance
    d   using the body most efficiently

7 Which two of the following parts form part of a wooden step ladder?

a String and step

b Tread and stile

c Tread and riser

d String and stile

8 When using a random orbital sander on hardwood surfaces, which of the following PPE options is most appropriate?

a Eye, nose, ear

b Ear, foot, eye

c Hand, ear, nose

d Hand, nose and eye

9 A triangular safety sign with a black border indicates which **one** of the following safety signs?

a Warning

b Prohibition

c Mandatory

d Information

10 The colour used to denote 110 voltage is

a red

b blue

c black

d yellow

INFORMATION, QUANTITIES AND COMMUNICATING WITH OTHERS 2

 LEARNING OUTCOMES

By the end of this chapter you should have developed a knowledge and understanding of:

- interpreting and producing building information;
- estimating quantities of resources;
- communicating workplace requirements efficiently.

INTRODUCTION

The aim of this chapter is for learners to be able to recognise and understand the various types of architects' and engineers' drawings used in the construction industry. It also explains the use of other documentation used to communicate information between various members of the building team, and explains current Building Regulations applicable to this area of study, following all the relevant health and safety law and good working practices.

SOURCES OF INFORMATION

Effective lines of communication in the building industry are vital to ensure that projects run smoothly, within budget and are completed within an agreed timescale. Communication begins on a building project with the first contact between the client and the architect to discuss a concept or idea, through to the site manager inducting tradesmen/women on to the site. Lack of communication between the client, the main contractor, designers, architects and different trades can result in costly mistakes and delays on a project. Effective communication between members of the building team is vital if changes are made to the contract documentation, or matters of health and safety arise on site. The following problems commonly occur in the construction industry as a result of poor communication:

- labour/tradespeople not on site and available at the right time and in the right sequence;
- materials not ordered in advance, resulting in delays on site; for example, carpenters waiting for the kitchen units to arrive so that the plumber can 'plumb in' the sink etc. to complete his second fixing;
- skips not ordered or emptied, resulting in stoppages;
- visits by the Building Control Officer are not requested in advance, delaying further progress on the build;
- changes to build details and contract documents, resulting in several sets of information being used by different members of the building team.

A line of communication can be as simple as a conversation between two parties, a memorandum (memo) on a notice board or even an employee's pay slip. Verbal dialect, hand signals and even body movement, posture and facial expressions are all methods of communication. Although we use these methods every day while undertaking work activities, there are several disadvantages. These include:

- they can often be misinterpreted;
- they are often misunderstood;
- there is no written evidence that can be referred back to at a later date.

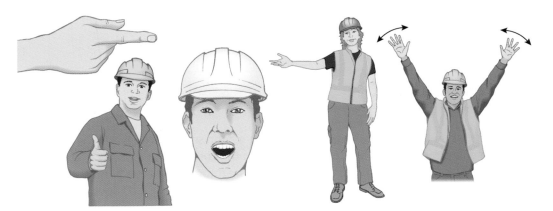

FIGURE 2.1 Methods of communication

The term 'written information' refers to all forms of documentation, including architects' drawings, sketches, programmes of work, etc., as well as text. Problems and queries arising throughout a construction project are usually passed through a hierarchy of people until the issue is resolved.

 FREQUENTLY ASKED QUESTIONS

▶ **What is a 'hierarchy'?**

A 'hierarchy' is term used to refer to the chain of command or pecking order on a construction site. The client is the most important member of the building team because they are usually funding the project; they are therefore always at the top of the ladder (see Figure 2.2).

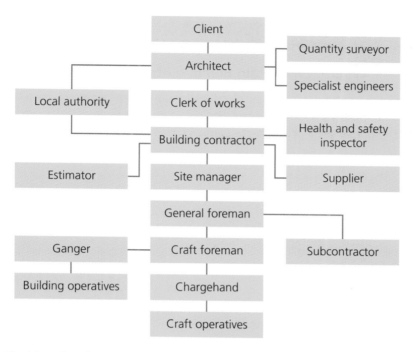

FIGURE 2.2 The hierarchy of a building team

The processes of controlling materials, labour and progress on a building site are usually down to one person – the 'site manager'. Although everyone on a construction site is usually working indirectly for the client, it is the site manager who will refer to the contract details to plan and organise the project. The most important sources of information a site manager will use are:

- architects' and structural engineers' drawings;
- bill of quantities;
- work programmes/schedules;
- specifications;
- manufacturers' information;
- conditions of the contract between the main contractor and the client.

These sources of information are compiled between the architects, the structural/services engineer and the quantity surveyor for the approval of the client before a project begins. When 'planning permission' and 'Building Regulations approval' have been granted by the local authority, the client will then pass these documents to the nominated main contractor. When an agreement has been signed between both parties, these papers are then referred to as the 'contract documents'. Any further changes or developments throughout the project must be in addition to the original agreement and are therefore an amendment. These changes to the original contract must be made in writing on a 'variation order' to prevent disputes when extra costs are claimed by the main contractor at the end of the project.

? FREQUENTLY ASKED QUESTIONS

▶ Where can I obtain Building Regulations information?

The local planning office will answer any questions you have regarding current Building Regulations. In most cases the architect and structural engineer will design the project, following the guidelines laid out in the approved documents below:

▶ Part A – Structure;

▶ Part B – Fire;

▶ Part C – Site preparation and resistance to moisture;

▶ Part D – Toxic substances;

▶ Part E – Resistance to the passage of sound;

▶ Part F – Ventilation;

▶ Part G – Hygiene;

▶ Part H – Drainage and waste disposal;

▶ Part J – Heat-producing appliances;

▶ Part K – Stairways, ramps and guards;

▶ Part L – Conservation, fuel and power.

When a project has been granted planning permission, Building Regulations approval must be sought to commence the build. Alternatively, the building work may start on a 'Building Notice' issued by the local authority, providing any work carried out complies with current regulations. At several stages throughout the building work, the Building Inspector will visit the project to ensure that the progress made satisfies the requirements of Building Regulations.

INTERPRETING INFORMATION

ARCHITECTS' DRAWINGS

BLOCK PLANS

Block plans identify the position of the building plot in relation to the surrounding area. They are normally drawn in scaled-down proportion of the real size, but rarely contain measurements. Block plans are used to submit information to the Planning Office in order to obtain planning permission.

SITE PLANS

Site plans are drawn to a bigger scale to illustrate the position of the proposed building on the plot. They usually contain basic information, including site dimensions, tree positions, drainage and main roads, etc.

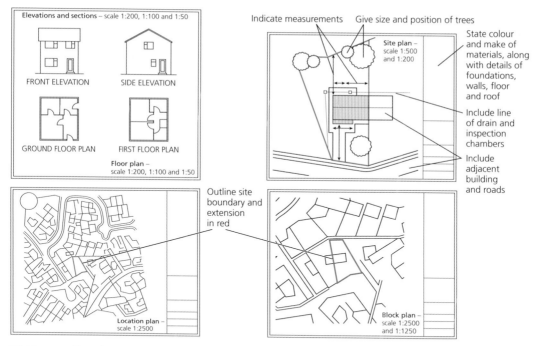

FIGURE 2.3 Site plans

ELEVATIONS

Elevations illustrate views of the building from all four sides to give a visual impression of the aspects. These are not working drawings and should not be used to construct the building.

SECTIONS

Sections through a building will be drawn by the architect to demonstrate the general construction of the floors, walls, ceiling and roof. Simple dimensions, such as room heights, and general notes are also contained within the drawings (see Figure 2.4).

FLOOR PLANS

Floor plans are a section through a building at approximately 1 metre above floor level. Their purpose is to indicate the layout of all the internal walls, internal and external doorways, windows and staircases within the proposed building.

DETAILED/TECHNICAL DRAWINGS

These are drawn by architects and structural engineers illustrating the information and calculations required to complete particular areas of the build. These may include:

- foundations;
- wall construction (e.g. brick and block cavity wall, timber framed);
- ground and upper floor construction;
- positions of any steel beams or load-bearing walls;

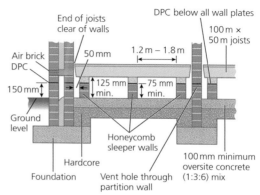

FIGURE 2.4 Construction detailing sections

- roof construction;
- eaves finishing detail.

RANGE DRAWINGS

Range drawings are used as references to detail the full 'range' of particular components; for example, a 'door range drawing' will illustrate the front views of all the internal and external doors, with basic information such as the overall dimensions (see Figure 2.5). They would also contain a simple referencing system to help identify the doors and their location on the floor plans. Range drawings are particularly useful when 'tendering' for a contract or placing purchase orders through the company 'buyer'.

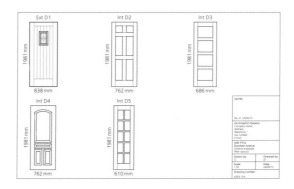

FIGURE 2.5 Example of a door range drawing

 FREQUENTLY ASKED QUESTIONS

▶ What does the term 'tendering' mean?

'Tendering' is a process conducted by the client or quantity surveyor on larger builds to determine the main contractor for a building project. A list of work required to complete a project is written by the quantity surveyor and forwarded to a number of building companies. This list is known as a 'bill of quantities'. Each company will itemise the costs for each phase of the build on the bill of quantities and return it for the client's approval.

TITLE PANELS

Title panels are sources of written information that should be contained on all forms of architectural and technical drawings. They are usually contained on the right-hand side of the main drawing and provide useful information, including:

- the name, address, telephone/fax and email address of the architect's or structural engineer's practice;
- job title – for example, the name and address of the client or project;
- drawing title – an explanation of the details drawn; for example, 'Building Regulations First Floor Plan';

- name of the author (the person who developed the drawing);
- name of the person who checked the drawing;
- the scale and size of the paper containing the drawing;
- date first drawn;
- drawing number;
- revision number or date.

'SCALED' MEASUREMENT

A scaled measurement is used to reduce the full size of an original item to a small enough measurement so that it will fit onto a single piece of drawing paper. This allows buildings or projects of any size to be drawn to a true representation of the original proportion. Scaled drawings are traditionally produced by hand on a drawing board with a range of drawing tools, which include a 'scale rule'.

The disadvantages of this method are that these drawings are slower to produce, they are not as accurate as electronic versions, and the paper will shrink and expand with changes in the climate. Nowadays they are regularly produced by architects, engineers and draughtsmen on 'AutoCAD®' computer programs. There are several advantages of having the drawings electronically; these include:

- images can be distributed quickly between members of the building team;
- the images can easily be magnified, manipulated and amended;
- AutoCAD® (computer-aided design) is 100 per cent accurate.

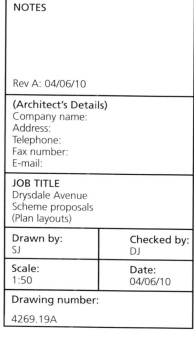

NOTES	
Rev A: 04/06/10	
(Architect's Details) Company name: Address: Telephone: Fax number: E-mail:	
JOB TITLE Drysdale Avenue Scheme proposals (Plan layouts)	
Drawn by: SJ	Checked by: DJ
Scale: 1:50	Date: 04/06/10
Drawing number: 4269.19A	

FIGURE 2.6 Example of a title panel

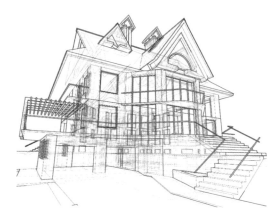

FIGURE 2.7 An example of an architect's drawing completed with a computer program

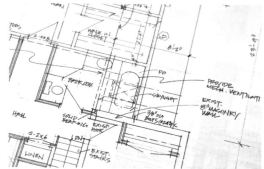

FIGURE 2.8 An example of an architect's drawing completed by hand

CONVERTING SCALE

Only essential information and measurements are usually contained on scaled drawings, other sizes are normally scaled directly from the images. This is simply achieved by referring to the title box to first establish the scale used to draw the pictures. Measurements can then be read from the drawing using the same conversion on a scale rule; alternatively, a standard metric rule can be used. In this case the size measured from the drawing must be multiplied by the scale. Here are some examples.

Example 1

A wall measures 40 mm on a drawing with a scale of 1:100

40 × 100 = 4000 mm

= 4 metres (this is the actual size of the wall)

Example 2

A window opening measures 7 mm on a drawing with scale of 1:50

7 × 50 = 350 mm

= 0.350 metres (this is the actual size of the window)

Example 3

If a floor joist measures 3.8 metres in length and has to be drawn to a scale of 1:50, the actual size it will be drawn will be 76 mm. This is simply calculated by breaking the 3.8 metres down into millimetres and dividing it by the scale size.

3.8 metres = 3800 mm ÷ 50 = 76 mm (this is the actual size of the floor joist on the drawing)

Whenever possible, any measurements specified on working drawings should always take priority, and scaling directly from them should be the last resort.

TRADE SECRETS

Do not assume that all drawings have been completed by the architect. Always check the title panel before scaling from the drawings, to ensure that the architect has not made a comment. In some cases the architect will provide instructions not to scale from the drawing, and all measurements are to be checked on site.

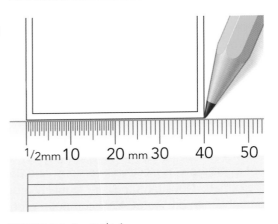

FIGURE 2.9 Example 1

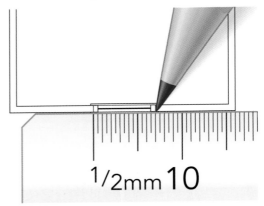

FIGURE 2.10 Example 2

DRAWING SYMBOLS AND ABBREVIATIONS

Drawing symbols and abbreviations are commonly used on architects' and engineers' drawings to prevent full explanations cluttering up the details. The symbols and abbreviations used by architects and engineers have been standardised by the British Standards Institute (BS 1192) to prevent confusion (see Figure 2.11).

Symbol	Meaning
	Asphalt/macadam
	Blockwork
	Brickwork
	Cement screed
	Concrete
	Damp proof course /membrane
	Earth (subsoil)
	Granular fill
	Glass sheet

Symbol	Meaning
	Hardcore
	Metal
	Plaster/render
	Plywood
	Stone
	Insulation
	Timber sawn – any type
	Timber hardwood – planed all round
	Timber softwood – planed all round

Symbol	Meaning
	Sink
	Bath
	Bidet
	Hot or cold waterdraw-off
CWC	Cold water cistern
HWC	Hot water cylinder
	Stop valve
WB	Wash basin
	Shower
	WC
CWT	Cold water tank
HWT	Hot water tank
	Calorifier
	Safety valve
	Radiator
	Towel rail
B	Boiler
C	Cooker
	Pump
	Thermostat
	Drain or sewer + flow direction
	Foul water
	Rainwater head
ST	Silt trap
RWP	Rainwater pipe
	Surface water
RWO	Rainwater outlet
G	Gulley
GT	Grease trap
VP	Vent pipe
G	Gas meter
	Plug in point
	Gas cock
G	Tap
	Gas valve

Symbol	Meaning
	Ventilation extract fan
	Ventilation supply fan
	Main control
	Electricity meter
2	Switch two-way
	Discharge lamp
	Bell
TV	Socket outlet television
	Cooker control unit
	Switch socket outlet
	Pull/pendant switch
	Wall lamp
	Push bell
R	Socket outlet radio
	Distribution board
	Switch
	Filament lamp
	Telephone (public)
	Immersion heater
	Existing contour 5.0 m
	Bank
	Building
	Fence (post + wire)
	Required contour 2.0 m
	Wall
	Road and pavement
	Gate
	Existing tree
	Tree to be removed
	New tree
	Existing hedge
	Proposed hedge

Single door (single swing)
Single door (double swing)
Side hung (folding)

Side hung
Top hung
Bottom hung
Point of arrow indicates hanging edge
Casement windows

Symbol	Meaning
	North direction
GL	Ground level
FFL	Finished floor level
BM	Bench mark
	Centre line
	Direction of rise
1234567	Staircase
1:10	Ratio (example – 1 in 10)
ext	External
int	Internal
C/C	Centre to centre

FIGURE 2.11 Drawing symbols and abbreviations

BILL OF QUANTITIES

A bill of quantities is a list of itemised materials, labour and parts required for a building project. The list is completed either by a 'quantity surveyor' or by an 'estimator', using the information and details contained in the architect's and engineer's drawings, the specifications and schedules. The bill of quantities is sent to a number of different companies at the tender stage to get a breakdown of estimated costs for the project. The breakdown of costs allows the client and project manager to make variations to the original contract documents throughout the project without having to re-tender.

WORK PROGRAMMES

Once all the tenders have been received, the client and quantity surveyor will review the costs submitted by the various companies and make an informed decision to award the contact. The company with the cheapest tender estimate is not necessarily the one that is chosen to complete the building work. There are other factors to consider; these include the following.

- Start date – the client's start date may not always suit the contractor's schedule. If possible the client may have to be flexible if they expect to use some larger, well-established companies.
- Quality of work – before awarding a tender to a company you should first carry out an investigation into the quality of previously completed projects and obtain references from other clients.
- Completion date – the client may instruct the quantity surveyor to request that a programme of work is submitted with each tender; this will provide details of the expected start and completion dates; in some cases the project may have to be finished within a designated time period.

TRADE SECRETS

If a company is short of work or able to start the project straight away, it is probably for a good reason. This may include:

- they are too expensive to win any other tenders;
- poor-quality workmanship.

Remember – it can take years to build a good reputation but only five minutes to lose one.

Item	Description	Quantity	Unit	Rate	Amount £	
	Preliminaries					
	Name of parties					
	Client Mr J Crouch					
	Quality Printing					
	Cornwallis House					
	Devon					
	Architect RDJ Contractors					
	Preambles					
	Woodwork					
	Supply and fit new impregnated sawn softwood joists to replace existing damaged joists					
A	Impregnated timber has been pressure impregnated with an approved preservative. Any timber cut on site must have a brush application of the same preservative in accordance with the manufacturer's instructions.					
B	50 mm x 200 mm joist					
C	75 mm x 200 mm joist					
D	Provide the provisional cost sum of *Five hundred and eighty pounds* £580 for the supply of impregnated sawn softwood joists.				580	00
E	Add for expenses and profit			%		
F	Include the provisional sum of *two hundred pounds* £200 for contingencies.				200	00
				£		

FIGURE 2.12 Sample bill of quantities

- Payment terms – in general, the contractor will stipulate their payment terms as part of their tender. Terms and conditions will vary between companies, although bigger projects are usually settled with 'interim' or 'stage' payments over the course of the build.
- Retention – a period of between three and six months is usually agreed between the contractor and the client to retain approximately 5 per cent of the final project cost. The 'retention' of money allows the client to inspect the work completed and ensure that any 'snagging' is completed to a satisfactory standard. If the contractor fails to complete any snagging, then the retention money is used to employ other contractors. On satisfactory completion, any outstanding payments are made to the main contractor.
- Penalty clauses – as previously mentioned, some projects will have to be completed within a certain time period before the client starts to incur losses. To prevent the contractor running over the expected completion time, a penalty clause is usually built in to the contract between both parties. Penalty clauses can amount to huge losses for the main contractor, who may pass on these costs to subcontractors. If the project looks likely to overrun, the employer usually offers incentives to the workforce, increases the working hours on site or employs further labour to complete the project on time.

To avoid costly penalty clauses, the main contractor will plan a programme of work at the start of the contract to track progress made through to the end of the build. There are several different types of programmes of work commonly used in the building industry; these include:

- Gantt charts;
- critical path analyses;
- bar charts;
- time lines.

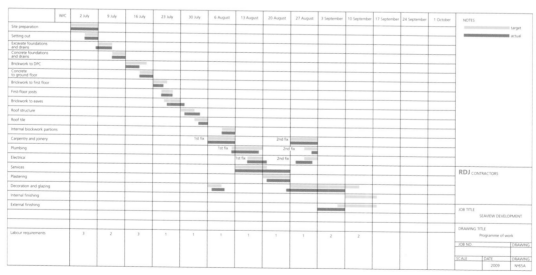

FIGURE 2.13 Example of a Gantt chart

Gantt charts

In simple terms, a Gantt chart is a programme of work designed by the site manager to complete the project in a timely manner. It consists of the starting and finishing dates along the top of the chart, with contingency weeks either end to allow for the project overrunning. These dates are broken down into the number of weeks the project is expected to last. Adjacent to this is a list of the different trades and phases of the build in the order they are expected to be introduced into the project. The projected target times are plotted on the chart for each trade, items of plant and equipment, as well as the various stages of the construction process. As progress is made, amendments may have to be plotted on the Gantt chart to indicate the actual stages of the building project. Adjusting the programme throughout the building work will allow the project manager to rectify delays caused at an earlier stage to complete the project on time.

SCHEDULES

Building drawings alone are unable to contain all the information needed for second-fix carpentry, and electrical and plumbing fitments; for example, internal doors will be shown on a plan and elevation drawings but rarely contain details regarding their design and use of ironmongery. To overcome this issue, 'schedules' are produced with a referencing system to the architect's drawings. In this case a door schedule may contain the following information:

- material used to construct the door (hardwood/softwood);
- type of glazing (if applicable);
- overall dimensions;
- type of door (flush, panelled, fully glazed, etc.);
- finish (painted, stained, etc.);
- types of ironmongery used (mortise lock, number of hinges, etc.).

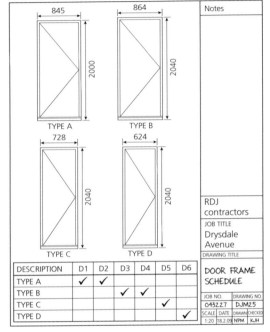

FIGURE 2.14 Example of a schedule

Schedules are produced by quantity surveyors to form a part of the tendering package used to estimate material and labour costs. They are also used throughout the building process to measure and order materials, check deliveries and help to identify the location of each item.

SPECIFICATIONS

As mentioned previously, it is impractical for an architect to be able to contain all the information needed to complete a building project on a set of drawings, so usually a document known as a 'specification' is used in conjunction. A specification is a written document that includes essential information that cannot be contained on the architect's drawings; for example:

- material information (e.g. dimensions, shape);
- finishes and quality;
- fixing methods;
- removal of materials from site;
- details of services (e.g. water, gas, electricity, telephone);
- recommended specialist suppliers;
- etc.

SPECIFICATION

(Architect's Details)

Company name;

Address;

Telephone number;

Fax number;

Email;

Site Address:

Job No:

1.0)   INTERNAL PARTITION WALLS

Stud walls to comprise of 100 mm x 50 mm treated softwood studs built off 100 mm x 50 mm sole plate and complete with 100 mm x 50 mm head plate. Provide noggins mid height. Face both sides with 12.5 mm plasterboard, joints taped and skimmed to form a smooth, level finish. All partitions separating rooms to be filled with sound-deadening insulation quilt. All timber to be preserved and pressure treated.

2.0)   STAIRCASE

Oak risers and treads between floors. Total rise as indicated on the stair details comprising equal risers and treads (minimum going of 225 mm) at a max pitch of 42°. Construction to comprise ex 32 mm strings, ex 30 mm treads, ex 12 mm risers and 94 mm x 94 mm straight stop chamfered newels. Handrails to be 900 mm above the pitch line. 25 mm x 25 mm oak vertical balusters at 100 mm centres to balustrades and flights where necessary. Landing to be provided with 1100 mm high balustrade comprising 25 mm x 25 mm oak vertical balusters at 100 mm centres.

3.0)   ROOF CONSTRUCTION

For roof structure layout see layout drawings. Generally prefabricated trussed rafters at 600 mm centres, designed, manufactured and installed in accordance with BS.5268. Roof bracing to be carried out in accordance with BS.5268 Part 3: 1985 and truss manufacturer's recommendations with a 38° pitch.

4.0)   LINTELS

Lintels to suit the size of opening and engineer's recommendations with minimum 150 mm bearing on either end. Paint underside of steel lintels with white paint over min. 2 coats metal primer and rust inhibiter.

FIGURE 2.15 Example of a specification

ACTIVITIES

Activity 10 – Interpreting and producing building information

Read through the following questions and answer them as fully as you can to help you develop your underpinning knowledge of this subject area.

1. What is a 'specification'?

2. List three different types of architect's drawings.

3. Explain the term 'tendering'.

4. What document itemises all the materials, labour and parts required for a building project?

5. Explain the terms 'retention' and 'penalty clause'.

MANUFACTURERS' INFORMATION

Manufacturers' information is usually distributed through catalogues and the internet to builders and the general public. Material specifications and design are regularly developing and updated in the industry, so it is important to understand these changes as they happen. Suppliers usually have staff members that are technically competent with specific materials, and in some cases their knowledge and advice can prove useful, saving time and money.

METHODS USED TO ESTIMATE QUANTITIES OF MATERIALS

ESTIMATING QUANTITIES

Tradesmen/women will be expected to calculate the quantity and cost of materials and labour needed to complete certain aspects of their job. This may range from a painter and decorator needing to work out the amount of wallpaper to cover a dining room, to a site carpenter needing to estimate the total length of skirting boards required for several rooms. In general terms these quantities and many more can be calculated using the following basic methods of mathematics (see Figures 2.16–2.19):

- size;
- area;
- perimeter;
- volume;
- percentage.

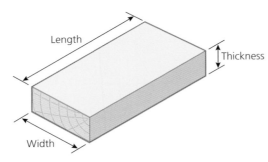

FIGURE 2.16 Size

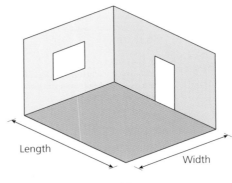

Length × Width = Area

FIGURE 2.17 Area

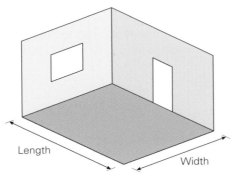

(2 × Length) + (2 × Width) = Perimeter

FIGURE 2.18 Perimeter

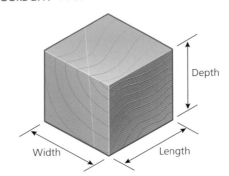

Length × Width × Depth = Volume

FIGURE 2.19 Volume

TRADE SECRETS

- Careful estimating of materials, plant, equipment and labour costs is essential to prevent over- or under-costing; for example, one decimal point in the wrong position on a tender could result in overestimating and losing the work. On the other hand, if the decimal point is in the wrong position in the opposite direction, this could result in underestimating, and monetary losses.
- It is common practice to add between 5 and 10 per cent on the quantity of timber-based materials to allow for saw cuts and waste materials when ordering.

Percentage %

Length of skirting | Answer equals 1% of the total length of skirting

625 ÷ 100 = 6.25 metres

Percentage of waste

1% of the total length of skirting | Total length of waste

6.25 × 5 = 31.25 metres

31.25 + 625 = 656.25 metres

Total length of waste | Total length of skirting required

Length of skirting

EXAMPLE

A carpenter requires 625 metres of skirting plus 5% for waste to complete a project. Prior to fixing the skirting the decorator needs to apply several coats of oil to seal the timber.

How many metres of skirting should the decorator oil?

FIGURE 2.20 Percentage

ACTIVITIES

Activity 11 – Estimating quantities of resources

Read through the following questions and answer them as fully as you can to help you develop your underpinning knowledge of this subject area.

A room measures 3.5 metres × 4.3 metres × 2.4 metres high.

1. Tongue and groove boards with a width of 140mm are required to cover the entire floor area. Calculate the quantity required.
2. Skirting boards are also needed. Calculate the quantity required.
3. Calculate an additional 5 per cent of skirting board for waste.
4. Calculate the volume of the room.

COMMUNICATING WORKPLACE REQUIREMENTS EFFICIENTLY

THE BUILDING TEAM

Throughout this book and while working in the construction industry you will often hear the term the 'building team' referred to. The building team is made up of all the key members of the design, planning and building stages of a project. The most important member of the team is the client, without whom the project would not be funded. Other members of the building team include those listed below.

ARCHITECT

The architect works closely with the client, the local authority and specialist engineers to design and plan buildings to the client's specifications. Once drawn, the plans are submitted with a planning application to the local planning office for 'planning permission'. Once planning permission has been obtained, the architect may then liaise with specialist engineers and manufacturers to design detailed drawings and a specification detailing the method of construction. These details are then submitted again to the local planning office to obtain 'Building Regulations approval'.

BUILDING CONTRACTOR

The main contractor is responsible for the day-to-day running and progress made on site. They are normally appointed by the client after submitting a tender for the intended works, and signing the contract documents. The building contractor regularly liaises with the architect and engineers to discuss issues encountered throughout the build.

BUILDING OPERATIVES

These are generally referred to as 'labourers' in the industry because of the range of work that they carry out. They usually support craft workers by lifting, moving and mixing a variety of building materials such as plaster and mortar. They may also dig trenches, lay paths, and operate machinery such as cement mixers, drills and pumps.

CHARGEHAND

These are general workers ranking just below the foreman with supervisory responsibilities on larger construction sites.

CLERK OF WORKS (COW)

The architect or client usually appoints this person as the client's representative on site. Their primary role is to ensure the quality of the materials used on the building work, and that the workmanship is in accordance with the specification and engineer's details.

CLIENT

The most important person involved in the building team, and usually the source of funding for the building works.

CRAFT FOREMAN

The craft foreman supervises skilled and unskilled labour on site, reporting to the general foreman. These types of foreman are normally very experienced and responsible only for their own craft workers.

CRAFT OPERATIVES/SKILLED WORKERS

The majority of the workforce on a construction site at any one time will be made up of skilled tradesmen/women. These workers have completed a period of several years' training to assess their competence as skilled workers before qualifying in their areas of expertise. Skilled workers are usually responsible to the trade foreman or the general foreman on smaller sites.

ESTIMATOR

Working directly for the main contractor, the estimator calculates the quantities of materials, plant and labour needed to complete a building project. They usually produce a list of these items on a document known as a 'bill of quantities' (see Figure 2.12). The bill of quantities may be sent to several subcontractors to complete the total cost for the building work.

FREQUENTLY ASKED QUESTIONS

▶ What does the term 'plant' mean?

The term 'plant' refers to the heavy machinery used during the construction process. Typical items of plant include:

- ▶ dumper;
- ▶ cement mixer;
- ▶ mini digger.

GANGER

This term is used for a person responsible for a group, or 'gang', of construction workers.

GENERAL FOREMAN

These operatives are responsible for coordinating a large team of construction workers, including the craft foremen and subcontractors. The general foreman reports directly to the site/general manager, and is partly responsible for hiring and firing of the labour on site.

FIGURE 2.21 Plant

HEALTH AND SAFETY INSPECTOR

The Health and Safety Inspector works for the Health and Safety Executive (HSE) to enforce the Health and Safety at Work Act 1974 (HASAWA). They may enter a site at any time throughout the building work to ensure that matters of health and safety are meeting with current laws and legislation. The Health and Safety Inspector has the right and power to:

- enter a premises without invitation;
- investigate the causes of incidents or accidents that have occurred on site;
- establish whether there has been a breach of health and safety law.

In addition to this, they can:

- take measurements, samples and photographs as evidence;
- record statements from employees;
- seize and make safe work equipment;
- dismantle or destroy dangerous machinery and equipment;
- inspect and copy documentation.

Any breaches of health and safety law can result in the following actions being taken by the Health and Safety Inspector:

- issue an *informal warning*, either written or verbally;
- issue an *improvement or prohibition notice* giving an employer the opportunity to rectify, change or destroy dangerous items of equipment or machinery or systems of work;
- *prosecute* companies or individuals responsible for endangering the lives of employees and the general public.

LOCAL AUTHORITY

The local authority is responsible for issuing planning consent and Building Regulations approval for a given project. At several stages throughout the building work a representative of the local authority, known as the 'building control officer', will visit the site to inspect the foundations and brickwork to damp-proof course level and wall plate level. Further visits will be made to the site by the building control officer as and when required. The purpose of each visit is to ensure that the building work is carried out as per the details submitted for approval at the planning stage. Any substandard work must be taken down and rebuilt to satisfy the building control officer and current Building Regulations.

QUANTITY SURVEYOR

The quantity surveyor works closely with the client to manage and control costs resulting from building work. S/he is also normally involved in the production of the bill of quantities and the appointment of the main building contractor.

SITE AGENT

The site agent, also known as the site manager, is appointed by the main contractor to manage the day-to-day running of a building project. S/he is also responsible for ensuring the health and safety of all site workers, general appointment of subcontractors and maintaining strict quality control. Site agents will also produce a programme of work to ensure the building project is completed within the terms of the contract agreement.

SPECIALIST ENGINEERS

These professionals will work alongside the architect to develop the plans and structural calculations needed for specialised non-conventional building work. Engineers may visit the site from time to time to ensure that any specially designed metalwork etc. is being installed as it was intended.

SUBCONTRACTORS

Subcontractors are commonly appointed by the main contractor to undertake part of the building work. In many cases, subcontractors are used by larger companies to reduce the risk of

FIGURE 2.22 A steel structure designed by a specialist engineer

employing full-time staff for the duration of a construction project. The danger of employing skilled labour is the potential for the specialised work to dry up, resulting in the employer having to pay wages to tradesmen and tradeswomen without using them to their full potential.

SUPPLIERS

Suppliers play a vital role in the construction process. Ensuring that materials, equipment and plant are available at the right time to purchase and hire requires good communication with the site manager/buyer. Phasing deliveries to site prevents materials being stored on site for long periods of time, taking up valuable space and becoming potential obstructions.

METHODS OF COMMUNICATION IN THE WORKPLACE

VERBAL COMMUNICATION

Verbal communication is probably the most widely used method of passing information and instruction from one person to another on a building site. Although this method of communicating is fast, enabling the workforce to react quickly, it is often misunderstood and misinterpreted. Communication between members of the management team is usually conducted through drawings, letters, memos, emails and 'minutes' of meetings that have taken place. These methods of passing information between members of the building team provide documented material that can be referred back to at a later date. This is especially important if disputes occur either throughout the build or upon completion.

 FREQUENTLY ASKED QUESTIONS

▶ **What does the term 'minutes' mean?**

'Minutes' are a written overview of a meeting. They are usually recorded by an administrator as a meeting progresses, accounting for the people present and those absent. Generally the structure and topics to discuss are written on an 'agenda' before the meeting takes place. Any responses to each item discussed are then recorded and written up logically after the meeting has finished – these are known as the 'minutes'. Copies of the minutes are sent to those who were present and absent from the meeting, for their records.

FORMAL BUSINESS LETTERS

These are used regularly to communicate information between members of the building team. Letters should be written in a clear, legible format and contain all the information required without being longer than necessary. The following guidelines are generally used to create business letters (see also the example in Figure 2.23).

- Addresses – the name and address of the person, company or organisation sending the letter should be written in the top right-hand corner of the page. The receiver's details are usually written on the left-hand side, just below the ending point of the other address.
- Date – this is written on the line below the last line of the address on either the right- or left-hand side.
- Greeting – 'Dear Sir or Madam' is used if you are unsure of the person you are sending the letter to, or alternatively 'Dear Mr (Mrs, Miss, Ms, Dr, etc.) Jones' if you know the title of the person. Never introduce a formal letter with the person's full name.
- Content of letter – the first paragraph usually explains the purpose of the letter, before leading on to the main text containing the relevant information. The final paragraph should explain the action required (if any) from the recipient.
- Ending – if you introduced the letter with 'Dear Sir or Madam' you should finish it with 'Yours faithfully'; if you started with the person's name, you should finish it with 'Yours sincerely'. Complete the letter with your signature and printed name underneath.

Large companies usually have an administrator to write the details of a dictated letter in shorthand before writing it up fully and signing it on behalf of the sender. This type of ending is normally identified with the initials 'PP' either before or after the signature. Some other common abbreviations found on formal letters are listed below:

- ASAP – as soon as possible;
- CC – carbon copy; this lets the receiver know that the letter has been duplicated and sent to more than one person;
- ENC – enclosure; this references documents contained within the letter;
- PP – per procurationem; this is Latin to explain that a letter or document as been signed on behalf of somebody else;
- PTO – please turn over;
- RSVP – répondez s'il vous plaît; this is a French phrase that translates to 'reply, please'.

FAX (SHORT FOR FACSIMILE)

Faxes are used regularly on small and large construction sites because the system is simple to set up and use with a telephone point. Messages, pictures and sketches can be sent and received on site very quickly with a fax machine; the disadvantage is that the images are in black and white. Any messages received will have the time and date recorded on the top or bottom of the fax page, along with the number of pages and the telephone number of the sender. Outgoing faxes will be recorded with a receipt printed off after a successful transfer has taken place.

EMAILS

Emails are normally processed through the computers in the site manager's office. They are advantageous because correspondence is clear, easily stored and accessible, which prevents the need for various unnecessary paper-based or 'hard' copies on site. Digital photographs

Mrs Architect
35 North Road
Bristol
BS12 7KT

Mr and Mrs Client
164 Lodge Avenue
Cardiff
CF24 8QR

16 February 2009

Dear Mr and Mrs Client

Ref: Development at 37 Sea View Heights, Little Town

Many thanks for your recent instruction regarding the changes to the design brief for the staircase position at Sea View Heights. I have made the appropriate alterations to the initial drawings, and have the pleasure of providing the revised layout of the proposed development. Please let me have your comments as soon as conviently possible so that we can submit a full planning application.

I look forward to your comments.

Yours faithfully

Mrs Architect

FIGURE 2.23 Formal business letter

FIGURE 2.24 Communication by Fax

FIGURE 2.25 Communication by Email

may also be taken on site of defects or progress made, and quickly uploaded onto a computer, before sending as attachments via email. The disadvantages of this method are that sketched images are difficult and slower to send through a computer system, and smaller sites may not have an internet connection.

TELEPHONE

Generally, telephones, fax machines and answer phones are combined units to save valuable space on site. Other similar methods of communicating via a phone include:

- two-way radios – used to transmit messages quickly between personnel on site, over short distances;
- mobile phones – used as an alternative to the two-way radios on site, with the advantage of being able to communicate verbally or with the use of text messages if the person leaves the site.

MEMORANDUM (MEMO)

Memos are used to record and pass information between operatives internally on construction sites. They normally contain only brief messages recorded by the site administrator from telephone calls or from notes passed between site workers about general information. A memo should be recorded on headed paper with the following information:

Telephone message
Date: Time:
Message for:
From:
Tel:
Message:
Message taken by:

FIGURE 2.26 Memorandum

- name of person recording the message;
- name of the intended recipient/receiver;
- date and time the message was recorded;
- the message.

POSTERS

Information contained on site message boards, posters and signs displayed around a construction site are all sources of important written instructions. Generally, site information is displayed at the entrance to the site to inform new personnel entering the area, in the site manager's office/hutment (hut) and in communal areas such as the site canteen. Displaying posters is a simple method of communicating best practice, as well as the dos and don'ts while on or around the site.

FIGURE 2.27 An information board

TIME SHEETS

Employees complete time sheets on a daily basis, logging the hours worked on each task while on a project (see Figure 2.28). The time sheets are normally completed for a whole week before employees and their line managers sign and date them before submitting to the site administrator. The information contained on the time sheets is usually input onto a computer database to monitor the progress made by the employees, and also account for expenditure and wages. They may also be referred to in the future to analyse the time taken on a particular project, and to plan upcoming programmes of work and contracts.

DAYWORK SHEETS

These documents (e.g. Figure 2.29) are normally completed by subcontractors to account for work completed on site that has not been estimated prior to starting; for example, additions or variations to the original contract details or specification.

RDJ contractors
Weekly Time Sheet

35 North Road
Bristol
BS12 7KT

Employee _Peter Smith_

For period _06/04/09 to 10/04/09_

Job name _Drysdale Avenue_

Date	Work carried out	Total hours
06/04/09	Brickwork to first floor	8
07/04/09	Brickwork to first floor	8
08/04/09	Roof structure	8
09/04/09	Roof structure	8
10/04/09	Roof tiles	8

Signature _____

Standard hours _____

Job overtime _____

Total _____

FIGURE 2.28 Time sheet

SITE DIARY

Entries into the site diary may be made several times throughout a day by the site manager to record the activities on site. The information contained in the site diary is normally duplicated and forwarded to the head office, and may also be used as evidence in the case of disputes between the main contractor, subcontractors, suppliers, etc. A typical site diary would include the following details:

- date and time of entry;
- adverse weather conditions;
- site visitors;
- delays/stoppages;
- late starts or subcontractors not attending the site;
- telephone/fax messages.

ORDERS/REQUISITIONS

Larger companies usually employ a 'buyer' who is responsible for sourcing and purchasing materials, equipment and plant for a construction project. The buyer would normally go through a process of sourcing the items through several companies to establish the most competitive quotes/prices, before completing a purchase order. Every purchase made should be documented on a form known as a 'requisition'.

RDJ contractors
Daywork Sheet

35 North Road
Bristol
BS12 7KT

Sheet no. _35/08_

For period _06/04/09 to 10/04/09_

Job name _Drysdale Avenue_

Work carried out
Second fixing to plot 8

Labour	Name	Craft	Hours	Gross rate	Total	
35/08	P. Smith	C & J	3	£25	£75	00
				Total labour	£75	00

Materials		Quantity	Rate	% Addition		
New door		1	£80	20	£100	00
				Total materials	£100	00

Plant		Hours	Rate	% Addition		
				Total plant	00	00

Note Gross labour rates include a percentage for overheads and profit as set out in the contract conditions	Sub total	£175	00
	VAT (where applicable) _N/A_ %	—	—
	Total claim	£175	00

Site manager/foreman _____
Architect _____

FIGURE 2.29 Daywork sheet

DELIVERY NOTES/RECORDS

Phased deliveries are normally made to a site at various times throughout the construction of a building. Upon the delivery of materials the driver will present a 'delivery note' containing the following details:

- items delivered;
- quantity of the goods;
- delivery address;
- company address;
- the date delivered.

Some suppliers and couriers prefer not use paper-based documentation for deliveries, and use electronic handheld notebooks instead. These are simply operated by the driver entering the delivery address into the notebook to bring up details of the order prior to the receiver signing the digital screen.

FIGURE 2.30 Hand-held electronic delivery notebook

Only authorised personnel should sign for deliveries on site after carrying out the following checks.

1. Check the delivery address on the delivery note to ensure that the correct goods are being delivered to the correct site.
2. Check the delivery against the original requisition (order).
3. Check the quantity. Large quantities of goods can often be overlooked if some items are missing.
4. Check the quality. Any damaged goods should either be sent back to the supplier or accepted with a comment made on the delivery note with a signature from the delivery driver as a witness.
5. Check the delivery has been made on the correct day. Phased deliveries to site prevent unnecessary storage for long periods of time.

SAFETY SIGNS

There are numerous amounts of different types of signage used in the workplace to convey information and instruction quickly and clearly. The Health and Safety (Safety Signs and Signals) Regulations 1996 place a legal responsibility on employers to display and maintain signs wherever there is a significant risk. British Standards BS5378: Parts 1 and 3: 1980 Safety Signs and Colours, has standardised the use of signs in the workplace so that they are interpreted in the same way, and have the same meaning. New members of staff that are unfamiliar with the safety signs used should have them explained as part of their induction.

Safety signs are usually identified by:

- shape;
- colour;
- pictograms;
- written information.

Safety signs fall into six different categories.

FIGURE 2.31 Prohibition sign

1. Prohibition – identified by a round, red and white sign, together with a pictogram in the middle, they mean you 'must *not* do'. For example, a sign with a picture of a mobile phone in the centre would mean 'you must *not* use a mobile phone'.
2. Mandatory – identified with a white pictogram on a blue background, they mean 'you *must* do'. For example, a sign with a picture of a pair of boots would mean 'safety footwear *must* be worn'.

FIGURE 2.32 Mandatory sign

FIGURE 2.33 Warning sign

3. Warning – identified with a black pictogram on a yellow background, they indicate a 'warning'. For example, a sign with a skull and crossbones would 'warn of toxic material'.

4. Safe conditions – identified with a white pictogram and text on a green background, they indicate 'safe conditions' or route. For example, a sign with a running stick man, an arrow and 'Fire exit' written, would indicate 'the direction of the emergency escape route'.

FIGURE 2.34 Safe conditions sign

5. Information – identified with text on a white background, they provide written information and instruction (e.g. Figure 2.35).

6. Fire fighting – identified with white text on a red background, they display the position of 'fire fighting equipment' – for example, fire blankets, fire extinguishers.

FIGURE 2.35 Information

FIGURE 2.36 Fire fighting

SITE MEETINGS

Every year the construction industry repairs and rectifies billions of pounds worth of defects, some of which are the result of poor communication, poor detailed drawings, incorrect and delayed information. Many of these problems could have been avoided if good management systems were in place to ensure effective lines of communication between the client, main contractor, subcontractors, etc.

General site meetings offer a very effective method of communicating between members of the building team. They are normally held regularly to freely discuss problems arising (and possible solutions) and to update/inform the client of progress made with the project.

There are several different types of meetings that will occur on site throughout the duration of a building project; these may include the following.

- 'General site meetings' are normally well structured and involve the client, main contractor, architect, structural engineer and the subcontractors. These meetings are normally held on site at regular intervals to discuss progress made, problems or issues that have arisen, and changes to the specification, drawings or contract documentation.
- 'Domestic site meetings' are held weekly between the main contractor, employees and subcontractors to discuss general issues, delays and the programme of work.
- 'Informal meetings' are often arranged at short notice to resolve problems arising as the build progresses. These types of meetings are unofficial and are usually conducted without a 'chairperson' or an agenda. The disadvantages of informal meetings are that they are not recorded and often result in misinterpreted information, mistakes and conflict between site personnel.

FREQUENTLY ASKED QUESTIONS

▶ What does a 'chairperson' do?

A 'chairperson' is the head of a meeting or committee. They are responsible for:

▶ arranging the date, start and finish times for the meeting;

▶ writing and distributing a programme for discussion, known as the 'agenda', to personnel invited to attend the meeting;

▶ appointing a person to record the points of discussion throughout the meeting; These are commonly referred to as the 'minutes';

▶ distributing a copy of the minutes to members that did not attend;

▶ making sure that the agenda of the meeting is followed in a controlled and orderly fashion.

STRUCTURED SITE MEETINGS

Well-planned meetings generally follow a similar structure, with specific points for discussion pre-planned and recorded on an 'agenda'. The agenda lists points for discussion and the order they will be addressed throughout the meeting. A typical agenda is structured as shown in the example that follows.

FIGURE 2.37 A site meeting

Agenda

1. *Members present* – names of the people actually attending the meeting.
2. *Apologies* – names of the people invited to the meeting but unable to attend. Minutes recorded at the meeting should be forwarded to these individuals to ensure they are kept up to date with the issues discussed.
3. *Matters arising from the previous meeting* – a copy of the minutes from the previous meeting should be available to review any action points previously raised and whether further action is required to resolve the issue.
4. *Discussion points* – several points or areas for discussion will be highlighted by the chairperson prior to the start of the meeting. Copies of the agenda will be circulated before the meeting to allow the client, architect, contractors, etc. to prepare for the areas for discussion and prevent the meeting overrunning its intended completion time.
5. *Actions* – discussion points at meetings usually raise issues to be resolved and therefore actions for individuals. These action points are usually agreed between the parties involved at the meeting and a deadline set for the points to be met; the actions are then reviewed at the next site meeting.
6. *Date for the next meeting* – dates are usually agreed at the end of a site meeting to ensure everybody is available.
7. *Any other business (AOB)* – usually members of the meeting are given the opportunity to raise and discuss any issues that are not on the agenda.

 ACTIVITIES

Activity 12 – Communicating workplace requirements efficiently

Read through the following questions and answer them as fully as you can to help you develop your underpinning knowledge of this subject area.

1. List five members of the 'building team'.
2. What is the role of the 'clerk of works'?
3. What is an 'improvement notice'?
4. List two advantages of communicating via a fax machine.
5. Explain the purpose of a site diary.

MULTIPLE-CHOICE QUESTIONS

1   Who would act as the architect's representative on site?
   a   Client
   b   Clerk of works
   c   Quantity surveyor
   d   Building control officer

2   The document referred to for supplementary information, such as the species of timber required, is the
   a   invoice
   b   site diary
   c   text book
   d   specification

3   The document which lists timber quantities and sizes used in the joinery machine shop is called a
   a   invoice
   b   cutting list
   c   working rod
   d   specification

4   Fourteen treads are required at 915mm in length, to be cut from oak boards 2.7m long. How many boards need to be ordered to complete this order?
   a   5
   b   6
   c   7
   d   8

5   Which **one** of the following scales would a workshop rod be drawn to?
   a   1:1
   b   1:2
   c   1:5
   d   1:10

6   **Over** estimating the quantity of materials required will
   a   increase work for the buyer
   b   decrease work for the buyer
   c   decrease the profit the contract will make
   d   increase the profit the contract will make

7   A joiner would record how long it has taken to assemble 14 door frames for a contract, on a

a   schedule

b   timesheet

c   workshop diary

d   estimate sheet

8   A 2m radius would be struck using a

a   compass

b   trammel

c   pair of dividers

d   scale of chords

9   Which part of the Building Regulations would be consulted prior to constructing a flight of stairs?

a   H

b   J

c   K

d   L

10 The type of paint required to prime casement windows prior to leaving the joinery shop would be found in the

a   schedule

b   specification

c   bill of quantities

d   drawing title box

BUILDING METHODS AND CONSTRUCTION TECHNOLOGY 2

CHAPTER 3

LEARNING OUTCOMES

By the end of this chapter you should have developed a knowledge and understanding of:

- the principles behind walls, floors and roofs;
- the principles behind internal work;
- materials storage and delivery of building materials.

INTRODUCTION

The aim of this chapter is for students to be able to recognise traditional and modern construction methods, and the principles behind them. It also looks at the some of the most common materials used in the industry, their methods of delivery and storage facilities. In addition, this chapter identifies and explains current Building Regulations applicable to this area of study, following all the relevant health and safety law and good working practices.

THE PRINCIPLES BEHIND WALLS, FLOORS AND ROOFS

The earliest stages of planning a building or structure usually begin with an idea and a brief; this is known as the 'conceptual design' stage. Clients will normally approach an architect to discuss their initial thoughts before developing the vision through to the 'preliminary design'. Architects will work closely with structural or civil engineers to ensure that the proposed designs will stand up to the forces and loads imposed upon them before the 'final design'. At this stage, the working drawings and structural calculations are normally submitted to the local authority for approval.

Buildings and structures are shaped by their design and construction methods because of the environment in which they exist. For example, a plot may sit in a historic village with listed buildings. The possibility of a high-rise concrete office block being granted planning permission would be slim. Good design ideas should to be sympathetic to the surrounding area and have as little impact on the environment as possible, while still meeting the needs of the client.

Developments in materials and construction methods have led to various types of structure being developed across the country, each one suited to demands of the location, local planning laws and Building Regulations.

TYPES OF BUILDING STRUCTURE

Building structures are usually designed with a combination of different building materials in order to perform the following functions:

- allow natural light and ventilation;
- allow people to work, live and play in them safely without risk;
- design (synthetic);
- provide security for the occupants and the materials contained within them;
- provide shelter;
- provide warmth.

Both residential (e.g. private dwelling) and non-residential (e.g. offices, shops) buildings are recognisable by the number of floors (known as 'storeys') over which they are constructed. Building structures can be divided into three categories:

1. high-rise (over seven storeys);
2. mid-rise (four to seven storeys);
3. low-rise (one to three storeys).

Note: low-rise buildings are further categorised into detached, semi-detached and terraced dwellings.

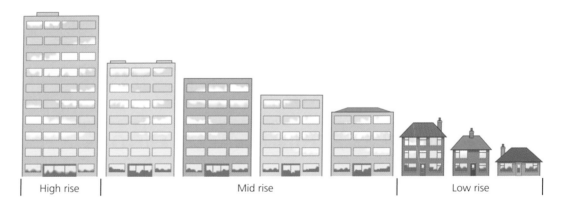

| High rise | Mid rise | Low rise |

FIGURE 3.1 Types of building structure

SUBSTRUCTURE AND SUPERSTRUCTURE

The weight of any building or structure must be fully supported at ground level with adequately designed and calculated foundations. Elements of a structure below damp-proof course (DPC), including the ground floor and foundations, are known as the 'substructure'. All the internal and external elements of a building above the substructure are referred to as the 'superstructure'. The components of the superstructure will distribute the weight (loads) of the building safely through the roof, walls and floors to the substructure (see Figure 3.4).

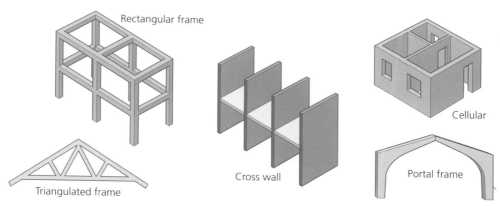

FIGURE 3.2 Elements of the superstructure

SOLID WALLS (WITHOUT CAVITY)

These are a fast, efficient method of building external walls. They have high 'U' values (thermal insulation), with the ability to retain heat in the winter months and keep the building cool during warmer periods. There are several methods commonly used to finish the surfaces on solid walls; these include:

- brick 'slip' systems;
- ceramic wall tiles;
- render;
- tile hanging;
- timber cladding.

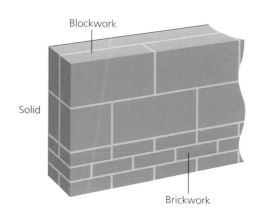

FIGURE 3.3 Solid wall

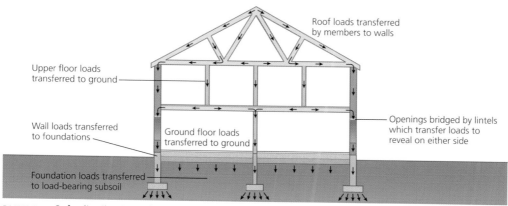

FIGURE 3.4 Safe distribution of loads via the superstructure

FREQUENTLY ASKED QUESTIONS

▶ What is a brick 'slip' system?

'Slips' are thin sections of bricks that are bonded to the plain surfaces of solid walls to give the appearance of being brick built. A 10 mm gap should still be maintained between the slips and filled with mortar with an application gun.

CAVITY WALLS

Walls consist of an inner and outer wall divided by a void, known as the 'cavity'. The walls are usually constructed with bricks and blocks, or two skins of blocks with render applied, or another method of wall covering. The masonry bricks and blocks used are usually porous, which will allow the water to penetrate through the walls only to the point of the cavity. The water or moisture then runs down the inside of the cavity and disperses at ground level through 'weep holes'. Cavity walls provide very good sound and thermal insulation when lined with cavity wall insulation. Independent single-skin walls may become unstable when they are built over one storey high. To improve the stability of double-skin walls they are connected to each other via non-corrosive 'cavity wall ties'. These are simply built into the brickwork courses between the two walls as the building progresses. Most wall ties are fitted with a plastic collar that allows the cavity wall insulation to be held tight against the inner wall, therefore preventing 'bridging'.

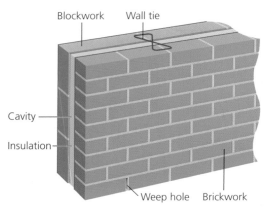

FIGURE 3.5 Cavity wall construction

FREQUENTLY ASKED QUESTIONS

▶ **What does the term 'bridging' mean?**

'Bridging' is a term given to moisture or water penetrating external walls across the void in a cavity to the inner skin. Bridging across a cavity wall will cause damp patches to appear on the inner walls.

TIMBER FRAME

Houses were traditionally built with heavy structural sections to form a skeleton frame, and the frames were then in-filled with bricks to complete the 'shell'. Modern timber frame buildings are normally constructed with timber internal frames clad with plywood to add strength, and a single skin of external brick or blockwork supported with 'wall ties'. Alternatively, the depth of the timber frames can be increased to the full thickness of the wall, and the building can be constructed without the need for brickwork above damp-proof course level. In all cases a suitable moisture and vapour barrier must be included to prevent the ingress of water and the onset of rot in the timber frames, as well as thermal and sound insulation to ensure current Building Regulations are met.

FREQUENTLY ASKED QUESTIONS

▶ What is a 'moisture barrier'?

Modern moisture barriers are paper-thin building materials, usually attached to the face of timber frame walls, or underneath the roof covering between the wall plate and ridge. They are used to ensure that the building remains dry by preventing water penetrating the exterior walls and roof. Moisture barriers also allow the building to 'breathe', by allowing stale moist air within the building to escape.

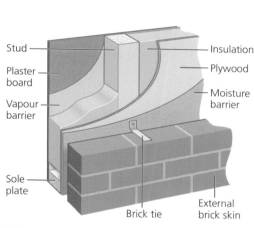

FIGURE 3.6

FIGURE 3.7

MODERN INSULATION MATERIALS

The early 1970s saw the development of a new idea of constructing buildings using 'structural insulated panels', or SIPs for short. The panels are a sandwich of two layers of oriented strand board (OSB) either side of a thick polyurethane foam core. The bond between all the materials results in extremely rigid panels, capable of supporting structural loads. SIPs are commonly used to construct whole buildings from the external walls and floors, up to the roof structure. Large SIPs require heavy lifting equipment to manoeuvre them into position on the building before they interlock with the other panels. There are several advantages of this method of construction; these include:

- speed of erection;
- no need for timber studs;
- no need for further insulation;
- no need for a vapour or air barrier.

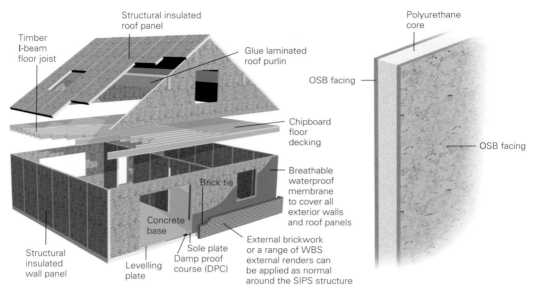

FIGURE 3.8 Modern insulation materials

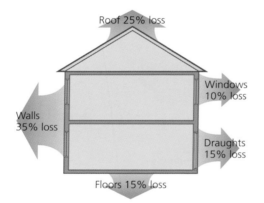

FIGURE 3.9 Energy loss

BUILDING METHODS

Structural and civil engineers are responsible for ensuring that the buildings and structures that they design in partnership with the architect are capable of withstanding the loads and stresses imposed on them.

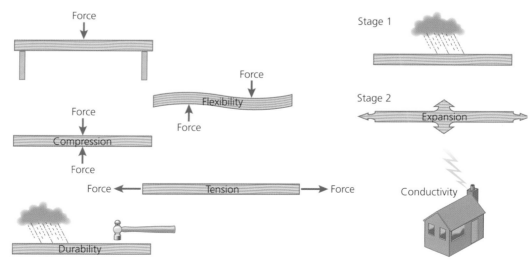

FIGURE 3.10 Loads and stress

SETTING OUT OF FOUNDATIONS AND WALLS

IDENTIFYING DIFFERENT TYPES OF CONCRETE FOUNDATION

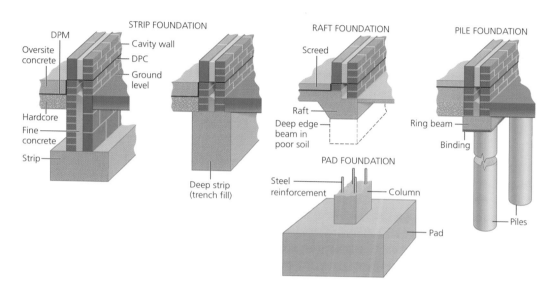

FIGURE 3.11 Different types of concrete foundation

There are several different types of concrete foundation commonly used in the construction industry. Each one is specifically engineered to support the dead load of the building, the type of soil in the ground and any other forces imposed upon the building. Strip foundations are designed to suit firm, stable ground conditions and are probably the most commonly used in the United Kingdom. Sites with soft ground or possibly on a hillside may require deep pile foundations to maintain stability.

SITE INVESTIGATION

A thorough investigation of a site will have to be carried out before any land can be built on, and the most suitable type of foundation can be determined. A surveyor would normally research the following areas before submitting a detailed report with recommendations to a structural engineer:

- previous use (brownfield site);
- contaminated land;
- mines or wells;
- type of soil;
- water levels in the ground;
- radon gas

▶ **What is 'radon' gas?**

'Radon' is a naturally occurring gas that develops in some ground conditions, particularly in the Cornish area of the UK. Exposure to high levels of the odourless gas can be a health hazard that can potentially lead to lung cancer.

FLOOR CONSTRUCTION

The method of construction for a floor in a building is normally determined by its position (lower or upper), the type of soil, site conditions (flat/elevated) and the displacement of the load/weight. Weak or unsuitable foundations and floors may lead to movement in the ground and potentially cause subsidence or cracking.

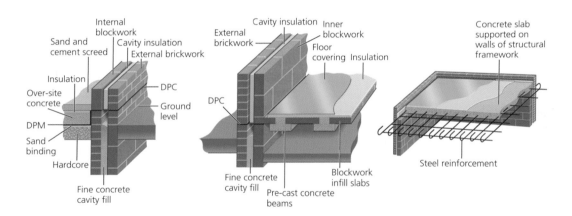

FIGURE 3.12 Methods of floor construction

HOLLOW TIMBER FLOORS

This method of floor construction is covered in detail in Chapter 6, Erect Structural Carcassing.

SCREED

Solid concrete, and beam and block floors are usually slightly uneven and unsuitable to accept a floor covering such as carpet. A screed is laid over the floor surface area and levelled manually with a long float, straight edge and spirit level. It consists of a semi-dry concrete mix of sharp sand and cement, usually containing an additive to slow down the drying time, therefore increasing the working time with the product.

DAMP-PROOF COURSE (DPC)

A DPC is normally built into the exterior brick and blockwork walls at least 150 mm above the exterior ground level. Its purpose is to provide a barrier to prevent moisture creeping up from the ground through the walls.

DAMP-PROOF MEMBRANE (DPM)

A DPM is normally built into the entire ground floor area of solid concrete floors. It is used to prevent moisture, damp and weed growth through the floors and lower portions of the internal walls.

ACTIVITIES

Activity 13 – The principles behind walls, floors and roofs

Read through the following questions and answer them as fully as you can to help you develop your underpinning knowledge of this subject area.

1. Sketch a section of a cavity wall and timber frame wall.

2. What do the initials DPC stand for?

3. Explain the purpose of a DPM.

4. Sketch a joist to demonstrate compression and tension.

5. Name one modern insulation material.

PRINCIPLES BEHIND INTERNAL WORK

PAINT COVERINGS

Internal walls are usually either lined with wallpaper or painted with water-based emulsion. Water-based paints are easily applied to walls and ceilings manually with a wide brush or deep pile roller. Working at height can be avoided in many cases when decorating high walls and ceilings if an extension pole is connected to the end of a roller. The disadvantage of applying paint with a roller or brush is the uneven results it produces. Many contractors now prefer to paint large surface areas with a spray system to achieve an even, smooth and flawless finish. All windows, mouldings and doors, etc. should be covered with masking tape and paper to prevent over-spraying and soiling. The time needed to prepare rooms for spraying is normally outweighed by the speed at which the non-toxic paint can be applied. Durable paints such as oil-based paints are usually applied with a brush and should not be applied with a spray system on site because of the risks the airborne paint can have to health.

BUILDING MATERIALS

AGGREGATES

Aggregates is a term used to describe different-sized crushed stone and minerals (e.g. fine sand, coarse sand, chippings). These materials are commonly used in the building industry to construct foundations, floors, beams and walls.

PLASTER

- **Lime plaster** – Lime plaster can be found on the internal, non-load-bearing walls of older buildings where it was used in conjunction with timber 'laths' to cover the surface of hollow walls. Laths are strips of 25 × 6 mm timber nailed horizontally across timber stud walls, with a gap of approximately 6 mm left in between. Plasterboard was not developed until the middle of the twentieth century so this method of 'lath and plaster' was the norm instead. The lime plaster was usually mixed with animal hair to improve its strength. Lime plaster is softer than modern gypsum products but can be 'worked' for longer periods of time before setting. The disadvantage of lime plaster is the extremely long periods of time needed between coats to allow it to dry fully; in some cases this could be up to 3–4 weeks. Lime plaster is sometimes used to construct new environmentally friendly buildings because it is a natural mineral mined from the ground.
- **Gypsum** – Gypsum is a natural product mined underground. It has been used in the construction industry since the nineteenth century, when it was added to lime-based plaster to reduce the setting times between coats. Gypsum has good hardening qualities that make it naturally resistant to fire and heat. It is now commonly used in plasterboard and as a replacement to lime traditionally used in plaster because of its quick drying times.
- **Browning and bonding** – Modern plaster is normally applied to walls and ceilings in two stages; these are render layer and finishing layer or 'skim'. Browning and bonding are normally grey or pink types of plaster, suitable for the first render layer; these are known as the 'backing' plasters. Bonding coats of plaster are required over absorbent surfaces such as brick or block walls to prepare them to take the thin layer of finishing plaster (skim). Applying the render between 9 and 12 mm thick to large areas requires a lot of practice and skill to achieve a flat surface.
- **Finishing plaster** – Finishing plaster can be applied over browning or bonding, or directly onto plasterboard. It is usually spread approximately 2 mm thick over the surface area; any thicker than this may result in cracking as it dries. When the plaster starts to dry it should be 'polished' with a float to complete a shiny surface ready to decorate.
- **Multi-finish plaster** – This is a finish plaster that can be applied to a range of backgrounds, including stone.
- **One-coat plaster** – One-coat plaster is an ideal product for 'patching' or repairing damaged walls. This type of plaster prevents the need to build up the thickness of the wall with several coats, thus speeding up completion times.

PLASTERBOARD

Before the 1940s, all hollow partition walls would have been covered in 6 mm thick lengths of timber (known as 'laths'), with 5–6 mm gaps in between, as a foundation to allow plaster to be applied. This method of cladding a partition wall is known as 'lath and plaster'. This method is rarely used now, but can be found in older buildings or used in restoration work.

Plasterboard is made from a gypsum core with lining paper on either side, and has been developed since the 1940s to replace the old method of lath and plaster. Its large sheet sizes make it quicker to cover the partition walls, and the flat surface reduces the labour time needed by the plasterer or dry liner. Plasterboard is available in thicknesses ranging between 9.5 and 12.5 mm through to 19 mm, and is manufactured in a variety of lengths and widths; some of these are listed below:

- 900 × 1800 mm;
- 1200 × 2400 mm;
- 1200 × 2700 mm;
- 1200 × 3000 mm.

Plasterboard is also available with square edges along all the sides; this is usually used for walls that require a skim coat of board finish plastering. The skim coat of plaster creates a seamless finish over the entire wall surface, masking the joints between the boards in preparation for a decorative finish to be applied. Plasterboard is also available with tapered edges manufactured on the two longest sides of the boards. After the sheets are installed, the joints between the tapered edges of the boards and the nail/screw fixing positions are then taped and filled with 'dry lining joint filler'. Once the filler has dried it is usually sanded flat, and then further layers of filler are applied until a perfectly flat surface is achieved. This method of wall boarding is known as 'dry lining'. Dry lining applied to partition walls avoids the need to plaster the whole surface.

Some of the types of plasterboard are listed below:

- Fire resistant (pink coloured core);
- Sound resistant;
- Thermal resistant;
- Vapour resistant/moisture resistant (green coloured core);
- Impact resistant (for use in hospitals, colleges, etc.)
- Flexible board (used on walls with internal and external curves).

CONCRETE

Concrete is a mixture of fine and coarse aggregate, water and cement, mixed to specified ratios to make an extremely strong material once cured. Pre-cast structural beams and lintels are formed with high-tensile steel reinforcing bars running through just above their lower face to increase their tensile strength and prevent cracking under load. Solid floors are also strengthened using similar methods, only this time the steel bars are bound together to make a web over the entire area before it is submerged under concrete.

METALS

Metals are commonly used in framed substructures of industrial buildings, offices and warehouses. The preformed metal sections are bolted and welded together in situ for the speedy erection of a building. This then allows the inner walls to be built in between the rigid 'skeleton' frame in preparation for the external covering. Steel joists are also commonly used in the industry to span long distances between walls to provide adequate support for shorter timber joists. They may also be used as lintels over doorways or window openings to support the imposed loads from the brick or blockwork above.

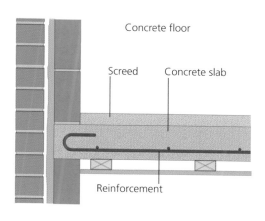

FIGURE 3.13 Concrete floor

SOFTWOOD AND HARDWOOD

These resources have been used to construct buildings for thousands of years because wood is a renewable building material and readily available. Timber-framed buildings have been commonly used to construct modern homes in the USA and Europe for many years. In recent years the building industry has grown in confidence with the resource and many companies and clients are experiencing the benefits. These include:

- increased productivity and speed of erection (example: a standard two-storey detached property frame can be erected and made watertight within five days);
- less disruption to the client;
- reduced building costs;
- less environmental impact.

GLASS

Information regarding different types of safety glass, single and double glazing, and installing glass are detailed in Chapter 4, First Fixing.

BRICKS AND BLOCKS

THERMAL BLOCKS

Thermal blocks are commonly used to construct the internal walls of offices, factories and houses. They are considerably lighter than conventional building blocks and easily cut with a handsaw, providing an efficient method of constructing partition walls. The exceptional thermal properties of the blocks mean that less insulation is required in the building. Although the blocks are lightweight, they can still be used to provide structural strength to a building. (*Note*: the exact load-bearing capacity for a wall constructed with thermal blocks should be obtained from a structural engineer.)

TRADE SECRETS

Remember — the difference between softwood and hardwood is not the strength of the timber. Timbers are categorised by their cellular structure, characteristics and species:

- *softwood trees have narrow needle leaves (coniferous);*
- *hardwood trees have broad leaves that usually drop in the autumn and winter months (deciduous).*

COMMON BRICKS

Common bricks are available in a vast range of different materials, colours and finishes to match existing brickwork or construct new. They are generally used only to build walls and columns if they are exposed because of the increased labour and material costs compared with other building resources. Careful consideration should be given to the type of bricks used in a given situation because some bricks are less dense and more porous than others, and will also be able to support heavier imposed loads.

CONCRETE BLOCKS

Concrete blocks are relatively inexpensive compared with facing bricks and thermal blocks, hence the reason they are commonly used in the construction industry to build the internal skins of cavity walls, etc. Concrete blocks are available in a range of different densities to suit the weight imposed upon them. A standard concrete block measures $440 \times 210 \times 100$ mm excluding the mortar joints.

ENGINEERING BRICKS

Engineering bricks are normally used to construct load-bearing columns and brickwork below damp-proof course (DPC) level because their superior strength and density make them resistant to frost attack. All engineering bricks should comply with British Standards before being used structurally. Both engineering and common bricks are manufactured in standard dimensions of $215 \times 102 \times 65$ mm, although more expensive handmade and recycled bricks may vary slightly.

ACTIVITIES

Activity 14 – The principles behind internal work

Read through the following questions and answer them as fully as you can to help you develop your underpinning knowledge of this subject area.

1. List three methods of applying paint finishes.

2. Describe the difference between concrete and thermal blocks.

3. Describe the difference between facing and engineering bricks.

MATERIAL STORAGE

ORDERING PLANT, EQUIPMENT AND MATERIALS

As materials, plant and equipment are required at different stages throughout a building project, the site manager or company buyer will refer to a 'programme of work' (programmes of work are covered in more detail in Chapter 2, Information, Quantities and Communicating with Others 2). Programmes of work are documents containing essential information about building projects, and include the following details:

- start and expected completion dates;
- periods of time each trade is expected to be working on site;
- actual time spent on each aspect of the build;
- significant phases of the work – for example, ground work, foundations, brickwork to damp-proof course (DPC).

While the programme of work is being drawn up, the 'lead' time for each item should be taken into account. In some cases suppliers may not have all the items or equipment in stock, so a period of delay may be incurred between the requisition (order) and the actual delivery to site. A site manager with good organisational skills will consider this factor, and make a note of the actual lead time required before ordering the items in advance, to prevent delays on site. Other factors to consider when organising a building project may include the following:

- availability of equipment and materials;
- availability of plant, due to breakdown, servicing or repairs;
- weather conditions/daylight;
- suitability of equipment or plant for the site conditions;
- availability of suitably trained personnel to operate the plant or equipment;
- access to the site and space to operate the plant or equipment;
- availability of a power source to operate the equipment;
- adequate labour and resources to unload the delivery;
- suitable assessments of the potential risk caused by unloading materials and equipment, and adequate controls in place to eliminate or reduce the danger and to ensure health and safety;
- suitable storage areas.

PHASED DELIVERIES

As mentioned previously, phasing the order of deliveries to site will prevent delays due to operatives waiting for materials, equipment and plant. These delays may have a knock-on effect that could result in the project overrunning the expected completion date. On the other hand, materials ordered too early in a construction project may result in there being insufficient space to store them and a potential obstruction or hazard. Materials inadequately stored may have to be moved several times before they are used, which normally results in them getting damaged, lost or stolen.

Construction materials such as paints, adhesives, plaster and cement. have a limited shelf life before they are opened, and an even shorter usable time after opening. Following these expiry dates the materials will start to deteriorate and 'go off' (set, cure or harden to a condition where they are no longer usable for the purpose for which they were intended). Such items should always be stored in date order, with the oldest at the front and then replaced with new stock at the back. This method of stock rotation is referred to as 'first in first out' (FIFO), and is used to prevent materials being stored at the rear of the stores or on shelves until they exceed their use-by dates. Large construction companies may employ a storeperson to control the stock levels and account for materials used. The storeperson will either use a 'tally book' to record the delivery of materials or a computer system on bigger sites. Materials requested by employees from a company's central store should be recorded on a 'requisition' (order form).

RDJ contractors
Deliveries Record

35 North Road
Bristol
BS12 7KT

Date <u>15 January 2009</u>

Job Name <u>Drysdale Avenue</u>

Supplier	Delivery information	Delivery note no.	Office use only		
			Rate	Value	
D. J. Building Supplies	Ready-mix concrete	3568			
D. J. Building Supplies	Plasterboard	3569			
			Total		

Site manager/foreman _____

Delivery records to be sent to head office weekly with delivery notes.

FIGURE 3.14 Deliveries record

Good communication between the site manager, company buyer and the suppliers could avoid materials and equipment being delivered at lunchtimes or last thing at the end of the working day when only limited labour is available. Some developments may be located in built-up areas or city centres where there is an increased risk of endangering the general public. The 'pre-tender health and safety plan' should identify the busiest times of day so that deliveries can be scheduled around these periods.

TAKING DELIVERY OF GOODS

Upon arrival at the delivery address, the supplier's driver will be expect to 'drop off' the goods and receive a signature on a delivery note or ticket as evidence that the delivery has taken place. In most cases delivery drivers are employed directly by the suppliers or delivery companies to deliver multiple 'drops' (deliveries of items to several addresses). The drivers are usually keen to unload the deliveries without delay before progressing on to complete their duties, so it is important that the person taking the delivery is prepared. In preparation, the site manager should ensure that adequate lifting equipment and labour are ready to unload the delivery with the correct safety measures in place.

TRADE SECRETS

Remember – some plant and equipment may have to be hired from suppliers. It is just as important to notify the suppliers of a convenient collection date as it is to order it in the first place. Failure to keep suppliers informed could result in the items having to be stored on site longer than necessary and additional cost incurred.

Manually unloading heavy items or large quantities of goods from the delivery vehicle should always be a last resort after considering all other mechanical options. Before personnel move or lift any delivered items manually, the site manager should ensure that they are aware of the risks involved by drawing their attention to the relevant method statements. All employees should take adequate measures to reduce the risk of harm to them by wearing the correct personal protective equipment (PPE) to comply with the Manual Handling Operations Regulations 2002. Suitable items of PPE may include the following items:

- safety footwear;
- hard hat;
- high-visibility clothing;
- gloves or gauntlets.

Before carrying out manual handling operations it is strongly recommended that suitable barrier cream be worn to protect against some of the products being handled. Upon completion and before eating, hands should be thoroughly washed with soap to remove any residue, and replenishing cream rubbed into hands to replace any lost moisture. Further manual work would require the application of additional barrier cream to seal and protect the surface of the skin. Remember, any item of PPE, including barrier cream, moisturiser and soap, should be provided free of charge by employers to their employees.

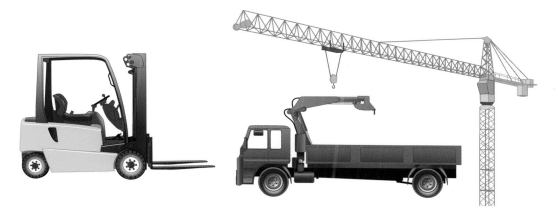

FIGURE 3.15 Unloading: mechanical options

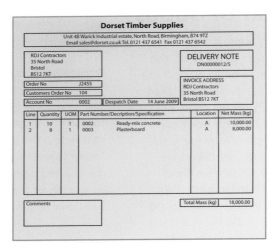

FIGURE 3.16 Delivery note

Further details about delivery notes and checking deliveries are covered in Chapter 2, Information, Quantities and Communicating with Others 2.

STORAGE AND PROTECTION OF MATERIALS

AGGREGATES

Large quantities of aggregates are normally delivered on the back of a truck and offloaded into divided areas known as 'bays'. This form of storage prevents the different types of aggregate mixing together to contaminate the products. Whenever possible, the base of the bays should be hardwearing, with a slight incline to allow water to escape. Alternatively, smaller quantities can be off loaded in bulk bags. This method avoids the need for bays to divide the different aggregates and the bags are simply cleared away after use.

BRICKS AND BLOCKS

Packs of bricks and blocks are usually delivered on pallets with plastic binding and wrapping to offer reasonable protection against the elements, including frost. The raised wooden pallets prevent them being stored directly on the floor, which may result in staining from salts contained in the soil, and moisture ingress. They also permit the forks on pallet and fork-lift trucks to slide underneath without obstruction, allowing future transportation from the storage areas closer to the building work. If individual bricks or blocks are delivered, they should be stacked in an alternating pattern no higher than the wrapped packs or that stated in the relevant method statement. Extra care should be taken when manually stacking and storing bricks and blocks to ensure that fingers do not get trapped and pinched between heavy blocks as they are being placed.

CEMENT, PLASTER, SAND, ETC.

Products affected by moisture, such as cement and dry plaster, are normally supplied in 25 kg moisture-resistant bags. These are the maximum weight bags that should be lifted manually, so only one bag should be carried at any one time. It is recommended that these types of product are stored off the ground in a dry, ventilated, lockable container. Generally, the bags should be stacked flat to prevent them from being perforated, and a maximum of five high, with a clear walkway between to gain easy access, in order to follow the 'first in first out' method.

DOORS

Expensive joinery products such as doors should always be stored in a dry lockable container until they are ready to be hung. Untreated soft and hardwood doors will twist, warp and absorb moisture very quickly if they are left open to the environment or stored on uneven surfaces. Some of this damage may not become apparent until after installation, when the doors may dry out, resulting in shrinkage, damage to the joints and warping. Mass-produced doors are usually covered with protective plastic with corner protectors, and should remain so until they are ready for installation. Whenever possible they should be stored flat, off the ground and supported on at least three 'bearers' with layers of cardboard in between each door to protect the faces. Purpose-made doors will usually be supplied with the 'horns' left on for removal on site just before their installation.

FLAMMABLES

Special precautions are required to store and handle pressurised containers such as 'gas' because of the risk of the substances leaking from the valves and potentially exploding. Incorrectly fitted valves and regulators, inadequate storage facilities and poor handling of pressurised cylinders are all hazards waiting to happen unless adequate controls are put in place. Every employer should ensure that assessments of the risks to health and safety are carried out before eliminating them as far as practically possible, or reducing them to an acceptable level.

Flammables should be purchased and stored on site only as and when they are needed, and should never be kept for long periods of time. When new containers are delivered to the site storage facilities, older cylinders should be rotated to the front. All pressurised cylinders should be stored vertically unless otherwise stated, and clearly labelled with the contents on their casing. They should also be stored:

- on a flat surface;
- under cover;
- with adequate ventilation;
- away from sources of heat and ignition;
- with restraints around the cylinders to prevent tipping;
- protected with 'valve caps' to prevent damage to the valves in the event of being dropped;
- in a well-signed area warning of hazards and precautions to be taken in that area.

GLASS

Clean and dry purpose-made racks should be used to store glass in a vertical position. Glass racks (also known as 'frails') should also have a slight lean on them to prevent the glazing tipping forward and to provide adequate support. Small foam sticky pads are normally attached to one side of the glazing panels before delivery to site. This prevents them sticking to each other when they are in storage, and reduces the risk of scratching occurring as a result of trapped dirt or grit.

INTERNAL TIMBER

Skirting, architraves, door linings, etc. are all examples of joinery quality timber used for second fixing. Internal timber is normally seasoned and moulded before installation to prevent the effects of shrinkage occurring. Whenever possible, they should be stored in the room or area where they are going to be fixed prior to cutting and fixing (second seasoning).

They should remain in the building until further movement has occurred in the timber and the 'equilibrium' moisture content has been achieved. All internal timber must be stored flat, off the ground on bearers, with piling sticks in between each layer to allow the air to flow around the stack.

IRONMONGERY AND FIXINGS

Desirable and expensive items such as ironmongery and fixings are likely to be stolen if they are left in unsecured areas for any length of time, or without an adequate store control system in place. If these items are stored in damp or wet conditions they may also start to show signs of deterioration. To prevent this happening they should be stored in dry, lockable containers and off the floor on shelves. The storage shelves should be clearly labelled for easy identification at a later date when they are required for use.

TRADE SECRETS

Whenever possible, heavy items such as ironmongery and fixings should be stored on the lower shelves in a storage area. This avoids unnecessary heavy lifting from the ground to the upper shelves.

PAINT, ADHESIVES, STRIPPERS, ETC.

Hazardous materials used in the construction industry are covered by the Control of Substances Hazardous to Health (COSHH) Regulations. The regulations place legal duties on employers to control the exposure of employees to chemicals and other substances. Employers should assess the risks involved with each product and provide employees with training, information and the correct PPE in order to use the substances safely without risk to themselves and/or others. Manufacturers and suppliers are required by law to provide 'safety data sheets' with each product. The safety data sheets are used as references for information regarding the safe handling, storage and use of a particular substance hazardous to health.

Hazardous materials decanted (poured) from large containers to smaller ones should be adequately labelled with their content and safety requirements.

PLASTERBOARD

Sheet materials should be stored under cover in a dry environment, flat, off the ground and on bearers, evenly spaced to prevent sagging. Alternatively, plasterboards can be stored vertically, provided that the bottoms of the boards are elevated above the floor. The disadvantage of this method is the potential to cause damage to the delicate edges and corners. If plasterboard is incorrectly stored and allowed to become damp, the plaster will become soft and difficult to cut cleanly when it is being installed and secured.

TIMBER-BASED SHEET MATERIALS

Timber-based sheet materials should be stored using the same methods as with plasterboard, although decorative or veneered boards should have their faces protected with cardboard. Alternatively, the best faces of the boards should be placed together to prevent scratching or staining of the surfaces.

WINDOWS

Plastic, aluminium and timber windows are rarely stored on site for long periods. Generally, they are installed by specialised window fitters who install the frames at the same time they deliver them to site. This prevents the items taking up valuable storage space for longer periods than necessary, and the potential to get damaged while on site. Any window frames stored on site should be secured under cover to protect against the elements, and adequately supported to prevent against twisting.

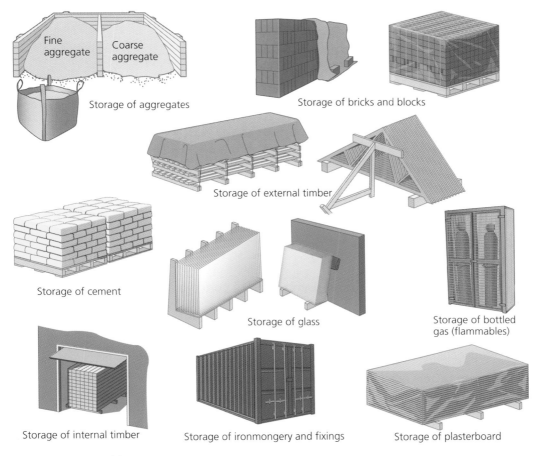

Fine aggregate | Coarse aggregate

Storage of aggregates

Storage of bricks and blocks

Storage of external timber

Storage of cement

Storage of glass

Storage of bottled gas (flammables)

Storage of internal timber

Storage of ironmongery and fixings

Storage of plasterboard

FIGURE 3.17 Materials storage

ACTIVITIES

Activity 15 – Materials storage and delivery of building materials

Read through the following questions and answer them as fully as you can to help you develop your underpinning knowledge of this subject area.

1. Explain the purpose of stock rotation.

2. Explain the effect on plaster if stored in damp conditions.

3. Why is it advisable to phase deliveries to site?

4. List the checks that should be carried out when a delivery is made to site.

5. How should internal joinery quality timber be stored on site?

MULTIPLE-CHOICE QUESTIONS

1   Which **one** of the following gives the range of storeys for buildings categorised as 'mid-rise'?
   a   2–5
   b   3–6
   c   4–7
   d   5–8

2   The foundations of a building up to the damp proof course are known as the
   a   sole plate
   b   ground works
   c   substructure
   d   superstructure

3   The type of brickwork bond used in the construction of cavity walls is
   a   header
   b   English
   c   Flemish
   d   stretcher

4   The thin sand and cement mix used to level a concrete slab is called a
   a   bed
   b   screed
   c   skim coat
   d   render coat

5   Common rafters are fixed at their lower end to the
   a   ridge
   b   crown
   c   sole plate
   d   wall plate

6   The first coat of paint applied to bare woodwork is called the
   a   primer
   b   leveller
   c   under coat
   d   premier coat

7   Softwood trees
   a   have needle-like leaves
   b   have broad spread leaves
   c   lose their leaves in the winter
   d   lose their leaves in the summer

8   Phased deliveries
  a   reduce the cost of the project
  b   increase the cost of the project
  c   reduce the requirement for storage
  d   increase the requirement for storage

9   Bags of plaster stored outside will
  a   last longer
  b   harden quickly
  c   be easier to mix
  d   be harder to mix

10   Which **one** of the following statements is true about steel fixings? They
  a   must be stored indoors
  b   must be stored outdoors
  c   have to be painted prior to use
  d   have to be painted following fixing

CHAPTER 4

CIRCULAR SAWS

 LEARNING OUTCOMES

By the end of this chapter you should have developed a knowledge and understanding of:

- setting up fixed and transportable circular saws;
- changing saw blades;
- cutting timber and sheet materials.

INTRODUCTION

The aim of this chapter is for students to be able to recognise the different types of circular saw and their component parts. This chapter also provides practical guidance on the safe methods used to set up, use and service/maintain them. Throughout this chapter references are made and explained regarding current machinery regulations applicable to this area of study, following all the relevant health and safety law and good working practices.

HEALTH AND SAFETY

Employers have a duty under the Health and Safety at Work Act 1974 (HASAWA) to provide employees with equipment and machinery that is safe to use. They must also ensure that employees are suitably trained and competent in the use of the machinery; this should be done by:

- providing information;
- training;
- instruction;
- supervision.

FIGURE 4.1 Supervision

New employees, even if suitably qualified, may need to undergo a period of refresher training, instruction and familiarisation. You cannot expect them to be competent in the use of all makes and models of woodworking machinery, so every employee must be assessed to establish their training needs.

FREQUENTLY ASKED QUESTIONS

▶ **If somebody is trained, doesn't that mean that they are competent?**

No, not necessarily. A person that has received training has to then prove their competence through testing. For example, a person may have been shown how to set up and use a circular saw, but that does not mean that they can set up and use the saw.

This system of training and testing will be repeated throughout Level 2 Bench Joinery.

PROVISION AND USE OF WORK EQUIPMENT REGULATIONS 1998 (PUWER)

PUWER gives practical guidance for the safe use of *all* manual and powered work equipment; these items may range from a microwave oven to a forklift truck. The Provision and Use of Work Equipment Regulations cover all sectors of work, not just construction. The aim of the Regulations is to ensure that *employers* provide equipment to their employees that:

- is regularly serviced;
- is maintained;
- is safe to use for its intended purpose;
- will not put people at risk.

RISK ASSESSMENTS

Employers have a statutory duty to carry out a thorough 'risk assessment' of all equipment in the workplace before use. All risk assessments should be carried out by a competent person(s) appointed by the employer; alternatively, an outside agency may be employed (risk assessments are covered in more detail in Chapter 1, Safe Working Practices). A risk assessment will highlight the risks or potential risks associated with a particular task, the people it will affect and measures needed to remove or control the risk. Once the control measures have been implemented they should be reviewed periodically, or if significant changes have occurred in the workplace. If a company employs five or more people, the risk assessment should be recorded in writing.

The Provision and Use of Work Equipment Regulations state that the following areas of a circular saw could potentially pose significant risks to operatives' health.

Noise

Noise is the level of sound, measured in decibels (dB), transmitted by the saw. Measures are required to be in place to control an operative's exposure where noise levels exceed 80 dB (e.g. ear protection, signage).

Wiring

It is essential that the saw has been correctly earthed by a qualified electrician and an isolation switch mounted independently from the machine. The mains power to the circular saw will run through the isolation switch; disengaging this switch allows the saw to be maintained, serviced or adjusted without risk of electrocution (any inspections carried out should be recorded in the machine's maintenance log).

FIGURE 4.2 Operating a circular saw

FIGURE 4.3 Bad practice (waste materials blown away)

Dust

Most woodworking machines will create a certain amount of dust when they are in use. Exposure to dust for long periods of time may cause skin disorders, asthma, nasal or lung cancer unless the correct personal protective equipment (PPE) is worn (dust mask, eye protection, gloves). In some situations fine concentrations of airborne wood dust can potentially explode if ignited (termed 'instantaneous combustion'), so it is important that the working area is kept clear at all times, especially around electrical equipment. Wood dust should, where ever practical, be collected with an extractor; this will prevent static dust becoming airborne again when disturbed.

FIGURE 4.4 Good practice (waste extracted away)

The Control of Substances Hazardous to Health Regulations (COSHH) recognise the hazard posed by wood dust and suggest extraction should be used as an effective tool to remove the waste from the area, therefore minimising the danger. (*Note*: the maximum exposure limit to wood dust is 5 mg/m³.) A dust extraction system will maintain its effectiveness only if it is regularly maintained and serviced. If the 'ducting' from an extractor becomes blocked due to it being either full or because there are foreign objects trapped within the system, it will lose suction. Any blockage within a dust extraction system is a potential fire risk and will have to be removed immediately.

There is a wide range of different kinds of dust extractor available for both static and transportable machines. Each system is specifically designed and tested by specialists to ensure it performs at optimum efficiency when one or more machines are in use at any one time. The working environment can be improved further with the use of an 'air filtration system'. Air filtration units are usually mounted at ceiling height in workshops and factories to extract airborne dust from the areas. The size, quantity and position of the units is determined and calculated by the volume of space requiring cleaning.

FREQUENTLY ASKED QUESTIONS

▶ What is a dust extraction 'system'?

Dust extraction can be as simple as a single-bag collection unit through to an extensive system of 'ducting', serving a dozen machines or more. The term 'ducting' refers to the lengths of pipes between the main extractor unit and the individual machines. The size of the ducting may be reduced between the main pipework and smaller machines to prevent a loss of suction and effectively remove the dust from the working area. Ducting is usually manufactured from galvanised metal and aluminium fittings; it can also range in size between 80 and 355 mm.

Dust extraction systems will normally have a number of 'blast gates' distributed between the end of the ducts and the machines that they are serving. Some dust extraction systems will lose their suction if all the blast gates are left open; generally only the machines in use should need extraction.

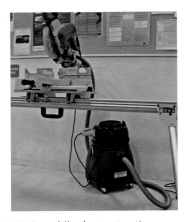

FIGURE 4.5 A mobile dust extraction

FIGURE 4.6 A Dust extractor

FIGURE 4.7 Blast gates

TRADE SECRETS

When you are choosing an extraction system, consider the environment and how you will dispose of your waste. There are some waste extraction systems that compress the dust and wood chippings into small square briquettes. The briquettes are then used as fuel for heating systems for the factory or workshop. Waste material can also be used for:

- animal bedding (no treated timber, some hardwoods or manufactured board material);
- composting;
- industrial spillage absorbent;
- man-made timber-based sheet materials.

STOPPING TIMES

Once a woodworking machine has been turned off, the moving parts generally continue rotating for a short period of time. The Supply of Machinery (Safety) Regulations 1992 state that the length of time a machine should take to stop should be no more than 10 seconds for new machines. New woodworking machines normally have an electronic braking device built into them; older machinery may require 'retrofitting' to bring the machine to a safe condition within the same period of time. 'Retrofitting' simply means adapting the machine to conform to current regulations; in this case the braking device is normally mounted on the outer body of the machine.

Some older machines may have a manual braking system; this is also an acceptable form of stopping the moving parts, provided it does so within the governed time.

WORKSHOP HAZARDS

It is essential that the machine shop/area:

- is free from trip and slip hazards, e.g. offcuts, sawdust, grease and dirt;
- has flat, level and non-slip floors directly around the machine;
- is planned so that machines have adequate space around them, ensuring the operator will not be knocked or distracted;
- has good natural or artificial lighting (poor artificial light may cast shadows on the machine and cause glare, which could be a potential hazard); at some high speeds saw blades can appear to become motionless – this is known as the 'stroboscopic' effect; twin tube light fittings are recommended to prevent this happening;
- has adequate working space and provision to store materials in use;
- is temperature controlled; the temperature in a machine shop must not fall below 16°C, and 10°C in a saw mill;
- is supplied with the *correct* fire extinguishers (e.g. carbon dioxide for electrical fires).

? FREQUENTLY ASKED QUESTIONS

▶ **What is the difference between a 'machine shop' and a 'saw mill'?**

After a tree has been 'felled' (cut down) it usually has to be sawn into smaller usable sections, a process known as 'timber conversion'. Timber conversion is carried out in a 'saw mill'. A saw mill is usually a lot larger than a machine shop simply because of the lengths of the materials being cut and the volume.

A 'machine shop' is normally paired with a joinery workshop. Its purpose is to prepare the sections supplied by the saw mill into planed and shaped sections. A machine shop usually contains some or all of the following:

▶ mortiser;

▶ tenoner;

▶ four-sided planer or through moulder;

▶ surface planer and thicknesser;

▶ spindle moulder;

▶ computer numerical control (CNC) machinery;

▶ circular saw;

▶ bandsaw;

▶ radial arm cross-cut saw;

▶ drum sander.

GUARDING

Poorly maintained guards or guarding that does not conform to PUWER pose a potential risk to the user. The HSE has the power to prosecute employers that provide machinery for their employees (including guarding) that is considered dangerous. The correct positioning of all the circular saw guards is stated in the HSE's Information Sheets and also in the HSE Safe Use of Woodworking Machines 'Code of Practice'. The main guards on a circular saw are depicted in Figure 4.8:

Both the *crown and nose guard* should be adjusted to a maximum of 10 mm above the top of the timber being fed; this will prevent the user's fingers passing between the timbers and guard.

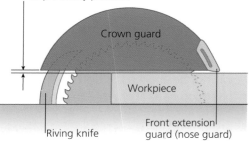

FIGURE 4.8 Crown guard

The *riving knife* maintains the separation of the cut and prevents the timber from closing in on the back of the saw, causing it to bind, and possibly throw the timber back at the operator. It also acts as a protection device to prevent the person 'pulling off' the back of the saw and coming into contact with the back of the saw blade. The circular saw should also be totally enclosed below the table to prevent exposure of the saw blade.

BRITISH STANDARD EMERGENCY STOP BUTTONS

In the event of a dangerous situation occurring while a machine is in use, an emergency stop button must be available to isolate the machine from the power source. Careful consideration must be given to the position of the emergency stop button on the machine. It should be within easy reach of the operator, but not where it could accidentally isolate the machine from the power. *Emergency stop buttons are designed for light use and should therefore only be used as last resort*; this will prevent unnecessary wear and ensure their safety and reliability. Emergency stop buttons should comply with British Standards; this means that they will be easily recognisable, with a red mushroom head on a yellow background. BS emergency stop buttons are operated by depressing the mushroom-style button to isolate the machine; the button is then reset by twisting the spring-loaded button until it rises. Emergency stop buttons are available with a locking mechanism that prevents the machine from being started without a key; this prevents unauthorised use.

FIGURE 4.9 British Standard stop button

FIGURE 4.10 Stop button with a security key

SAFETY MARKING LABELS

Employers must ensure that every woodworking machine displays the necessary markings to ensure employees' health and safety; this will include:

- the safe working speed of the machine (displayed on the machine if possible);
- the safe working speed of the saw blade (displayed on the body of each saw blade);
- the minimum diameter blades allowed to be used *must* be displayed on circular saws; this will ensure that the speed of the blade (the 'peripheral' speed) does not exceed safety limits.

Note: the manufacturer's information and service schedule should be referred to if there is any doubt due to unclear markings.

CODES OF PRACTICE

Codes of practice are approved documents available from the Health and Safety Executive. There are many different codes of practice available for different regulations. Each one will give practical advice on how to comply with the Regulations – for example, 'Safe Use of Woodworking Machinery – Approved Code of Practice and Guidance'.

The codes should not be confused with the law – they only given advice on ways to comply with the law; alternative safe methods can be used provided that they meet with PUWER. Further details are available on 'Information Sheets' for specific machinery from the Health and Safety Executive.

RECAP

HEALTH AND SAFETY AT WORK ACT (HASAWA)

'Secure the health, safety and welfare of all persons at work'

PROVISION AND USE OF WORK EQUIPMENT REGULATIONS (PUWER)

'An employer that provides work equipment must ensure that it is safe to use'

APPROVED CODES OF PRACTICE (ACOP)

'Gives practice advice on how to comply with the law'

FIGURE 4.11 HASAWA flowchart

CIRCULAR SAW DEFINITION

The term 'circular saw' refers to a round metal disc with shaped teeth around its perimeter. A circular saw can be mounted and powered in either a portable power tool or a static machine. The size, shape and amount of teeth will be determined by the machine or power tool it is used in, its intended use and the material being cut.

Chop saw

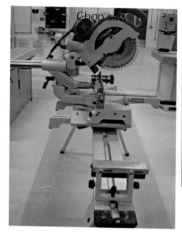

Chop saw

Biscuit jointer

Circular saw

FIGURE 4.12 Portable power tools with circular saw blades

Static circular saws are usually driven by larger motors than portable powered tools; therefore they are capable of cutting larger sections of solid timber and sheet materials with ease. Static circular saws are usually used only in saw mills and machine shops for production work; their weight and overall size make them impractical to transport to site. There are several different types of static circular saw, each one designed to either cut along the grain (ripping) or across the grain (cross-cutting). Other machines are specifically designed to cut man-made boards or timber-based sheet materials. These machines may have a smaller secondary circular saw blade in alignment with the main blade; this is known as a 'scoring' saw. A scoring saw can usually be raised and lowered so that it just protrudes above the surface of the saw table (also known as the bed), so that it cuts the surface of veneered, laminated or melamine sheet materials. Scoring saws are normally only used on panel, dimension and wall saws, to prevent the expensive finished surfaces of the sheet materials from breaking out as the circular saw blade passes through the underside of the board.

FIGURE 4.13 Panel saw

FIGURE 4.14 Damage to the underside of the board

TYPES OF CIRCULAR SAW

Table or fixed bed rip saw

Circular bench saw

Transportable circular bench saw

Transportable wall saw

FIGURE 4.15

This type of saw, the main focus of this chapter, can be used for a variety of tasks, including:

- ripping;
- cutting to length (with a sliding fence attachment);
- angled cutting with the use of jigs and tilting the blade;
- cutting wedges and firrings (used to create the fall on flat roofs).

Circular saw blades can range in size from 100 mm for a scoring blade, up to 2.97 m (9 feet) for a rip saw used to convert trees in a saw mill. Generally, the most common sizes used in the construction industry range from 350 to 600 mm.

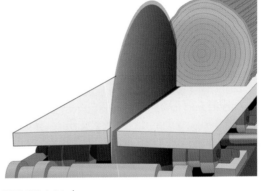

FIGURE 4.16 Log saw

Panel/dimension saw

These types of machine are designed to cut timber-based sheet materials to size. They each have a large lightweight 'bed' attached to the left-hand side of the circular saw; this enables the weight of the material to be balanced across the machine table. The bed is able to slide along the length of the machine, thus allowing the sheet material to be trimmed and cut to width. Panel/dimension saws are available in four standard sizes: 1600 mm, 2200 mm, 3200 mm and 3800 mm. This relates to the length the bed can travel along the side of the main saw table. They also have the facility of an additional scoring saw blade and the ability to tilt to 45°. In general, this is a very versatile machine that is normally used in the production of joinery and shopfitting items.

Wall saw

A wall saw is capable of all the aforementioned operations but has the advantage of taking up less floor space; this is particularly useful for smaller workshops. A wall saw is normally only used to cut timber-based sheet materials. It functions by simply positioning the panels on a wall rack, before adjusting the circular saw to the desired position. The saw is then pulled over the face of the sheet material to cut it to the required dimension.

Cross-cut saw

As the name suggests, this saw is used to cut across the grain of timber to the required length. Some machines are capable of cutting timber up to 125 mm in thickness and 700 mm in width. Most machines have the ability to raise and lower the height of the saw blade over the timber; this action allows the saw to be used for cutting housing joints. It is normally used in conjunction with a fence with adjustable length stops.

? FREQUENTLY ASKED QUESTIONS

▶ **What is a 'fence and stop'?**

A *fence* is a fixed guide used to support an item of timber. Fences provide a solid platform to rest the timber against while it is being machined or cut. They are commonly used on all items of woodworking machinery, including rip and cross-cut saws. It is common practice to attach a tape measure along the length of the fence to use as a guide; this prevents repetitive measuring.

A *stop* is simply an adjustable block that can be moved along the length of a fence. An 'offcut' of timber, securely fixed in position with a 'G' clamp, can be used to create a stop. Alternatively, manufactured metal stops can be purchased; these are usually more accurate because they interlock with the fence and can easily be flipped over when they are not in use.

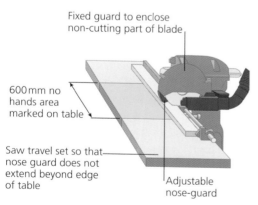

Fixed guard to enclose non-cutting part of blade

600mm no hands area marked on table

Saw travel set so that nose guard does not extend beyond edge of table

Adjustable nose-guard

FIGURE 4.17 Cross-cut saw

FIGURE 4.18 Stops used on a panel saw

Radial arm saw

This type of saw is similar to a cross-cut saw. Although they are both used to cut across the grain of timber, a radial arm saw is more versatile. Radial arm saws are normally used to cut smaller sections than cross-cut saws and therefore tend to be slightly smaller and lighter in weight. In

simple terms, it is best described as a portable circular saw mounted on a long 'arm' that overhangs the base of the machine that it is mounted on. Timber is then fed between the radial arm saw and the base on the machine to the required position, and then the saw is drawn across the timber by the operator to cut the timber to size. The saw is controlled with the use of a handle attached to the motor and saw assembly. Some radial arm saws have the start and stop switches mounted on the handle of the saw for easy use. They may also have a spring coil attached to the cast iron arm; this allows the saw to return automatically to its starting position.

FIGURE 4.19 Radial arm saw

FIGURE 4.20 Spring coil

Radial arm saw features

As mentioned previously, this saw has many features besides straightforward cross-cutting. Radial arm saws are capable of cutting up to 610 mm in width, 110 mm in depth and 920 mm in length when repositioned to rip timber to width. When the saw has been adjusted to cut across the grain at an angle, the capacity to cut wide boards is reduced. The saw can be easily and quickly adjusted with the use of fixed levers and stops to make the cuts shown in Figure 4.21. (*Note*: The saw blade will have to be changed to suit the operation undertaken.)

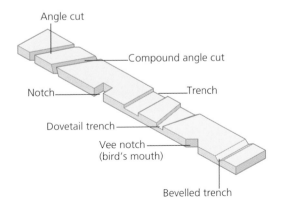

FIGURE 4.21 Cuts

TRADE SECRETS

A study by the HSE of 1000 accidents occurring on woodworking machines showed that 35 per cent happened on circular saws. The majority of these accidents could have been avoided if the guards provided were used and positioned correctly. The majority of these accidents resulted in the loss of fingers as the timber was being 'hand fed' into the machines (Figure 4.23); these types of machine are considered to be 'high risk'. The risk of accidents occurring on woodworking machines can be greatly reduced if 'powered feed rollers' are used. Once they are set up, they eliminate the need for the machinist to position their fingers anywhere near the cutting edges. Feed rollers can also improve the quality of the machined timber by running the material through the machine at a consistent speed.

Mitre cutting

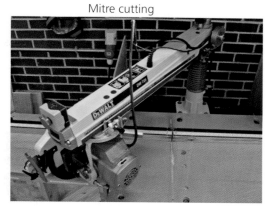

Square cutting

FIGURE 4.22

FIGURE 4.23 Hand-fed timber

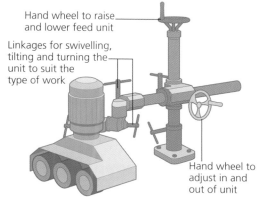

Hand wheel to raise and lower feed unit

Linkages for swivelling, tilting and turning the unit to suit the type of work

Hand wheel to adjust in and out of unit

FIGURE 4.24 Powered feed rollers

Circular bench saw – component identification

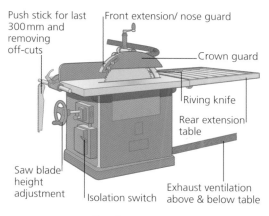

Push stick for last 300mm and removing off-cuts

Front extension/ nose guard

Crown guard

Riving knife

Rear extension table

Saw blade height adjustment

Isolation switch

Exhaust ventilation above & below table

FIGURE 4.25 Circular saw and outfeed table

Crown guard

A crown guard is positioned over the circular saw to minimise the amount of the blade visible; it also reduces the risk to the operator. Crown guards on modern machines are designed with an extraction outlet built in; this is a very effective point to remove the sawdust. The crown guards on transportable circular saws are normally attached to the riving knife, and adjusted by raising and lowering the height of the saw blade.

Note: 'under no circumstances should the safety guards provided on a machine be removed or altered' (PUWER 1998).

Extraction outlets

Extraction outlets are positioned at strategic points on a machine to remove the maximum amount of waste possible. It is vital that these points are checked regularly and kept clear to maintain an effective extraction system.

Fine adjustment screw

This allows accurate alignment of the fence position.

Finger plate

The finger plate is loosely fitted within the bed of the machine along one side of the saw blade. The finger holes in the finger plate allow it to be removed without the need for any service tools. When it is removed, it allows easy access into the body of the machine to adjust, maintain and service the blade and riving knife.

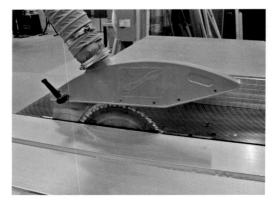

FIGURE 4.26 Crown guard

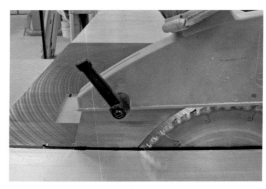

FIGURE 4.27 Extraction outlet

FIGURE 4.28 Removal of the finger plate

Mouth piece

The mouth piece is positioned directly in front of the saw blade, at table-top level. Its purpose is to narrow the gap between the circular saw blade and the metal table, and prevent damage to both parts. As circular saws are started, they begin to build up their speed until they reach the maximum revolutions per minute (RPM). During this start-up period, large-diameter saw blades are likely to wobble slightly before reaching their maximum speed and perfect balance.

Nose/front extension guard

The nose guard is mounted over the front edge of the crown guard with an adjustment wing nut. It is used in addition to the main protection devices as a lightweight fine adjustment to minimise the gap between the underside of the crown guard and the top of the timber being cut.

Outfeed table

This is used to provide additional support to the timber or sheet material as it exits the back of the circular saw after cutting. Outfeed tables should extend at least 1200 mm in length beyond the centre of the circular saw blade. Any person employed to 'take off' (remove) material at the back of the saw should remain 1200 mm away from the blade and avoid reaching over the table. The outfeed table also provides rear support for the timber being cut.

Packing pieces

Packing pieces are very similar to the 'mouth piece' in the front of the saw bed, only they are positioned along both sides of the blade. Over a period of time the packing pieces will become worn and will have to be replaced. Excessive wear will cause the gap between the side of the saw and the packing pieces to grow; this may lead to smaller 'offcuts' slipping between the gap during use. A build-up of material slipping through the table bed at this point may cause the dust extraction outlet to clog up; larger offcuts may act as a wedge against the blade, forcing it to jam to a halt.

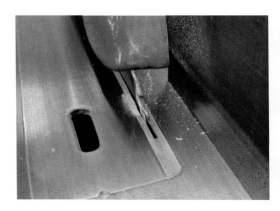

FIGURE 4.29 Mouth piece

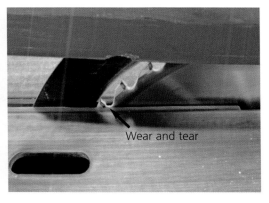

Wear and tear

FIGURE 4.30 Wear and tear on packing pieces

Push sticks

Push sticks are used to apply pressure and firmly hold the material in position as it is being pushed through the circular saw. They prevent the need for the machine operator to put their fingers too close to the saw blade while it is rotating. Push sticks should be stored on the machine on which they are going to be used so that they are within easy reach of the machine operator. They should be used to feed timber through a circular saw that is shorter than 300 mm, or for the last 300 mm of longer pieces. They should also be used to remove the cut timber between the saw blade and the rip fence, unless the timber is 150 mm in width or bigger. Push sticks should be a minimum length of 300 mm plus the handle; this usually amounts to 450 mm over all. (*Note*: the machinist's hands should not be in line with the circular saw blade as material is being fed through the saw. This reduces the risk of the operator's hands slipping towards the teeth on the blade.)

Rip fence

The rip fence is used to guide and control the width of the timber being cut. The correct positioning of the rip fence is essential to prevent the timber jamming and resulting in a poor finish to the sawn edge as it is fed in to the saw blade.

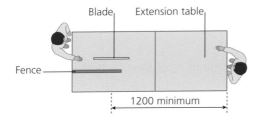

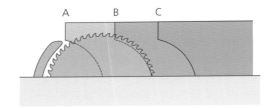

Position A - will cause the final portion to jamb
Position B - correct position
Position C - will cause the final portion of the saw cut to be unguided, and therefore result in a poor finish

FIGURE 4.32 Rip fence

Typical push stick

FIGURE 4.31 Push sticks

Riving knife

The riving knife should be made of ridged steel construction and accurately aligned directly behind the circular saw blade. The purpose of the riving knife is to prevent timber 'binded' on the saw blade as it is being cut; this is a result of the width of the saw cut (the 'kerf') being reduced as fresh

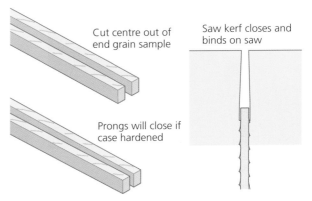

Cut centre out of end grain sample

Saw kerf closes and binds on saw

Prongs will close if case hardened

FIGURE 4.33 The kerf closing behind the riving knife

timber exposed by the saw cut moves. A riving knife should be 10 per cent thicker than the width of the kerf, and have a shaped/rounded front edge to guide it through the saw cut and prevent it from 'binding'. The riving knife must be adjusted to suit the diameter of the circular saw blade being used. The Approved Code of Practice states that the maximum distance between the riving knife and the saw blade should not exceed 8 mm at the table-top level. It also states that, with blades greater than 600 mm in diameter, the riving knife should be at least 225 mm above the table surface. For blades less than 60mm diameter the top of the riving knife should not be more than 25mm below the top of the saw.

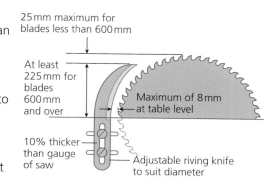

FIGURE 4.34 Setting up a riving knife

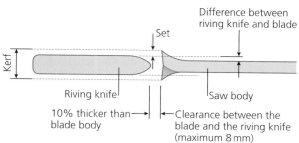

FIGURE 4.35

FREQUENTLY ASKED QUESTIONS

▶ What is the 'kerf'?

The 'kerf' is a term given to the width of a saw cut and should not be confused as being the thickness of the saw blade. The teeth on a circular saw blade will protrude on each side, giving a clearance for the 'plate' and preventing jamming.

YOUNG PEOPLE AT WORK

All types of industrial machinery are considered to have an element of risk to the user. The level of risk depends on the following factors:

● young person (under the age of 18);
● supervision;
● instruction;
● experience;
● training;
● competence;
● familiarity with the machinery;
● authorisation.

Young people are permitted to use low- and high-risk machinery provided that they do so as part of their training, and thereafter under supervision. There is a greater risk of injury to younger users, because they may not be at a suitable level of maturity and may lack experience; they may also not be as physically able as a mature adult. (*Note*: maturity must be demonstrated and not just achieved in age.) Employers have a duty under the Health and Safety at Work Act (HASAWA) to ensure that young people are not employed to carry out tasks that are beyond their physical and psychological capabilities.

INSTRUCTION AND TRAINING

The Provision and Use of Work Equipment Regulations (PUWER) require employers to provide all the necessary instructions, information and training for the safe use of machinery in the workplace. Where appropriate, written information should be available for employees regarding all matters of health and safety; this may be in the form of 'method statements'.

Examples of training records

✓: Sheet 1 – List of authorised machine operators

The authorised trainer of _____ is _____

                     (the company)   (name of trainer)

Date _____

I certify that:

(a)   I have carried out training, as indicated on the machines listed.

(b)   I am satisfied that the people named below have demonstrated competence in the operation of the machines listed and have met all the training objectives for those machines, including:

    (i)   correct selection of machine for type of work to be done;

    (ii) purpose and adjustment of guards and safeguards;

    (iii) correct selection and use of safety devices – push-sticks, push spike, jigs and work-holders;

  (iv) practical understanding and application of legal requirements;

  (v)   safe working practices to include feeding, setting, cleaning and taking off.

Operator's name	Circular rip saw	Cross-cut saw	Dimension saw	Surface planing machine	Thickness planing machine moulder	Single-ended tenoner	Spindle moulder	High-speed router	Four-sided planer/	Narrow band saw	Band re-saw	etc
J Brown	✓	✓	✓	✓	✓	✓						
D Smith	✓	✓	✓	✓	✓					✓		
C White	✓	✓										

FIGURE 4.36 Training records

Everyone involved in the machining process must be adequately trained and informed in all matters of health and safety; these people include:

- the machine operator;
- the person 'taking off' material from the back of the machine;
- the person who services or maintains the machinery.

Employers that provide woodworking machinery for their employees to use must ensure that a suitable process for implementing and recording training is in place. The 'Safe Use of Woodworking Machinery – Approved Code of Practice and Guidance' gives examples of ways to record the level of training given and the range of machinery.

It is essential that people employed to use machinery at work have completed a period of training and demonstrated competence to satisfy their employers. A person that has demonstrated competence will be able to:

- Select the safest machine and tooling for the task;
- Demonstrate safe methods of working;
- Correctly adjust guarding to minimise the risk;
- Demonstrate strong knowledge and understanding of their legal responsibilities.

TRAINING SCHEDULE

'Unfamiliar with the machine or have no wood machining experience'

Step 1 – *Assessment of the operator's training needs*

Step 2 – *Training*

Step 3 – *Reassess the trainee*

Step 4 – *Competence proven to the employer*

Step 5 – *Authorisation given and recorded*

FIGURE 4.37

TRAINING SCHEDULE

'Experienced in the use of woodworking machinery'

Step 1 – *Is the machinist experienced on the machine?*

Step 2 – *Provide training (if needed)*   **Step 2** – *Assessment of the operator's training needs*

Step 3 – *Assessment of machinist*   **Step 3** – *Provide training*

Step 4 – *Competence proven to the employer*

Step 5 – *Authorisation given and recorded*

FIGURE 4.38

MACHINE MAINTENANCE AND SERVICING

It is essential that machinery is regularly maintained and serviced to ensure an efficient state and prevent unnecessary wear. If a machine breaks down, it could be costly in terms of damage to the machine and unused labour, due to repairs and lost production time. Poorly maintained machines may deteriorate to an unsafe condition and put the users and people in the immediate area at risk; this is against the law and could lead to the HSE prosecuting the employer.

The exact amount of servicing and maintenance necessary will vary between machines and the amount of use. Woodworking machinery should be maintained in accordance with the manufacturer's maintenance instructions and schedule; these documents will detail the type of maintenance work required and the frequency. Service schedules should be kept up to date and any maintenance recorded in a log. Both items should be kept close to the machine or maintenance area.

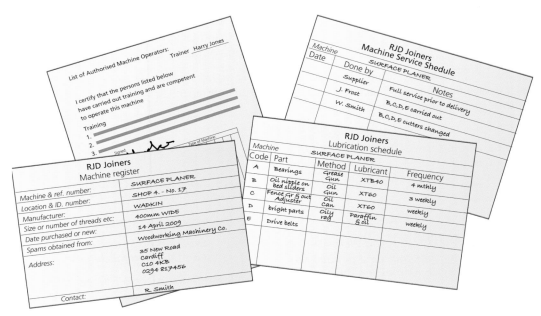

List of Authorised Machine Operators: Trainer Harry Jones

I certify that the persons listed below have carried out training and are competent to operate this machine

Training

1.
2.
3.

Signed

RJD Joiners
Machine register

Machine & ref. number:	SURFACE PLANER
Location & ID. number:	SHOP 4. - No. 17
Manufacturer:	WADKIN
Size or number of threads etc:	400mm WIDE
Date purchased or new:	14 April 2009
Spams obtained from:	Woodworking Machinery Co.
Address:	35 New Road Cardiff C10 4KB 0294 817456
Contact:	R. Smith

RJD Joiners
Machine Service Shedule
SURFACE PLANER

Machine Date	Done by	Notes
	Supplier	Full service prior to delivery
	J. Frost	B,C,D,E carried out
	W. Smith	B,C,D,E cutters changed

RJD Joiners
Lubrication schedule
SURFACE PLANER

Code	Part	Method	Lubricant	Frequency
A	Bearings	Grease Gun		
B	Oil nipple on bed sliders	Oil Gun	XTB40	4 mthly
C	Fence Gr & out Adjuster	Oil Can	XT60	3 weekly
D	bright parts	Oily rag	XT60	weekly
E	Drive belts		Paraffin & oil	weekly

FIGURE 4.39 Machine service schedule

? FREQUENTLY ASKED QUESTIONS

▶ **Why do you have to record all maintenance and servicing carried out?**

You are *not* required by law to keep a maintenance log, but advised to do so if one is available. A maintenance log will provide details to other users of the machine of the type of work carried out and future actions required.

MAINTENANCE SCHEDULES

'Planned'

The manufacturer's handbook will provide details of the machine's maintenance schedule, together with the period of time between services and routine inspections. A planned service would include:

- greasing and oiling of moving parts;
- checking, adjusting and replacing worn or damaged parts;

FIGURE 4.40 Servicing a circular saw

- checking guards and safety devices are working correctly over their full range;
- general cleaning.

'Condition-based'

Worn or damaged parts should be noted and ordered during the planned maintenance; these parts are then replaced at a more convenient time (e.g. changing saw blades).

'Emergency'

Regular servicing and maintenance will reduce the likelihood of an emergency breakdown occurring. Unplanned stoppages are costly to employers through lost labour time, emergency engineers' expenses and missed deadlines or delivery dates. Poorly serviced machines will function less accurately and reduce productivity; they could also put the user at risk.

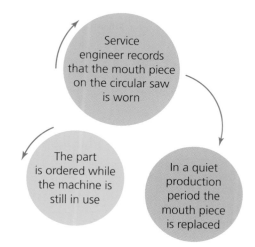

FIGURE 4.41 'Condition-based' maintenance

ROUTINE INSPECTIONS

Routine visual checks should be carried out on all woodworking machines before use to ensure that they are in good working order and a safe condition. The inspections should be carried out by a competent and authorised person, and preferably the person about to use the machine. During this time particular attention should be paid to the following areas:

- extraction ducting – should be free from splits, dust build-up and blockages, and kinks;
- dust extraction bins or bags – below maximum capacity and capable of collecting the waste from the next job;
- floor area around the machine – should be free from obstructions and dust, and should be non-slip;
- start, stop and emergency stop buttons – securely fixed to the machine, operate correctly and undamaged;
- guards, push sticks and safety devices – undamaged, fully functional and safe to use;
- rip fence – moves freely along its full range;
- table surface – clean and clear of waste material and offcuts;
- saw blade faults – as illustrated below.

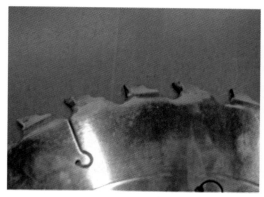

FIGURE 4.42 Saw blade with damaged or missing teeth

FIGURE 4.43 Build-up of resin

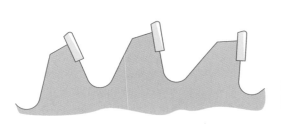

FIGURE 4.44 Blunt or dull cutting edge

FIGURE 4.45 Black eyes

TRADE SECRETS

Machine and hand tools with blunt cutting edges are referred to in the trade as 'losing their edge'. It is not always easy to identify tooling that has 'lost its edge', especially if you are inexperienced or a trainee.

If increased effort is needed while pushing material through a saw, this is normally a result of the circular saw blade being blunt; other signs are:

- *increased breakout on the underside of the material being cut;*
- *during the ripping operation, the material drifts away from the rip fence;*
- *the saw blade becomes unbalanced and wobbles due to overheating;*
- *poor-quality saw cut;*
- *burning or scorching of the material during cutting.*

ACTIVITIES

Activity 31 – Setting up fixed and transportable circular saws

Read through the following questions and answer them as fully as you can to help you develop your underpinning knowledge of this subject area.

1. What do the initials PUWER stand for?
2. What is an 'approved code of practice'?
3. Name one effective method of removing dust from a working area.
4. All moving parts on a circular saw are required by the law to stop within how many seconds?
5. What should the minimum temperature be in a machining area?

CHANGING CIRCULAR SAW BLADES

The exact process of changing a circular saw blade will differ between manufactured machines, although the principles are very similar. Circular saw blades are manufactured with either one central hole that locates over the drive shaft or a secondary hole just off the centre. The secondary hole is positioned over the drive pin to secure the blade in position and prevent the saw from slipping while it is in motion. When a saw blade is changed and relocated over the drive shaft, it is important to pull the saw blade back against the drive pin to ensure it is correctly positioned while tightening the nut.

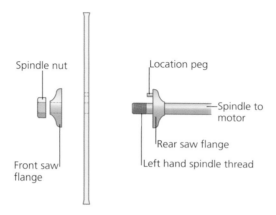

FIGURE 4.46

The location holes through the circular saw blades will vary in diameter between machines; the size of the hole is referred to as the 'bore' size. It is important that the location hole suits the spindle or drive shaft perfectly. If the bore size is too small it will not fit over the spindle; if it is too big, the blade will not rotate centrally while it is in motion, possibly resulting in a poor finish and increased stress on the machine parts. Bore sizes will be stated in the machine manufacturer's handbook and on the 'plate' of the circular saw blade.

 FREQUENTLY ASKED QUESTIONS

▶ **Older machines seem to have an unusual 'bore size'; can you still get blades to fit these machines?**

It is quite common for some older or imported machines to have imperial-sized parts (e.g. ¼ inch, ½ inch). The most common metric bore sizes are 16 mm, 20 mm and 30 mm. Saw blades with metric holes can be adapted to suit imperial machines; this is normally achieved by inserting metal 'bushes'.

SERVICE TOOLS

All woodworking machinery is usually purchased and supplied with a selection of basic service tools. Each tool is designed specifically to fit the component parts of each machine. Using other tooling may result in poor fitting and could potentially damage the parts; this would also be a potential hazard for the service engineer.

CIRCULAR SAW BLADE SELECTION

Circular saw blades are specifically designed and shaped to cut through timber and timber-based sheet materials, both effectively and efficiently. It is important to consider the following factors before selecting the most suitable circular saw blade:

- type of material being cut (e.g. hardwood, softwood, veneered sheet material);
- operation (cross-cutting, ripping, multifunction);
- scoring (panel, dimension and wall saws only);
- finish required (general purpose, high-quality/extra-thin kerf).

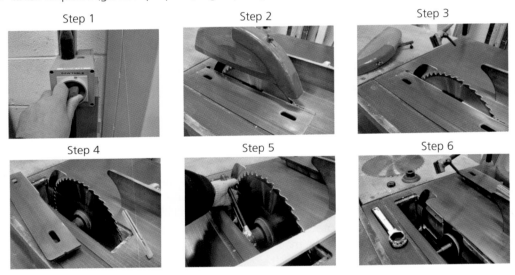

Step 1

Step 2

Step 3

Step 4

Step 5

Step 6

FIGURE 4.47 Changing a circular saw blade

IDENTIFICATION OF PARTS

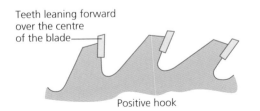

Teeth leaning forward over the centre of the blade

Positive hook

Teeth leaning backward behind the centre of the blade

Negative hook

FIGURE 4.48 Circular saw blade with positive rake

FIGURE 4.49 Circular saw blade with negative rake

TYPES OF SAW BLADE

Generally, circular saw blades have been manufactured with a parallel plate with teeth shaped and bent on either side of the body; this clearance is known as the 'set'. The set on the saw gives clearance to the body of the blade as it cuts through the material; this prevents the saw from binding and overheating as it cuts. The amount of set on a blade will vary depending on the operation and materials being cut. If the set is too much, the saw blade will produce a poor finish, require increased effort to feed the material through and produce a wider 'kerf'. If the set is too little, it will result in the material jamming and being forced back towards the operator; this is known as 'kick back'.

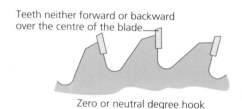

Teeth neither forward or backward over the centre of the blade

Zero or neutral degree hook

FIGURE 4.50 Circular saw blade with zero degree rake

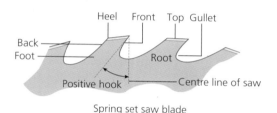

Spring set saw blade

FIGURE 4.51 Tooth terminology

FIGURE 4.52 TCT blade

Spring set blades are rarely used in industry nowadays because they quickly lose their sharp edge, especially when abrasive hardwoods and sheet materials are being cut. Tungsten carbide tipped (TCT) saw blades have now replaced spring set blades, and are commonly used in the construction industry. Tungsten is heat fused to the ends of the teeth on a saw blade because it is extremely hard; it also maintains its cutting edge and set for long periods of time.

SAW TEETH

The shape of the teeth is determined by the material on which they are going to be used.

RIP SAW BLADES

- If the 'hook angle' of the teeth is steep, it will have a deep gullet to collect the waste and be very effective in cutting through softwood. Although the edge on the teeth is extremely sharp, it is very weak and could break if used to cut hardwood.
- The 'hook angle' should be reduced to 20° for multi-purpose cutting of hardwood, softwood and panel materials. The lower hook angle means that the speed at which the material is fed into the saw must be reduced (feed speed).
- Hook angles of 10° should be used to cut panelled materials, including wood veneered boards. This type of circular saw will commonly have a minimum of 60 teeth on a 350 mm diameter blade.

PERIPHERAL SPEEDS

The 'peripheral speed', or 'rim speed', is the speed at which the circumference of a saw blade runs. If the peripheral speed of a circular saw blade is high, it will result in a poor-quality finish and compromise the health and safety of the machine operator. If the speed is too slow, it will make the process of cutting the material difficult and will normally require increased or excessive force to push the timber or sheet material through the saw; 50 metres per second is considered to be the most effective. The peripheral speed for a saw can be established by the calculation below.

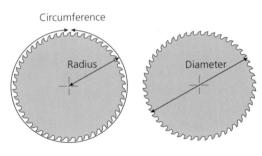

FIGURE 4.53

(*Remember* – the circumference of a circle is equal to 3.142 times the diameter.)

Example calculation

Circular saw circumference × spindle speed

= peripheral speed in metres per minute ÷ 60

= peripheral speed recorded in metres/second

If you are in any doubt as to the spindle speed and the suitable peripheral speeds for a circular saw, these can be found in the manufacturer's handbook.

 ACTIVITIES

Activity 32 – Changing saw blades

Read through the following questions and answer them as fully as you can to help you develop your underpinning knowledge of this subject area.

1. How often should circular saws be serviced?
2. Who should carry out servicing on a circular saw?
3. What item needs to be removed from the bed on a circular saw to gain access to the riving knife and blade?
4. What is the minimum length of a push stick?
5. How can you identify faults on a circular saw blade?

CONVERTING TIMBER

While preparing to cut sections of solid timber on a circular saw, you must analyse the shape of each piece and look for timber defects, these may include dead knots, pockets of sap and splits. It is highly unlikely that longer lengths of natural timber will be perfectly 'true' (straight) or without an element of 'cupping', especially if the material is sawn. Consideration for the shape of the timber before cutting will save timber, avoid mistakes and protect the operator from the results of the timber 'kicking back' and 'snatching'. Snatching is the result of the timber being unsupported as it is fed into the saw. For example, the timber being used may have a bow; if this is fed into the saw with the bow side up (the 'crown'), it will be unsupported across a large area of the timber. As the teeth on the saw blade begin to cut into the timber, this will force the timber downwards onto the saw bed; this is known as 'snatching'.

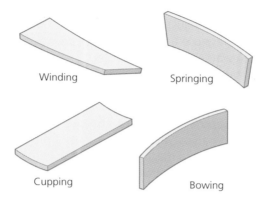

FIGURE 4.54 Defected timber

FREQUENTLY ASKED QUESTIONS

▶ What is 'case hardening'?

Case hardening is a timber defect that occurs during the drying out of the timber after it has been converted. It is difficult to identify the defect until it has been recut after seasoning; it normally results in the saw cut (kerf) closing as it passes through the saw blade, and jamming on the blade. This is due to the timber being dried out too quickly and leaving a high level of moisture in the centre of the timber.

JIGS

Circular rip saws can be used for a number of operations besides ripping and cross-cutting. They are extremely versatile woodworking machines and, when they are used in conjunction with 'jigs', can accurately produce repetition work, with consistent results. Care should be taken when producing jigs to avoid using materials that could damage the saw blade if contact is made during its operation. Made-made sheet materials such as plywood and medium-density fibreboard (MDF) are usually used to manufacture jigs because they are both durable and stable.

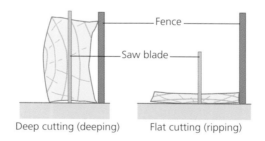

FIGURE 4.55

RECAP

SAFE WORKING PRACTICE ON CIRCULAR SAWS

- *Always* adjust guards to the lowest possible height.
- *Always* use the safety devices provided (e.g. push sticks).
- *Always* use dust extraction.
- *Always* report faults or defects found.
- *Always* isolate the power from the machine before setting up or adjusting.
- *Never* use machinery under the influence of alcohol or drugs.
- *Never* use a machine with loose clothing, jewellery or long hair.
- *Never* adjust, alter or walk away from the machine while the saw blade is still in motion.
- *Never* use a machine without the correct training, information and authorisation.
- *Never* use woodworking machinery without the correct personal protective equipment (PPE).
- *Never* use a machine without being authorised to do so.
- *Never* distract or talk to an operative (skilled worker) while they are operating machinery.
- *Never* use the machine in an unsafe condition.

 ACTIVITIES

Activity 33 – Cutting timber and sheet materials

Read through the following questions and answer them as fully as you can to help you develop your underpinning knowledge of this subject area.

1. What is a 'jig' used for?
2. Explain the meaning of 'case hardening'.
3. Sketch the following timber conversions: 'flatting' and 'deeping'.

MULTIPLE-CHOICE QUESTIONS

1 When a circular saw is switched off, within how many seconds must the blade stop?
  a 5
  b 10
  c 15
  d 20

2 The guarding of circular saws is a requirement of which one of the following?
  a WaHR
  b PPER
  c PUWER
  d RIDDOR

3 A push stick should be used for the last
  a 200 mm of the cut
  b 300 mm of the cut
  c 400 mm of the cut
  d 500 mm of the cut

4 At table-top level the distance between the riving knife and the saw blade should not exceed:
  a 4 mm
  b 8 mm
  c 12 mm
  d 16 mm

5 A machine with a broken guard should be
  a sold
  b used with care
  c labelled unsafe for use
  d used if no other machine is available

6 Which **one** of the following hook types is required for a circular saw blade designed to rip timber?
  a Bill
  b Barbed
  c Positive
  d Negative

7   Which **one** of the following types of saw is small in diameter and cuts on the underside of the material to prevent breakout?

   a kerf
   b crown
   c raking
   d scoring

8   The aid required to cut wedges safely and to a consistent shape is called a

   a jig
   b box
   c saddle
   d harness

9   Before changing a saw blade, the machine must be

   a cleaned
   b wedged
   c isolated
   d serviced

10 What percentage should the riving knife be thicker than a circular saw?

   a 10 per cent
   b 20 per cent
   c 30 per cent
   d 40 per cent

PRODUCE SETTING-OUT DETAILS FOR ROUTINE PRODUCTS

CHAPTER 5

LEARNING OUTCOMES

By the end of this chapter you should have developed a knowledge and understanding of:

- interpreting information for setting out;
- selecting resources for setting out;
- setting out for bench joinery and site carpentry.

INTERPRETING INFORMATION FOR SETTING OUT

WORKING DRAWINGS

Understanding written forms of communication is vital to prevent misinterpretation, wasted time and costly mistakes. Draughtsmen such as architects, engineers and designers are responsible for producing initial drawings following a design brief from the client, before forwarding these details to local planning departments for approval and eventually to the main and subcontractors. (Further information regarding architects' and engineers' drawings and specifications is provided in Chapter 2 – Information, Quantities and Communicating with Others.) Joinery companies usually receive architects' plans and a brief specification directly from the architect, the principle contractor or the client, particularly if they are managing the project themselves. Because joinery items are rarely structural, the information received normally consists of design details rather than assembly drawings. It is usually the role of the workshop manager to liaise with the person/s at the source of the information to clarify details, and also to ensure that the design information provided will translate into working drawings ready for production. The initial stage of deciphering a specification and architects'/designers' drawings is to establish the component details and overall dimensions; this is then redrawn by the 'setter-out' or joiner onto a component detail drawing.

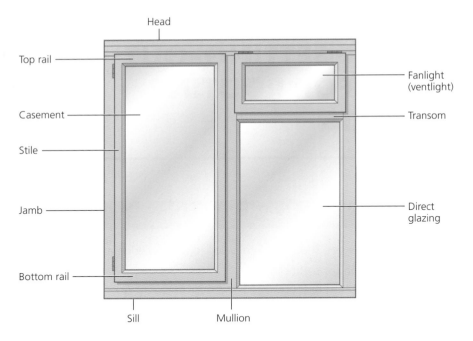

FIGURE 5.1 Component detail drawing (known as a rod)

The setter-out will usually use the component drawings to determine the most efficient method of assembly. These details are then communicated to the machinists and joiners (production members) via assembly drawings and cutting lists. The information contained in the assembly drawings should be no more than the minimum required to produce the components; any further information may clutter the drawing and is also a waste of resources. In general terms, assembly drawings allow joinery items to be produced following the design details and specification from the architect or client. These types of drawings are often referred to as 'working drawings' because of their practical application.

RODS

Rods are simply full-scale drawings of the height and width of joinery items and usually contain a section through the middle. They are normally produced if a complex item of purpose-made joinery is required or multiple components require marking out. Each component is normally laid on the setting out to enable critical lines, such as the shoulders of joints, to be transferred. Using a rod to mark out rather than measuring individual components speeds up the process, improves accuracy and provides consistency between joinery parts.

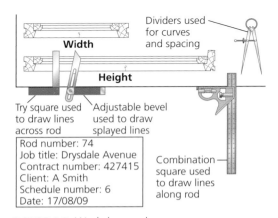

FIGURE 5.2 Workshop rod

TRADE SECRETS

Setting out workshop rods on paper should be avoided because they will absorb the moisture in the environment, causing them to expand. The amount of movement will depend on the type of paper used, the size of the rod and the level of humidity in the workshop. Movement in the paper will interfere with the accuracy of the working drawing and possibly lead to mistakes.

CUTTING LISTS

Cutting lists are normally produced by the setter-out in the drawing office upon checking and completion of the assembly drawings. They are used to list all the components, dimensions and quantities of the materials required to complete a particular project, and in some cases details of second-phase machining. In addition to these details each project will have a unique reference or job number printed on the cutting list, along with the date and names of the person who completed and checked the information. Copies of cutting lists are usually distributed from the setting out office to the workshop foreperson, and eventually to the machinists. The machinists will use the cutting lists to prepare the materials ready for either the joiners or in some larger companies the marker-out.

Machinists preparing planed joinery and quality timber normally begin the process by referring to a cutting list for the exact finished dimensions of each item. Although every component is usually itemised on one or more cutting lists, it is usually the responsibility of the machinist to calculate the most economical way of converting the material into manageable sections. In

Rod number: 74
Job title: Drysdale Avenue
Client: A Smith
Date: 17/08/09
Contract number: 427415

Cutting list									
Item number	Description	Quantity	Material	Cut sizes			Finished sizes		
				L	W	Th	L	W	Th
1	Head	1	Mahogany	70	95	700	75	100	700
2	Sill	1	Mahogany	70	120	700	75	125	700
3	Jambs	2	Mahogany	70	95	1000	75	100	1000
4	Top rail	1	Mahogany	450	45	90	50	50	450
5	Bottom rail	1	Mahogany	450	70	500	50	75	450
6	Stiles	2	Mahogany	900	45	45	900	50	50

FIGURE 5.3 Cutting list

addition to the finished dimensions on a cutting list, the setter-out will normally provide the 'sawn sizes'. The sawn dimensions are slightly bigger than the 'finished sizes' to allow the timber to be reduced to provide a planed smooth surface. Each component is normally identified throughout the machining process with a unique reference number, which is marked on its end. The component reference number is normally identified on the cutting list for easy identification of each item by the machinists and joiners. Failure to clearly identify every component throughout the machining process could lead to mistakes and wasted time resulting from having to reset machinery. The danger of having to machine timber once a machine has been adjusted, is the possibility of marginal differences between batches or 'runs'.

? FREQUENTLY ASKED QUESTIONS

▶ What is a 'marker-out' and 'second-phase machining'?

Upon preparation of the timber, some larger joinery companies find it more efficient to employ experienced joiners to mark out the timber components prior to returning them to the machine shop for 'second-phase machining'. These employees are referred to as a 'marker-out'. During the second stage of machining, the timber may be rebated or moulded, or simply have the joints cut before forwarding to the bench joiners in the workshop.

ACTIVITIES

Activity 16 – Interpreting information for setting out

Read through the following questions and answer them as fully as you can to help you develop your underpinning knowledge of this subject area.

1. What other information is normally required on a timber cutting list besides the length and section sizes?
2. What is the purpose of a workshop rod?
3. List three examples of draughtsmen.
4. Define the role of a 'setter-out'.
5. Explain the disadvantage of using setting-out workshop rods on drawing paper.

SELECTING RESOURCES FOR SETTING OUT

Timber is a natural resource that is generally divided into two categories:

- Hardwood (deciduous);
- Softwood (coniferous).

The species of trees in each category is generally identified and divided by their method of growth, the shape of the crown of the tree and the density of the timber. It is a common mistake to assume that hardwoods are identified by their hardness and softwoods by their softness; in fact some species of softwood are harder than some hardwoods and vice versa. The range of species of hardwoods extends to approximately 100 times more than softwoods but not all are suitable for a given situation. In general, most hard- and softwoods will be suited for internal use, but may rapidly deteriorate in external positions. Some tropical hardwoods are becoming endangered due to de-forestation; this problem has caused some timber prices to dramatically increase and the use of veneered boards to become ever more popular. Softwood can generally be purchased commercially in a range of standard widths and thicknesses, with the lengths increasing in 300mm increments (1.8 m, 2.1 m, 2.4 m, and so on). Some of the most commonly available sizes of commercial sawn softwood sections are listed below:

Typical sizes of commercial sawn softwood

19×50 mm			50×50 mm			
19×75 mm			50×75 mm		75×75 mm	
19×100 mm	22×100 mm	25×100 mm	50×100 mm	63×100 mm	75×100 mm	100×100 mm
19×125 mm	22×125 mm		50×125 mm	63×125 mm	75×125 mm	100×125 mm
19×150 mm	22×150 mm	25×150 mm	50×150 mm	63×150 mm	75×150 mm	100×150 mm
					75×175 mm	100×175 mm
			50×200 mm	63×200 mm	75×200 mm	100×200 mm
		25×225 mm	50×225 mm	63×225 mm	75×225 mm	100×225 mm
			50×250 mm		75×250 mm	100×250 mm
						100×275 mm
			50×300 mm		75×300 mm	100×300 mm

Note: The larger among these sizes are difficult to obtain and as such command a premium price.

The cost and shape of hardwood trees has determined the method of stocking these species at timber merchants. Modern methods of timber construction result in the edges of the sawn boards retaining a portion of the outer bark known as the 'waney edge'. Although the bark can easily be removed whilst straightening the edges of the boards, this will result in the loss of a substantial amount of usable timber. Timber merchants commonly offer a service for removal of the uneven edge otherwise known as the 'wane', but usually pass the labour and waste material costs on to the customer. Owing to the nature of hardwood, the widths and lengths of the trunks will vary considerably, resulting in difficulties when calculating the value of each board. To overcome this problem hardwoods are commonly supplied with the wane attached to the boards and the price calculated per cubic metre. To cut down on transport costs and to make packing easier, most timber is shipped 'square-edged' rather than 'waney-edged'.

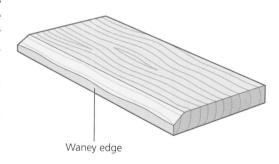

Waney edge

FIGURE 5.4 Wane

? FREQUENTLY ASKED QUESTIONS

▶ **How are the sizes of hardwood boards determined if they contain 'wane'?**

The width of a board containing wane is usually measured at several points along the length of the board before average dimensions are determined.

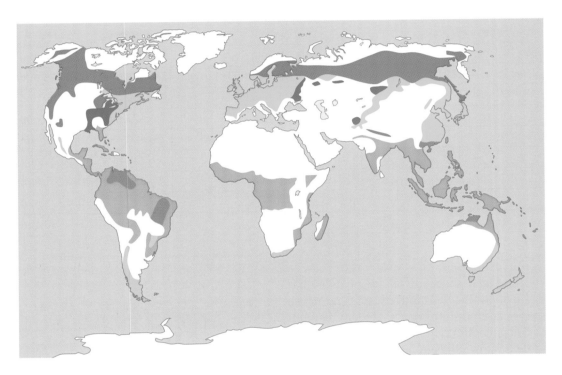

 Coniferous (arctic and subarctic)

 Broad-leaved deciduous (temperate)

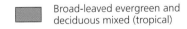 Broad-leaved evergreen and deciduous mixed (tropical)

Mixed coniferous and broad-leaved deciduous (temperate)

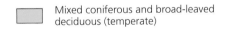 Broad-leaved evergreen (tropical)

FIGURE 5.5 Sources of hardwood and softwood

TIMBER (HARDWOOD)

ASH (AMERICAN)

- Characteristics – white with pale brown, mostly straight grain and strong;
- Common uses – tool handles, sports equipment, joinery and boat building;
- Durability – perishable;
- Source – United States of America and Canada;
- Weight – 690 kg/m³;
- Workability – moderate.

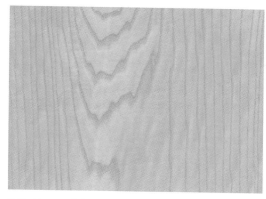

FIGURE 5.6 Ash

BALSA

- Characteristics – very lightweight and soft, with a light cream appearance;
- Common uses – model making and insulation;
- Durability – perishable;
- Source – South America;
- Weight – 160kg/m³;
- Ease of use – easy.

FIGURE 5.7 Balsa

BEECH (EUROPEAN)

- Characteristics – whitish brown with a straight, even grain. Steamed beech is pinkish brown;
- Common uses – internal joinery, cabinet making and veneered man-made sheet materials and wooden hand tools such as mallets and gauges;
- Durability – perishable;
- Source – Europe;
- Weight – 720 kg/m³;
- Workability – moderate.

FIGURE 5.8 Beech (European)

FREQUENTLY ASKED QUESTIONS

▶ **What is the difference between 'steamed' beech and standard beech?**

Traditionally, beech used for furniture making was treated to a process of steaming in a kiln within a few days of conversion. The combination of heat and moisture usually takes the tension out of the boards and turns standard or 'white beech' an attractive shade of pink/brown.

CHERRY (AMERICAN)

- Characteristics – deep red, turning brown with age and a light, straight grain. Medium density;
- Common uses – internal joinery, veneered man-made sheet materials and furniture;
- Durability – moderately durable;
- Source – United States of America and Canada;
- Weight – 595 kg/m³;
- Workability – easy.

FIGURE 5.9 Cherry (American)

ELM (AMERICAN WHITE)

- Characteristics – light, reddish brown with a straight, sometimes interlocking (refractory) grain;
- Common uses – internal joinery, boat building and furniture;
- Durability – moderately durable;
- Source – United States of America and Canada;
- Weight – 570 kg/m³;
- Workability – moderate/difficult.

FIGURE 5.10 Elm (American White)

? FREQUENTLY ASKED QUESTIONS

▶ What is 'interlocking' grain?

The mass of a tree's cell structure constitutes the grain of the wood. In general, the tree's cells run along the length of the trunk resulting in long, even and straight grain. Some species of trees twist and turn along their length during their growth causing the cells to deviate from the main axis. The result of this distortion is referred to as 'interlocking grain'. Interlocking grain is often very difficult to work (machine, plane, chisel, etc) and usually requires highly skilled, experienced joiners with razor-sharp specialist tools to achieve a smooth finish. One hand tool regularly used to finish timber containing interlocking grain is a 'cabinet scraper'.

Cabinet scrapers

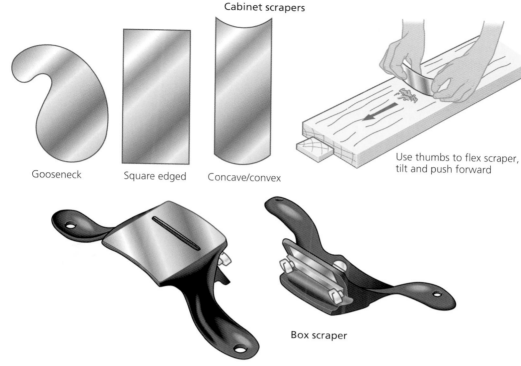

Gooseneck   Square edged   Concave/convex

Use thumbs to flex scraper, tilt and push forward

Box scraper

FIGURE 5.11 Cabinet Scraper

MAHOGANY (BRAZILIAN)

- Characteristics – medium density, reddish brown with an even grain;
- Common uses – internal and exterior joinery, veneered man-made sheet materials and panelling;
- Durability – durable;
- Source – Central and South America;
- Weight – 560 kg/m³;
- Workability – moderate.

MAPLE

- Characteristics – white with a straight, open light-brown grain;
- Common uses – interior joinery, flooring and veneers for man-made sheet materials;
- Durability – moderate;
- Source – United States of America and Canada;
- Weight – 640 kg/m³;
- Workability – easy.

FIGURE 5.12 Mahogany (Brazilian)

FIGURE 5.13 Maple

IROKO

- Characteristics – very dense, golden to medium brown appearance with a high natural oil;
- Common uses – general exterior joinery and garden furniture;
- Durability – very durable;
- Source – West Africa;
- Weight – 660kg/m;
- Workability – moderate/difficult.

OAK (EUROPEAN)

- Characteristics – medium density, light brown with a distinct grain pattern and figuring;
- Common uses – external carpentry and joinery, panelling and flooring;
- Durability – durable;
- Source – Asia, Europe, North Africa;
- Weight – 725 kg/m³;
- Workability – moderate/difficult.

FIGURE 5.14 Oak (European)

 FREQUENTLY ASKED QUESTIONS

▶ What does 'figuring' mean?

Timber is often distinguished by its colour, weight, density and grain. The shape or pattern of the grain within a section of timber is mainly due to the method of conversion. For example, a trunk that has been cut 'tangentially' will have a distinctively attractive grain, with the annual growth rings resembling flames. Alternatively, if the trunk has been 'quarter sawn' the grain will be considerably straighter.

SAPELE

- Characteristics – reddish brown appearance with stripy, interlocking grain;
- Common uses – general internal and external joinery;
- Durability – durable;
- Source – West Africa;
- Weight – 640kg/m³;
- Workability – difficult.

SYCAMORE

- Characteristics – medium density; White–light yellow, with mostly straight grain and some figuring;
- Common uses – internal joinery, furniture and flooring;
- Durability – medium;
- Source – Europe and North America;
- Weight – 640 kg/m³;
- Workability – average.

FIGURE 5.15 Sycamore (European)

TEAK

- Characteristics – golden brown with a high volume of natural oils;
- Common uses – high quality interior and exterior joinery, and furniture;
- Durability – durable;
- Source – Far East;
- Weight – 660kg/m³;
- Workability – good.

UTILE

- Characteristics – pink–brown, with a striped, interlocking grain;
- Common uses – interior and exterior joinery, flooring, plywood and veneered timber-based sheet materials. It is also commonly use as a mahogany substitute;
- Durability – durable;
- Source – Africa;
- Weight – 660 kg/m³;
- Workability – difficult.

FIGURE 5.16 Utile

TIMBER (SOFTWOOD)

CEDAR (WESTERN RED)

- Characteristics – relatively soft timber, with a reddish brown appearance that fades to silver–grey after exposure to the weather for long periods;
- Common uses – exterior boarding, cladding;
- Durability – moderate durability;
- Grown – United States of America, Canada, United Kingdom, New Zealand;
- Weight – 380 kg/m³;
- Workability – good.

FIGURE 5.17 Cedar (Western wood)

DOUGLAS FIR

- Characteristics – reddish brown in colour; straight grained with few knots;
- Common uses – plywood, flooring, exterior joinery;
- Durability – moderate durability;
- Grown – United Kingdom, Canada, western America, western Australia and New Zealand;
- Weight – 490 kg/m³;
- Workability – good.

FIGURE 5.18 Douglas fir

HEMLOCK

- Characteristics – light brown with a straight grain and few knots;
- Common uses – joinery and construction work;
- Durability – non-durable;
- Grown – United Kingdom, Canada and United States of America;
- Weight – 500 kg/m³;
- Workability – good.

FIGURE 5.19 Hemlock

LARCH

- Characteristics – light-red heartwood with pale cream sapwood. Generally straight grained with a coarse texture;
- Common uses – joinery, boat planking and railway sleepers;
- Durability – moderately durable;
- Grown – North America, North Asia and Europe;
- Weight – 580 kg/m³;
- Workability – moderate.

FIGURE 5.20 Larch

PARANA PINE

- Characteristics – light brown with red streaks and a fine texture;
- Common uses – internal joinery (particularly staircases) and furniture;
- Durability – non-durable;
- Grown – Argentina, Brazil and Paraguay;
- Weight – 545 kg/m³;
- Workability – good.

? FREQUENTLY ASKED QUESTIONS

▶ **What is the difference between 'heartwood' and 'sapwood'?**

Sapwood can be located towards the outer portion of a tree's trunk and branches. It is easily distinguishable in some hardwoods due to its light-coloured appearance against the darker heartwood. Trees use the porous sapwood to distribute water absorbed by the roots through the trunk and branches. The cell structure of the sapwood has thin walls and therefore has the ability to lose and absorb water quickly; therefore it is prone to excessive shrinkage and expansion after conversion.

REDWOOD (EUROPEAN)

- Characteristics – light-yellow, resinous timber with distinguishing grain;
- Common uses – joinery, furniture and construction;
- Durability – moderately durable;
- Grown – Asia, Europe and United Kingdom;
- Weight – 510 kg/m³;
- Workability – moderate.

EUROPEAN WHITEWOOD (ALSO KNOWN AS 'NORWEGIAN SPRUCE')

- Characteristics – straight, even and open grained with a pale cream appearance;
- Common uses – internal joinery, studwork, floor joists;
- Durability – non-durable;
- Grown – Scandinavia;
- Weight – 510kg/m³;
- Workability – good.

SPRUCE

- Characteristics – straight grain with an even texture;
- Common uses – plywood, oars, masts, construction and joinery;
- Durability – non-durable;
- Grown – Europe;
- Weight – 400 kg/m³;
- Workability – good.

YELLOW PINE

- Characteristics – yellow to pale brown in colour; very stable with a straight, even grain;
- Common uses – panelling, boat building, furniture and construction;
- Durability – non-durable;
- Grown – East Canada and United States of America;
- Weight – 425 kg/m³;
- Workability – good.

FIGURE 5.21 Redwood (European)

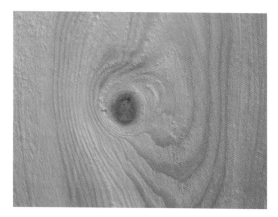

FIGURE 5.22 Spruce

FIGURE 5.23 Yellow pine

YEW

- Characteristics – very tough and hard softwood with orange–red heart wood and light-yellow sapwood;
- Common uses – interior joinery, furniture, wood turning;
- Durability – durable;
- Grown – Asia, North Africa, western and central Europe;
- Weight – 680 kg/m³;
- Workability – difficult.

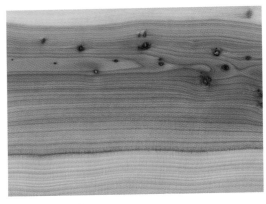

FIGURE 5.24 Yew

TIMBER-BASED MANUFACTURED BOARDS (MAN-MADE BOARDS)

Timber-based manufactured boards have been developed since plywood was introduced in the early part of the nineteenth century, closely followed by particle boards to provide an alternative to solid wood. Timber-based engineered boards such as plywood, chipboard and medium-density fibreboard (MDF) provide a relatively cheap and stable material that is resistant to warping and splitting under normal conditions. Today man-made boards are commonly used in the mass production of affordable furniture, floors and wall panelling to name just a few. Timber-based boards have evolved in recent years with the use of moisture and fire-resistant materials, moulded, perforated and faced boards. The use of decorative foils and real timber veneers create simulated solid materials that are sometimes difficult to distinguish from the real thing.

FIGURE 5.25 Edge banding machine (type: Ambition 1650 FC; manufacturer: Brandt (Germany))

Timber-based manufactured boards are divided into three categories:

1. laminated boards;
2. fibreboards;
3. particle boards.

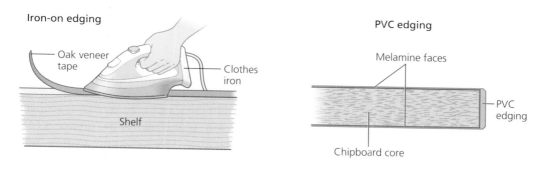

Iron-on edging

Oak veneer tape

Clothes iron

Shelf

PVC edging

Melamine faces

PVC edging

Chipboard core

Hardwood edging

Laminate

Plywood or particle board

Edge build-up

FIGURE 5.26 Edge finishes

 ## FREQUENTLY ASKED QUESTIONS

▶ How are the edges of foil and veneered boards finished?

Veneered and foil-wrapped man-made boards are usually supplied with decorative finishes on their face sides and not along their long and short edges. Some suppliers stock a limited range of narrow manufactured boards with finished edges, although these are normally only suitable for shelving or similar applications. In most cases the edges of decorative boards are uneven with a slight overhang of the veneers or foils applied to the faces during the manufacturing process. Before an edging can be applied to a man-made board it has to be re-cut to provide a perfectly square, undamaged surface.

There are a variety of different materials that can be used to finish the edges of man-made boards, including:

▶ 'Iron-on edging' – 1 mm thick and self-adhesive, it is available with real wood and plastic finishes cut to length off a roll and applied with a hot iron under light pressure. Iron-on edging can be used to ensure that the edge of the board will not encounter excessive wear;

▶ PVC – 2–2.5 mm thick with pencil-rounded edges. Normally applied with an 'edge-banding machine'. As the edging is applied during this process, hot adhesive is fed between the edge of the board and the back of the edging; it cures in seconds as it cools. PVC edges have a strong resistance to knocks and are therefore commonly used for commercial uses such as desk tops and counters;

▶ Solid timber edging – This may be applied in a variety of different thicknesses depending on its use. Timber edges can also be applied with an edge bander or manually for complex shaped boards. Solid edges have a strong resistance to damage and are also easily repairable, unlike other types of edging.

LAMINATED BOARDS

PLYWOOD

Plywood is constructed with a number of thin layers of timber known as 'veneers' or 'plies' laminated (bonded) together. The number of plies used in a sheet of plywood is determined by the total thickness of the board and an odd number of layers is used to achieve the overall finished dimension. Plywood is constructed with an odd number of plies so that the grain is running in the same direction on both sides of the board; it also allows the plywood to be evenly balanced whilst still maintaining its stability. The outer layers/plies are usually better quality timber compared with the middle of the board; these are referred to as the 'faces'. The veneers of timber underneath the faces are usually bonded perpendicular (at right angles) to each other; this provides the strength to the plywood and eliminates the risk of shrinkage and expansion in the length and width of the board. Timber-based manufactured boards such as plywood are often preferable as opposed to solid timber because they are:

- stable over width, length and thickness;
- readily available in large sizes;
- less likely to deteriorate (providing the appropriate material has been selected for use);
- easier to cut to size and shape;
- free from defects such as splits, shakes, cupping, etc.;
- cost efficient.

Standard dimensions

Plywood is available in a limited range of standard widths and lengths, as listed in Table 5.1.

Length and width
2440 mm × 1220 mm
3050 mm × 1220 mm
3050 mm × 1525 mm
1525 mm × 3660 mm
1900 mm × 4000 mm

Thickness
3, 4, 5, 6, 8, 9, 12, 15, 18, 21, 24, 27, 30 mm

TABLE 5.1 Standard sizes for plywood

The grain on the faces of plywood sheets usually runs parallel to the longest edge, but is also available from some stockists across the width of the board. Manufacturers normally identify the direction of the grain by specifying the side it runs parallel to first, for example: a sheet of plywood 1220 mm × 2440 mm will have the grain running across the width of the sheet.

FIGURE 5.27 Direction of grain on 1220 × 2440mm plywood

Grading

The finish of plywood will vary significantly depending on its intended use, for example:

- interior;
- exterior;
- faced (decorative);
- softwood;
- hardwood, etc.

The quality of plywood is normally determined by the face appearance of the surfaces, the number of veneers and the amount of defects on the interior and exterior layers of the board. In general terms, the more layers contained within the plywood the stronger the sheet. The performance of plywood will vary depending of the type of adhesive used to bond the layers together and the quality of the plies. The grading of the plywood is normally marked on one face with a label; this will specify the quality of the plies used as well as the type of adhesive between each layer and the species of timber used to construct the board. The quality of the plies is usually graded in Europe (Russia, Poland, Finland, etc.) from A to D, 'A' being a virtually defect-free, smooth and superior condition; 'D' being a plywood that may have some small holes, splits, knots and discolouration. In some cases only one face will need to be premium 'A' quality and the other side a lower grade such as 'B'; in these cases the plywood would be labelled A/B. Decorative plywood will be graded according to the type of veneer used on the face sides; for example ash veneer may be used on both sides of a sheet of plywood; in this case the plywood would be graded A/A. If the ash veneer is only used on one side and a balancing veneer on the other then it may be graded A/B.

FREQUENTLY ASKED QUESTIONS

▶ **What will happen to interior grade plywood if it is used in an exterior position?**

The adhesive used to bond the plies together between the interior plywood has a low resistance to water. If moisture is absorbed into the timber layers whilst it is either used externally, or internally in areas of high humidity, the layers will 'delaminate'. The term 'delaminate' refers to the failure of the bond between plies and the lifting of the layers to cause the plywood to fall apart.

Types of plywood

1. **Interior-grade plywood (INT)** – is usually bonded together during manufacture with urea–formaldehyde adhesive, which is only appropriate for dry conditions. The arrangement of the plies within the plywood also prevents this type of man-made board from being used for structural purposes. INT normally has at least one good-quality face suitable for finishing with paint, varnish or veneer/laminate. The use of a lower quality veneer on the reverse sides of the boards reduces the cost of the plywood; this is especially useful for projects when only one face side will be seen, for example wall panelling, flooring and encasing services. Interior plywood is commonly available with a standard range of decorative finishes such as hard- and softwood veneers, applied to

either both faces of the boards or one side with a balancing veneer on the reverse. A large proportion of INT is produced in regions of Asia (often referred to as 'far eastern plywood') and imported from countries such as Malaysia and Indonesia.

2. **Exterior grade plywood (EXT) or moisture resistant (MR)** – is suitable for use in most positions where it may be exposed to moisture and humidity such as kitchens or bathrooms. The quality of the adhesive used between the plies will determine the amount of exposure to the elements the plywood can withstand before it starts to deteriorate and delaminate. Standard exterior-grade plywood is normally manufactured with 'melamine urea-formaldehyde', which is only semi-durable in extreme conditions. If further resistance to cold and extreme heat is required then 'weather- and boil-proof plywood (WBP)' is commonly used. Any plywood that is open to the elements or water ingress should be protected with good-quality water-resistant paint or varnish. WBP plywood is commonly used in the construction industry for sheds, cladding and decking.

3. **Marine plywood** – is an expensive premium-grade sheet material that has been developed for the marine industry to withstand complete submersion in water. The laminates contained within the plywood usually consist of hardwoods such as mahogany, Douglas fir or western larch. The grading of the surface and inner plies is usually far better, with no gaps or voids between the layers for water to settle. Marine plywood is usually bonded together with a 'phenolic' adhesive which is both completely moisture resistant (MR) and boil resistant (BR). The quality of the adhesive and timbers used, together with the grading standards results in a durable man-made sheet material.

4. **Structural plywood** – usually consists of the two layers in the centre of the board with their grain running in the same direction as each other, resulting in increased strength in one direction. The direction of the two veneers used to construct the core of the plywood results in the grain running perpendicular to each other on the faces if an odd number of layers are used. This is normally overcome with the use of an even number of plies on all structural plywood.

5. **Shuttering/sheathing plywood** – is normally used in the construction industry by 'shuttering carpenters' to construct concrete formwork (shuttering boxes). It is usually lower quality than other plywood, with softwood veneers and one unsanded face bonded together with moisture-resistant adhesive. Although the faces of the shuttering plywood are not decorative, the pattern of the grain in timber such as 'Douglas fir' can be transferred onto the surfaces of the concrete to create a feature. Smoother surfaces can be achieved on the concrete with the use of 'birch plywood'. Alternatively, higher quality repetitive shuttering jobs may require plywood with resin treatments for optimum performance, allowing the components to be reused without deteriorating.

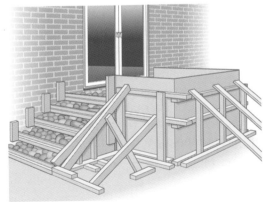

FIGURE 5.28 Shuttering box

6. **Flexible plywood** – is very similar to other plywood products with the exception of the number and thicknesses of the plies, giving it complete flexibility along the direction of the grain. Flexible plywood is normally constructed with three layers. The two outer faces both run in the same direction to each other and are usually substantially thicker than the core; these give the board

its flexibility whilst the thin layer dividing the faces provides the strength to the sheet. Flexible plywood is commonly available in 2440 mm × 1220 mm sheet sizes and thicknesses ranging between 3, 5, 8 and 16 mm, with the option for the grain to run along the length or across the width of the sheet. Complex radial shapes can easily be formed with flexible plywood down to 25 mm in radius with thin sheets; in general terms the thinner the sheet material the more flexible the sheet will become without rupturing (damage). Specialist equipment is not required to form shapes with this man-made board, but it will only retain its shape if it is securely fixed around a rigid structure (known as a 'former') or if it is bonded across its entire surface to another sheet to achieve the desired thickness. Flexible plywood is a cost-effective solution to building curved counters, reception desks etc. by reducing labour time associated with other more rigid materials, such as standard plywood. If the plywood is formed around a tight convex radius the grain may separate slightly to create small gaps along the length of the grain; this is normally covered with a finished veneer or laminate. Alternatively the relatively smooth surface of the plywood can be 'grain filled' and sanded to a smooth surface in preparation for staining or painting.

FREQUENTLY ASKED QUESTIONS

▶ What are 'shuttering boxes'?

Shuttering boxes are used to form moulds capable of holding concrete whilst it sets. When the concrete has completely cured the temporary fixings are removed from the shuttering box to reveal the casting. Castings are commonly formed on site (in situ) to repair or replace existing components or structures, for example: walls, window sills, staircases and paths; this improves the accuracy of the casting and prevents transporting of heavy concrete forms. A well-designed shuttering box will be completely rigid and maintain its shape after the concrete has been poured; it will also contain suitable fixings that can easily be removed without damaging the mould and allow the shuttering box to be reused.

Concrete products may also be cast in factories prior to delivery to site; this method of manufacture is known as 'pre-cast'.

BLOCKBOARD AND LAMINBOARD

Blockboard is made up with approximately 19–32 mm blocks glued together, with multiple layers of hardwood veneer 'cross-bonded' (alternating direction of the grain in the veneers) over both faces. It is rarely used in the construction industry these days because of cheaper alternatives, including MDF and plywood. Blockboard should only be used internally in non-structural positions because the majority of the grain in the board runs in the same direction, causing a weakness. In general, it has a strong resistance to warping

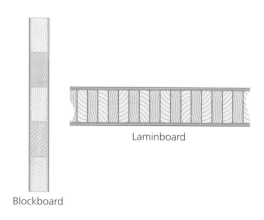

FIGURE 5.29 Blockboard and laminboard

and has the advantage of being lighter than standard MDF and plywood. The blocks in the board are usually lower grade softwood and commonly have voids between them in their length and width, which may cause difficulties when fixing. The edges of the boards usually have to be finished with softwood or hardwood edging strips to provide a suitable surface for finishing. Laminboard is constructed in a similar way to blockboard, with the only difference being the width and quality of the 3–8 mm blocks. The superior quality of laminboard is preferred by joiners and cabinet makers for high-class cabinet work, shopfitting and barfitting.

FIBREBOARDS

Fibreboards are manufactured using wood fibre broken down to a pulp and usually mixed together with resins before applying heat and pressure to bond the board together. The amount of pressure applied to the board during manufacture not only determines its thickness but also it density. The following fibreboards are commonly used in the construction industry for general use as well as purpose-made joinery:

FIGURE 5.30 MDF

- medium density fibreboard (MDF);
- hardboard.

MEDIUM-DENSITY FIBREBOARD (MDF)

Unlike other timber-based man-made boards, MDF is manufactured with fine wood fibres which result in panels without grain, knots or natural defects. The fibres of the boards are bonded together during a dry process of manufacture with a mixture of wax and resin under pressure and high temperature. MDF is not only stable and uniformed through the dense core – it is also an ideal substrate for veneers and laminates. MDF is commonly used by 'do it yourself' (DIY) enthusiasts as well as in the construction industry; this is partly due to the fact that it is a relatively inexpensive resource and readily available. Most panel suppliers carry a variety of different thicknesses, including 3, 4, 6, 9, 12, 15, 18, 22, 25, 30, 38, and 50 mm boards. Local builders' merchants normally stock a limited range of these thicknesses with an overall sheet size of 2440 mm × 1220 mm; other less common sizes are available from specialists including 3050 mm × 1220 mm and 2620 mm × 2070 mm. MDF can easily be cut, machined and moulded just like solid wood, although the resin used to bond the fibres together can blunt the teeth and cutters very quickly. This can be lessened for high-quality volume production with the use of 'tungsten'- or 'diamond'-tipped tooling. Once cut, drilled or moulded the fine particles usually become airborne, which can be hazardous if breathed in or if they come into contact with the eyes. This can be minimised if the correct safety precautions are followed as stated on the product's accompanying safety data sheet. In most cases preventative measures for the use of MDF and other man-made boards usually include the use of extractors, air filtration systems, disposable respirators/masks and barrier cream.

TRADE SECRETS

Respiratory diseases such as occupational asthma are reportedly affecting thousands of people working in the construction industry every year. The Health and Safety Executive (HSE) has recently reported that many of these people are failing to adequately protect themselves against hazardous materials such as hard- and softwood dust by wearing 'nuisance' dust masks (see Figure 5.31). These types of masks should only be used when dusts are not a hazard and they are not considered to be protective devices. Nuisance masks are often incorrectly provided by employers as a cheaper alternative to disposable respirators. When selecting a suitable protection device always:

- seek advice from your supervisor;
- read any relevant method statements or safety data;
- only use approved personal protection (PPE) with CE marks.

The types of MDF on the market today include:

1. **Moisture-resistant (MR)-grade MDF** – Standard MDF has many different uses in the construction industry including panelling, skirting and window boards but will absorb moisture if it is exposed to damp or humid environments such as in bathrooms and kitchens. In these positions MR-grade MDF should be used to prevent swelling and deterioration; this can be identified with a green-coloured core through the middle of these boards.

FIGURE 5.31 Nuisance dust mask

2. **Exterior-grade MDF** – is manufactured to provide a higher resistance to water and the extreme elements in exposed positions such as fascias, exterior mouldings, sign boards and shop fronts; this can be distinguished by its 'grey' core. Exterior-grade MDF has a long life expectancy provided it is adequately sealed along all its edges as well as the faces with a suitable exterior-grade coating before being exposed to the weather.

3. **Flame-retardant (FR) MDF** – has been developed with the use of flame-retardant chemicals to conform to Building Regulations to protect people, property and materials from the spread of fire. FR MDF was formally classified as '0' and '1', but has now been reclassified by its euro classes 'B' and 'C', respectively, to comply with BS 476 parts 6 and 7 of the Building Regulations. This simply means that it is suitable for symmetrical non-load-bearing positions, providing 30 minutes' fire resistance if it is not painted or covered with any materials that would compromise this rating. FR MDF is only suitable for non-structural internal use in completely dry areas, and should be conditioned for several days before use to ensure that any joints between adjoining boards remain tight after fixing. As with other flame-retardant products, FR MDF is easily distinguishable by its 'pink' coloured core. Flame-retardant MDF is being increasingly specified for use in hospitals, offices, schools, cinemas and clubs for the following applications:

- wall linings;
- ceilings;
- partitions;
- panelling.

4. **High-density fibreboard (HDF)** – is very similar to standard MDF with the exception of the increased density of the core; this also makes the board slightly heavier in weight. HDF has been specifically developed for kitchen and bedroom furniture manufacture, allowing the face and edges to be deep moulded without heavily raising the fibres of the core. The smoother finish of the moulded HDF is suitable for oil, solvent and water-based paint finishes. The stability of the HDF also makes it a suitable substructure for melamine foil and wood veneer coverings. The different types of HDF are as follows: LDF ultralight (20 per cent lighter than standard MDF), bendy MDF, 200–320 grit for sanding veneers, 150–240 grit for sanding moulded edges of standard MDF (raised fibres), profile wrappings (foils and veneers) and melamine-impregnated foils.

5. **Hardboard** – this is a relatively cheap material used regularly by joiners during the manufacture of carcasses and drawer bases; only one face is normally visible for these uses so standard hardboard with one smooth face is usually preferred. Alternatively 'duo-faced' hardboard can be used if two smooth faces are required. In areas of high moisture, 'tempered' hardboard should be used; these boards consist of a mixture of resin and oil impregnated into standard material. Tempered hardboard is stronger than standard hardboard, making it more resistant to scratches and abrasions. In addition to these varieties of timber-based sheet materials decorative, moulded and perforated panels are also manufactured for a range of different uses. Generally speaking hardboard of between 1.5–3 mm is used for normal operations but is available in a full range of up to 12 mm thick and 2440 × 1220 mm overall sheet dimensions.

FIGURE 5.32 Hardboard

6. **Medium board** – this board is divided into two categories – 'low' and 'high' density – and is manufactured using a similar process to hardboard. Low-density fibreboard (LM) is commonly used for notice/pin boards, partitions and acoustic screens, and high density (HM) for insulation in panelling, office screens, partitions and also under flat roof coverings.

PARTICLE BOARDS

1. **Oriented strand board** – otherwise known as 'OSB' – has several common uses, including site hoardings and decking on flat roofs etc. There are two different types of OSB: 'standard' and 'conditioned'. Conditioned-grade OSB is more suitable for use under damp or wet conditions. OSB is generally manufactured with three layers, each layer containing long strands of pine laid in one direction. The middle layer of strands is normally laid perpendicular to the two outer layers, therefore producing a strong, rigid board suitable for many first fixing tasks.

FIGURE 5.33 Oriented strand board (OSB)

2. **Chipboard** – this is widely used in both the manufacturing and construction industries for a number of applications including kitchen worktops, fire doors and flooring. There are two different classes of chipboard: 'low' and 'high' density. Low density or 'standard grade' as it is also known, has a density of approximately 635 kg/m³; this makes it suitable for most dry, non-load-bearing positions such as general joinery and furniture. The fine wood chips that are used to form standard chipboard are evenly distributed throughout the boards and bonded together to achieve a uniformed single

FIGURE 5.34 Chipboard

layer. If standard-grade chipboard becomes exposed to water or moisture it will swell and distort, and will not return to its original shape, even after drying out. An alternative material to this is 'flooring-grade' chipboard; this has an increased density of approximately 640 kg/m³ to provide a much stronger and harder-wearing board suitable for floors. Flooring-grade chipboard is available in both standard and moisture-resistant grades for internal use in areas of high humidity, such as kitchens and bathrooms. It consists of three layers: the inner coarse layer, the fine particles and additional resin of the two outer layers, providing a smooth finish. It usually contains machined tongue and groove edges to enable strong joints in their length and width, therefore reducing the risk of movement between the boards and resulting in squeaking. Flooring-grade chipboard is commonly available in half-sheet sizes measuring 2400 × 600 mm and either 18 or 22 mm thick. Chipboard is considerably weaker than other materials such as plywood; it is also prone to damage around its brittle edges if it is unprotected, which may sometimes cause problems when joining the tongues and grooves together.

MATERIAL DEFECTS

Timber is a natural resource that will last for many years in both internal and external positions providing that is correctly converted, seasoned and treated prior to installation and regularly maintained thereafter. Failure to use suitably prepared timber will see the rapid decline in the timber appearance and strength due to one or more of the following defects:

- Natural defects;
- Seasoning defects;
- Insect attack;
- Dry and wet rot (fungal attack).

TRADE SECRETS

Ironmongery buried below the surfaces of old timber can sometimes be difficult to find without a thorough inspection. Any objects remaining within the timber are a hazard and could potentially cause serious damage to machinery and the operator. The most efficient method of establishing whether or not foreign objects are contained within a section of timber is with the use of a hand-held 'metal detector'.

Whilst selecting new timber for use it is vital that a simple visual inspection of all the faces is carried out to ensure it is free from defects; this is especially important when reusing older timber. Imperfections and foreign objects such as nails, screws and staples are commonly discovered both on the surfaces and buried deep within the timber.

Cup shakes

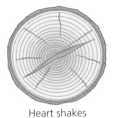
Heart shakes

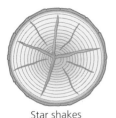
Star shakes

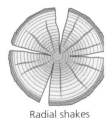
Radial shakes

FIGURE 5.38 Shakes

SEASONING DEFECTS

1. **Bowing** – refers to the curvature of the timber along its length, on the face side. It usually occurs in timber immediately after conversion due to the stresses within the trunk and the shape of the tree. Bowing could also occur in straight-grained timber if it is unsupported over long spans, which may eventually lead to the sagging. Stacking timber on a flat, level surface with bearers and piling sticks during seasoning and storing is essential preparation to prevent the irreversible effects of bowing.

FIGURE 5.39 Bowing

2. **Case hardening** – As timber dries out it will lose moisture and shrink slightly. If the timber is dried out too quickly it will stretch around the swollen core, causing it to seal the timber. The difference in moisture content between the core and the surface will cause tension and stress in the fibres that may not be visible on the surface. Difficulties usually occur with case-hardened timber when it is sawn, planed and moulded, resulting in warped and twisted timber.

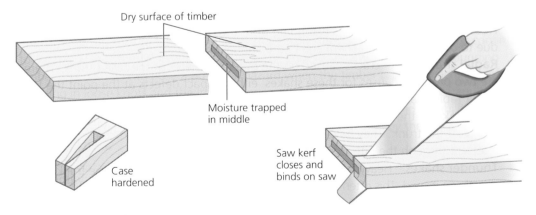
FIGURE 5.40 Case hardening

3. **Cupping** – The angle of the growth rings across the section of timber after conversion will determine the amount and direction of the distortion during and after seasoning. The term 'cupping' is used to describe the dish shape across the width of the timber as a result of existing stresses during air or kiln drying and the fact that timber shrinks most tangentially.

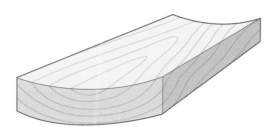

4. **Splits** – often occur because of tension in the trunk being released at the point it is converted into usable sections. These smaller sections have little or no resistance to the tension once converted, so the fibres

FIGURE 5.41 Cupping

usually separate along the length of the timber, causing splitting and shakes. Further splitting can occur as a result of drying the wood out too fast during the seasoning process. Shallow splits on the surfaces and ends of the timber are known as 'checks' and are usually completely removed during machining.

TRADE SECRETS

Excessive splitting along the length of wide hardwood boards can reduce their value. To prevent this from happening some timber merchants secure large steel staples into the end grain to bridge the gap created by the split in order to minimise the damage. Some suppliers paint the ends of the boards.

5. **Twisting/warping and winding** – are terms used to describe the movement between one corner of a board in relation to the general plane of the rest of the board. The distortion can be a result of a number of possible factors including poor storage of the timber, as well as the release of the tension and stresses in the fibres during conversion and seasoning.

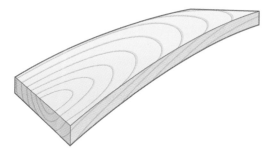

FIGURE 5.42 Twist

6. **Springing** – this is a curve along the length of the board as a result of poor conversion and irregular shaped grain.
7. **Collapse** – Timber that has been rapidly kiln dried (seasoned) may result in the molecular cells collapsing; as a result its shape will become distorted. Once collapse has occurred in timber it is impossible to reverse the process, and the timber is usually no longer suitable for joinery products.

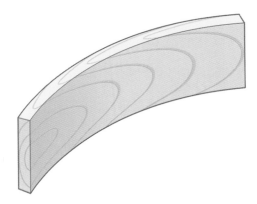

FIGURE 5.43 Springing

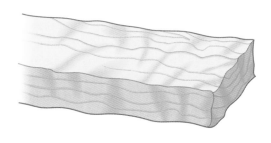

FIGURE 5.44 Collapse

8. **Honeycombing** – this occurs in timber if the outside of the board is rapidly dried during seasoning, the result being a high moisture content in the middle of the board. If timber is not dried to the point that it has an even moisture content, then the outer surface seals itself. Once this occurs the substantially higher moisture content in the centre of the board will begin to dry, which in turn will result in cavities and splitting as the timber dries and shrinks. The damage usually follows the pattern of the 'medullary rays', not along the length of the grain in the timber. The effects of honeycombing will not be visible in the timber until the board has been converted to usable sections after seasoning.

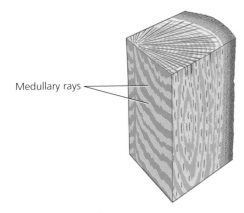

Medullary rays

FIGURE 5.45 Medullary rays

? FREQUENTLY ASKED QUESTIONS

▶ What are 'medullary rays'?

Medullary rays are groups of storage cells that run from the middle of the tree to the 'cambium' layer just under the bark.

INSECT INFESTATION ON TIMBER

In general, any timber discovered to have dozens of tiny holes bored into its surface, is usually considered to have 'woodworm'. Woodworm is not a specific species of insect, rather a generic name given to any wood-boring insect at its development stage. There are many different species of wood-boring insects; these include:

- powder post beetle;
- common furniture beetle;
- death watch beetle;
- house longhorn.

Adult wood-boring beetles usually lay offspring known as 'larvae' in the surface cracks and deep grain of certain seasoned hard-, and softwoods. Studies have shown that timber containing 'sapwood' rather than 'heartwood' is more susceptible to widespread infestation as sapwood is less dense and contains a ready food source. When laid, the larvae are white in colour and only approximately 1 mm in length. They normally burrow down into the surface of the timber and remain there for months as they grow into fully developed adult beetles. At this stage they will resurface by boring back through the face of the timber, leaving a trail of exit holes and wood dust ('frass'). Badly infected areas of timber are usually destroyed by the insects turning the sound timber into crumbling powder.

Furniture beetle

Powder post beetle

Death watch beetle

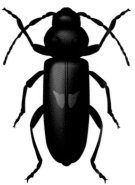

House longhorn beetle

FIGURE 5.46 Beetles

ERADICATING INFESTED TIMBERS

Wood-boring beetles are commonly discovered in furniture, flooring and the structural timbers of old buildings. Infected timbers should be replaced with treated wood, whilst the remaining uninfected timbers should be treated with insecticides or fumigation to control the potential for re-infection. Infected waste materials should be immediately removed from the site and correctly disposed of at a waste management depot to prevent the contamination of other timbers in the building.

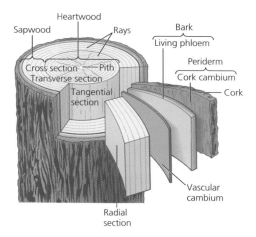

FIGURE 5.47 An insect attacking sapwood

DRY AND WET ROT (FUNGAL ATTACK)

Dry and wet rot can potentially be found in all areas of older buildings, causing cosmetic and structural damage amounting to thousands of pounds in repair bills. It is important to be able to recognise the different types of wood decay, treat them correctly, and prevent them from reoccurring.

WET ROT

Wet rot is a common problem found in timber with a high moisture content, such as:

- the back of wooden window frames;
- along the sill or jambs on door frames;
- leaking roofs;
- along the ends of joists;
- behind toilets, sinks and baths;
- behind washing machines, dishwashers, etc.

FIGURE 5.48 Damage caused by rot

Detecting wet rot

Vulnerable areas at risk of wet rot should be regularly inspected for early signs of deterioration of the timber. Damaged paintwork, discolouring and smell in the timber are all tell-tale signs and should be investigated further. This can simply be done by inserting a sharp knife into the timber; if the end of the knife disappears it is highly likely that wet rot is present.

Treating infected timber

It is vital that the source of the water damage is located and repaired before any repairs take place to prevent the timber from being affected again. Voids created in the construction of buildings should be adequately ventilated to prevent stagnant air and moisture deteriorating the timber components. This is commonly discovered in voids between suspended timber ground floors in older properties. Wet rot is easily treated by cutting out the damaged areas until sound timber is discovered. Smaller areas can be spliced with new sections of timber to replace the damaged sections, and treated with preservative and several coats of wood primer, undercoat and top coat. Minor areas can be treated with an 'epoxy-based repair kit' following the manufacturer's instructions. If it is suspected that the high moisture levels may reappear, then the timber should have a wet rot treatment applied. If the problem extends to structural timbers such as the roof or floor joists, then professional advice should be sought to ensure that the maintenance does not affect the integrity of the building.

DRY ROT

Dry rot is a much more serious problem than wet rot, and is often referred to as 'building cancer' by tradesmen and women in the industry, because of its potential to travel through walls and destroy timber structures. Unlike wet rot, dry rot is a fungus that grows in damp timber with a moisture content above 28–30 per cent and also in dark, unventilated areas, attacking mouldings such as skirting,

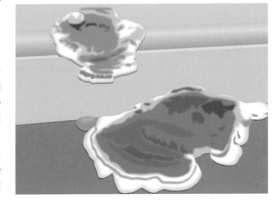

FIGURE 5.49 Dry rot

flooring, etc. Dry rot is often discovered in voids behind timber walls etc., and will often go unde-
tected for a long period of time before the later stages of growth; this is when the
mushroom-shaped fruit bodies start to appear.

? FREQUENTLY ASKED QUESTIONS

▶ **Why is dry rot referred to as such if it is not dry at all?**

It is referred to as 'dry rot' because the fungus is capable of transporting moisture from
other sources metres away to attack dry timber.

Identifying dry rot

There are several stages that the rot will go through as it develops and starts to attack the
timber:

1st **stage** – white sheets simulating cotton wool appear on the face of the infected timber;

2nd **stage** – the sheets develop into fungal strands;

3rd **stage** – large flat mushroom-like fruiting bodies grow across the infected areas;

4th **stage** – red–brown spores are produced by the mushrooms;

5th **stage** – the infected timber will begin to develop deep cracks along and across the
grain of the timber;

6th **stage** – a musty, damp odour starts to develop.

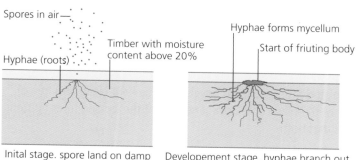
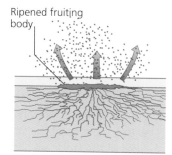

FIGURE 5.50 Stages of dry rot

Treating infected timber

Generally, specialist companies are normally used to treat infected properties because of the
risks associated with the materials used to eradicate the problem. They are usually better
equipped and have the expertise to carry out thorough risk assessments to comply with the
Control of Substances Hazardous to Health (COSHH) Regulations 1988.

Wherever possible timber lintels and infected joists etc. should be disposed of away from the site and replaced with steel to prevent new timbers being re-infected. Dry rot thrives on damp or wet timber with little or no ventilation; if these elements can be removed then it will cease to grow, although it can still remain dormant for years after. Dry rot should be cut out from the infected areas and at least 1 m past the last signs of timber decay, and replaced with pressure-treated timber. In areas where it is not possible to remove the damaged timber the dry rot must be treated with a chemical- or water-based fungicide. Brushing the treatment over the dry rot should be avoided, because it will only cure the surface area. Deeper penetration can be achieved by injecting the fungicides into the core of the timber. Alternatively fungicidal paste can be used to spread over the infected areas, allowing the fungicidal oil contained in the paste to penetrate deep into the timber, providing the surface is not too wet.

MAINTENANCE OF MARKING-OUT TOOLS

Regular inspection, cleaning and maintenance of marking-out tools is essential to prolong the life expectancy of the equipment; it will also ensure that it performs as it is designed. This section highlights some of the more commonly used marking-out tools and simple care and maintenance requirements:

FIGURE 5.51 Sliding bevel

1. **Sliding bevel** – A sliding bevel comprises of two parts – the stock and the blade. The blade is connected through a slot to the stock and held in position with a thumbscrew, a wing nut or the preferred method of a locking lever. The angle between the stock and the blade can be adjusted by loosening the locking lever to duplicate angles from one position to another. Quality sliding bevels are usually manufactured with sealed rosewood stocks, hardened and tempered steel blades and brass fittings. Lower quality tools have moulded plastic stocks, aluminium blades and chrome-plated fittings. Sliding bevels must be kept clean and free of adhesive on the face and edges of the blade and stock. Ensure that the locking lever tightens within the area of the stock and that both sides of the stock are aligned.

2. **Box square** – Box squares are commonly used by joiners and cabinet makers for marking out, as well as checking and transferring 90-degree and 45-degree angles around adjacent perpendicular faces. They may also be used as a guide to rest the face of a chisel against to form precision mitres and scribed joints. Box squares are usually made of cast steel or aluminium, so require little maintenance other than keeping clean, dry and stored

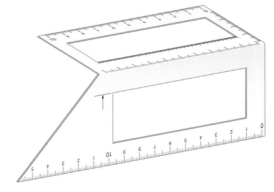

FIGURE 5.52 Box square

to prevent accidental damage. Joiners very often make their own out of a stable seasoned hardwood such as beech or mahogany; as these wear they will need to be re-trued to maintain their accuracy.

3. **Compass** – There are two parts to a compass: the centre point used as a pivot and a pencil secured on the opposite leg. Adjusting the distance between the two points allows different radii to be drawn; the maximum radius is normally determined by the length of the compass. Compasses are frequently used to set out curves and circles on joinery items on workshop rods. Occasionally the bolt and nut used to hinge the compass together may work loose through regular use and should therefore be checked, and if necessary tightened regularly to maintain accurate setting out.

FIGURE 5.53 Dividers

4. **Dividers** – These are instruments used by draftsmen for setting out, transferring measurements and of course dividing lines into equal segments. Dividers closely resemble a compass, with the only difference being the absence of a pencil contained on one end, and the adjustment usually carried out via a thumbscrew.

5. **Marking knife** – Marking knives are used to cut lines across the fibres of the timber whilst marking out, rather than using a pencil. Cutting the fibres using this method improves the accuracy of the marking out and results in exceptional joint cutting with sharp edges. Using a marking knife along the length of the grain should be avoided, as this will result in the fine taper cutting edge following the figure of the grain rather than the line required. Marking knives are generally produced approximately 150 mm long with rosewood handles and carbon steel blades. A bevel is usually ground on one side of the blade, allowing the surface of the opposite side to rest tightly against the square etc. while marking out. They are available both right and left handed. On occasions the edge on the blade will need to be honed to regain the razor sharp cutting edge, and from time to time the grinding angle will also have to be reproduced.

6. **Tape measure** – Tape measures are probably the most frequently used hand tools by bench joiners. They are commonly available with both metric (metres and millimetres – m/mm) and imperial (feet and inches – '/") measurements. The film-coated metal blade with the dimensions marked is usually concealed within the body of the tape measure and held in place with a coiled spring. When in use, the blade (tape) is withdrawn from the body of the lock to the required length and held in place with a 'blade lock' to allow it to be easily read without retracting. The 'hook' end of the tape measure is designed to move slightly along the length of the blade to compensate for measuring both internally and externally. Care should be taken to control the speed that the blade is retracted into the body of the tape measure to ensure that the hook end does not get damaged. This is usually achieved by engaging the brake button on the body of the tape measure to cushion the action of the retracting blade. Continued use and retraction of the blade against the body of the tape may result in the rivets securing the hook end becoming loose; this will then cause inaccurate reading to be determined from the blade. It is

common practice by bench joiners to use a 5 m tape measures for routine joinery products; although long tapes of 8 m are also available they are rarely used because of their weight and overall size. All tape measures regardless of their length have a slight curve on their blade to add strength and prevent it from bending whilst it is extended. Generally, longer tape measures have wider blades and an increased curvature to support their extension to between 3 and 4 m before collapsing.

7. **Pencil** – The lead that was traditionally used in pencils has now been replaced with graphite. Graphite is not only safer to use than lead, it also produces smoother and less abrasive lines. Pencils are normally split into two categorises – hardness (H) and blackness (B). Further shades of pencils range through each category from one (1) to nine (9), nine being the most extreme. For example:

   - a pencil labelled '1H' will be the softest in the range;
   - a pencil labelled '9B' will produce the darkest line in the range.

   Generally, pencils labelled '2H' are used for setting out etc. because they produce an accurate line. This grade of pencil is normally unsuitable for marking-out joinery items because it will fail to maintain its fine point, and therefore requires frequent sharpening. In the construction industry it is common practice to use a '2H' pencil for the general marking out of soft- and hardwoods as well as timber-based boards.

FIGURE 5.54 Pencil grades

FIGURE 5.55 Carpenters' pencil

8. **Protractor** – Protractors are used by draughtspeople, joiners and carpenters to measure and mark out angles in degrees onto drawings and components. Semi-circular protractors are the most commonly used in the industry to measure angles ranging from zero to 180 degrees. Complete 360-degree protractors are available but can be problematic and less accurate when used in conjunction with a sliding bevel to transfer angles. The problem occurs because the stock of the sliding bevel is unable to sit against the flat surface of the 'baseline'.

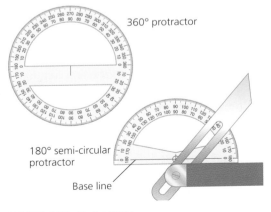

FIGURE 5.56 Protractors

TRADE SECRETS

Whilst working at height, carpenters commonly lose pencils due to them rolling off working platforms etc. To overcome this problem square 'carpenters' pencils' are used. Carpenters' pencils are usually medium grade and therefore too soft for joiners to use for setting and marking out.

9. **Rule** – Steel rules are commonly used by joiners for accurate marking out of joints, grooves and rebates, etc. Although imperial measurement is rarely used in the construction industry these days, the dimension is usually marked along one face of standard rules with metric on the other. Quality rules are normally manufactured in steel or aluminium and vary in length from 100 to 300 mm. As with all hand tools regular cleaning and wiping over with a clean cloth will prolong the life of the tool, but additional care should be given to the edges of a rule to prevent damage through poor storage and neglect.

10. **Scale rule** – Scale rules are used by tradespersons to either draw full-sized components to a smaller size whilst maintaining their proportion, or to translate scale dimensions from an architect's or engineer's plan back to full size. Scale rules are commonly available with between four and eight different scales along each edge; if a greater range of scales is required then triangular rules may be used. Triangular rules have up to 12 different commonly used scales over three colour-coded faces for easy reference and greater versatility. For further details about scale drawings and converting scale, refer to Chapter 2 – 'Information, Quantities and Communicating with Others'.

FIGURE 5.57 Scale rules

11. **Square** – There are several different types of squares used by draughtsmen to set out drawings, including:

   ● **Tee squares** – Used to mark vertical and horizontal lines at right angles along the width and length of the drawing paper. Traditionally tee squares would have been made from high-quality hardwoods. Today they are manufactured from aluminium, with at least four rivets used to secure the stock to the rule to accurately maintain 90 degrees. Careless handling and storage of a tee square could result in the block being knocked 'out of square'; if this does occur, attempting to repair it should be avoided and in most cases it should be discarded.

   ● **Set squares** (45/45/90 degrees and 60/30/90 degrees) – The two different types of set squares, are identified by their one right angle (90 degrees) and the remaining corners equalling 45 degrees each (90/45/45 or 90/30/60). The most commonly used set squares are produced from plastic with tapered edges for improved accuracy when marking out and when using ink pens.

   ● **Adjustable squares** (Further information on these can be found in Chapter 7 'Manufacture Routine Joinery Products'.)

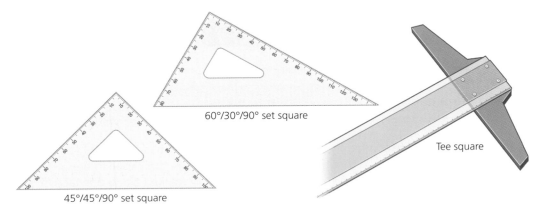

60°/30°/90° set square

Tee square

45°/45°/90° set square

FIGURE 5.58 Tee squares and set squares

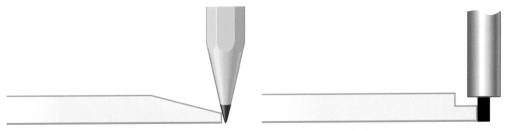

Tapered edge – pencil use

Rebated edge – pen use

FIGURE 5.59 Using a square with a pencil or ink

 ACTIVITIES

Activity 17 – Selecting resources for setting out

Read through the following questions and answer them as fully as you can to help you develop your underpinning knowledge of this subject area.

1. Explain the term 'wane' with the aid of a sketch.

2. A 'box square' is commonly used for what operation?

3. Explain how the defect 'thunder shakes' occur.

4. Divide the following timbers into softwoods (coniferous) and hardwoods (deciduous):
   i.   Balsa;
   ii.   Spruce;
   iii.   Maple;
   iv.   Parana pine;
   v.   European oak;
   vi.   Hemlock;
   vii.   Sapele;
   viii. Larch;
   viiii. Cedar.

5. Explain one method of finishing the edge of a decorative-faced man-made board.

SETTING OUT FOR BENCH JOINERY AND SITE CARPENTRY

ORGANISING RESOURCES FOR SETTING OUT

Manufacturing joinery products requires careful planning and sequencing to achieve the most economical use of labour and resources. Inefficient scheduling by line managers may lead to delays in materials, 'down time' for joiners and machinists, and possibly missed deadlines. From time to time changes may occur to the client's specifications, or additional items required compared to the original contract documentation that undoubtedly causes unforeseen delays. Upon approval of the changes and additional costs a 'variation order' must be agreed and completed between the client and the contractor. It may be beneficial to integrate the additional items halfway through production of the original contracted work rather than waiting until completion as this may prevent having to reset machinery etc. several times to repeat the processes required for production.

Once all the design details from the specification and architects' drawings have been finalised, the materials are normally ordered in advance of setting out to prevent delays once the process of production has begun.

SETTING OUT WORKSHOP RODS

It is common practice to set out workshop rods on timber-based boards such as MDF and hardboard with several coats of white emulsion to increase the definition of the lines and show them more clearly. The smooth surfaces of these boards can be easily repainted upon completion and reused again very quickly with the use of water-based paint. Setting out on rigid boards rather than paper avoids the likelihood of damage to the edges of the rod, whilst it is either in use or storage. The firm edges of the boards also allow setting-out tools to be positioned against them to transfer angles etc. from the rod to the timber.

Whenever possible a site survey should be carried out to check the dimensions and levels on the architect's drawings against the actual positions on site. It may not always be possible to undertake a site survey, especially if the items of joinery are being built-in to the structure of the building rather than fixed-in.

CRITICAL POSITIONS

A completed workshop rod will illustrate a section through the height and width of joinery items with section details for each of the components. Each timber component is normally laid on the workshop rod to transfer critical positions from the setting out stage onto the faces of the timber to prevent repetitive measuring and marking out of components.

The following positions are considered essential to transfer from the setting out stage onto the timber to ensure the overall dimensions are correct and the main components are located in the correct positions:

- overall width;
- overall height;
- shoulder positions;
- glazing sizes.

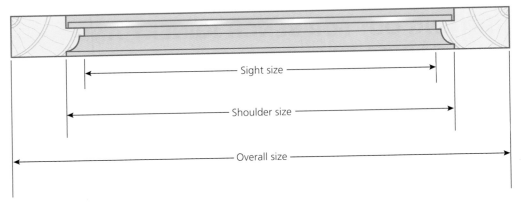

FIGURE 5.60 Critical positions

SEQUENCE OF SETTING OUT ROUTINE JOINERY PRODUCTS

As mentioned previously, the efficient sequencing of setting out, marking out, etc. will improve productivity and profit margins. The following stages illustrate and explain the methods used by joiners to set out routine joinery products, although the technique will be very similar with more complex items:

- **Stage 1** – Ensuring that only lightly weighted construction lines are used: mark a parallel line along the length of the workshop rod equal to the height of the joinery item;
- **Stage 2** – Square the overall height positions across the width of the paper equal to the thickness of the joinery item;
- **Stage 3** – Mark a line parallel to the edge of the rod and equal to the thickness of the joinery component;
- **Stage 4** – Repeat the process of setting out for the width just above the height section, ensuring that the top and one side of the width sections align;
- **Stage 5** – Mark the total width of each component onto the height section before squaring the lines across the width of the rod onto the width section;
- **Stage 6** – Mark any glazing rebates or grooves required onto each section;
- **Stage 7** – Continue to mark any mouldings or glazing beads etc. onto the workshop rod;
- **Stage 8** – Remove any unwanted lines to prevent overcomplicating details on the setting out;
- **Stage 9** – Complete the setting out by adding weight to the lines with hatching on the end sections to improve the clarity of the drawing, and dashed lines to illustrate hidden details;
- **Stage 10** – Add a title panel to the setting out (for further details on 'title panels', refer to Chapter 2 – Information, Quantities and Communicating with Others');
- **Stage 11** – Produce a cutting sheet/ironmongery and timber orders.

EXAMPLES OF SETTING OUT FOR ROUTINE JOINERY ITEMS

DOORS

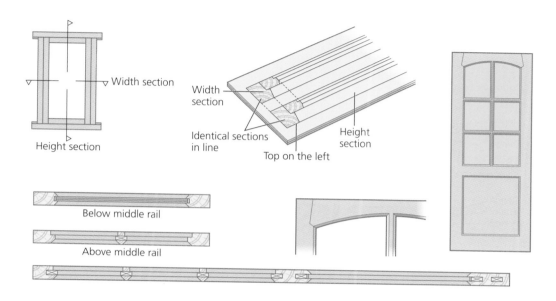

FIGURE 5.61 Setting out doors

FRAMES

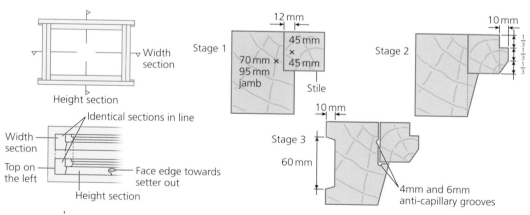

FIGURE 5.62 Setting out door linings and loft hatches

LINING

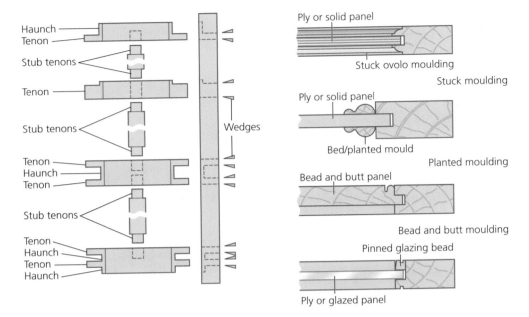

FIGURE 5.63 Setting out door and window frames

UNITS AND FITMENTS

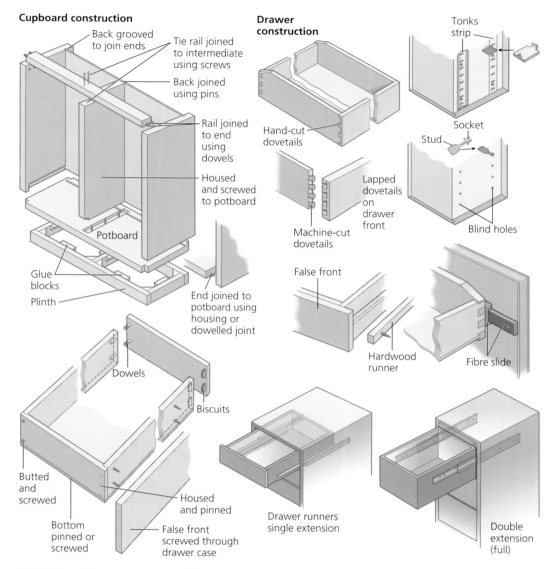

Cupboard construction

- Back grooved to join ends
- Tie rail joined to intermediate using screws
- Back joined using pins
- Rail joined to end using dowels
- Housed and screwed to potboard
- Potboard
- Glue blocks
- Plinth
- End joined to potboard using housing or dowelled joint
- Dowels
- Biscuits
- Butted and screwed
- Bottom pinned or screwed
- Housed and pinned
- False front screwed through drawer case

Drawer construction

- Hand-cut dovetails
- Machine-cut dovetails
- Lapped dovetails on drawer front
- False front
- Hardwood runner
- Fibre slide
- Drawer runners single extension

- Tonks strip
- Socket
- Stud
- Blind holes
- Double extension (full)

FIGURE 5.64 Setting out units and fitments

STAIRCASES

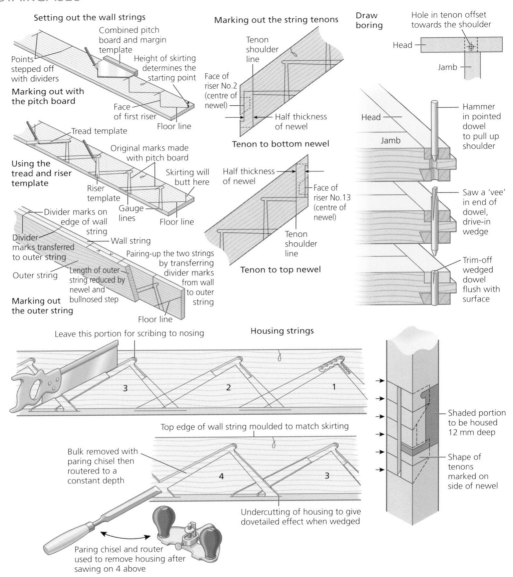

FIGURE 5.65 Setting out staircases

 ACTIVITIES

Activity 18 – Setting out for bench joinery and site carpentry

Read through the following questions and answer them as fully as you can to help you develop your underpinning knowledge of this subject area:

1. List three critical sizes when setting out.
2. Explain the term 'weighted lines'.
3. Describe the effects of poorly managed procedures.
4. Sketch the joint between the top rail and stile on a panelled door.
5. Draw a typical title panel for a workshop rod.

MULTIPLE-CHOICE QUESTIONS

1   Which **one** of the following is a commercially available sawn timber size for softwood?
    a   225mm × 50mm
    b   235mm × 50mm
    c   245mm × 50mm
    d   255mm × 50mm

2   Which **one** of the following best describes ash?
    a   Medium brown oily softwood
    b   Medium brown oily hardwood
    c   White to creamy brown softwood
    d   White to creamy brown hardwood

3   Which **one** of the following is a commonly available MDF board size?
    a   600mm × 600mm
    b   600mm × 1200mm
    c   2000mm × 1000mm
    d   2440mm × 1220mm.

4   A 'Norfolk latch' is used to secure which one of the following door types?
    a   Jib
    b   Fire
    c   Ledged
    d   Revolving

5   Softwood sawn boards are available in lengths increasing in increments of
    a   100mm
    b   200mm
    c   300mm
    d   400mm

6   Which **one** of the following grades of pencil is most suitable for use when setting out?
    a   2B
    b   2H
    c   6B
    d   6H

7   The core colour of flame-retardant MDF is
    a   pink
    b   blue
    c   green
    d   yellow

8 Which one of the following is **not** a timber defect?
 a Dry rot
 b Wet rot
 c Red stain
 d Blue stain

9 A rail measuring 20mm on a drawing, which is scaled at 1:10, has a true dimension of
 a 2mm
 b 20mm
 c 200mm
 d 2000mm

10 The type of hardwood required for a door would be indicated on the
 a drawing
 b schedule
 c portfolio
 d specification

MARK OUT FROM SETTING-OUT DETAILS FOR ROUTINE JOINERY PRODUCTS

 LEARNING OUTCOMES

By the end of this chapter you should have developed a knowledge and understanding of:

• producing marking out efficiently;
• producing accurate marking out.

PRODUCING MARKING OUT EFFICIENTLY

The process of making out purpose-made joinery products will differ between manufacturers depending on the size of the company and quantity of items required. It is common practice for small joinery works to employ joiners capable of setting out rods for 'one-off' specialist work, as well as marking out. Sequencing the initial stages of manufacture in this manner prevents difficulty in communicating complex information and ideas from one person to another. The process of setting out, marking out and manufacture may be made more efficient if routine products are being produced or larger numbers of craft workers are employed to undertake different tasks. Joinery companies commonly allocate different tasks to employees to improve productivity by training them to specialise in a specific area. Dividing the process of manufacture into different stages increases output to meet the demands of the industry whilst maintaining the ability to complete within given timescales. The following sequence of events is typical during the manufacture of routine joinery products:

• **Stage 1** – The 'setter-out' completes the workshop rod and a cutting list while referring to the architect's details, specification and site survey details. (*Note* – details regarding timber cutting lists can be found in Chapter 5 – Interpreting Information for Setting Out);

 TRADE SECRETS

Whenever possible, supply the machinists with a detailed drawing to accompany the cutting list, especially if the product being manufactured is a complex design. This will allow them to reference the drawing to clarify the positioning of the components being machined.

To avoid overcomplicating setting out and cutting lists, each part may be simply labelled with a reference or item number.

- **Stage 2** – Timber is machined to size by the 'machinists' following the information contained on the cutting lists;
- **Stage 3** – Jointing details and component sections are transferred from the rod to the timber by the marker out;
- **Stage 4** – The components are returned to the 'machinists' for secondary machining including jointing, rebates, grooves and mouldings;
- **Stage 5** – The timber components are returned to the 'bench joiners' to 'dry fit' before sanding and final assembly.

? FREQUENTLY ASKED QUESTIONS

▶ What does the term 'dry fit' mean?

The term 'dry fit' is often used by joiners to describe the assembly of an item of joinery without the use of adhesive. It is good practice to assemble products dry during manufacture to check the fit of each joint and the overall sizes against the original setting out.

It is may also be necessary to disassemble the joinery prior to pressure treating with preservative. This method of preserving the timber ensures that all of the exposed surfaces are protected, therefore prolonging the life expectancy.

PRODUCING ACCURATE MARKING OUT

SELECTION OF MATERIALS

ADHESIVES

Today the range of wood adhesives is extensive, but careful selection is vital to ensure the suitability of the adhesive for the materials being used, the environment and the situation. Before using any product the manufacturer's instructions and The Control of Substances Hazardous to Health Regulations (COSHH) 'safety data sheets' should be read and understood. The details contained within these documents will explain the limitations for its use, as well as the measures that should be in place to minimise the risk to health and safety through the following:

- handling and storage;
- exposure controls and personal protection (PPE);
- disposal;
- transportation.

Types of wood adhesive

1. **Animal glue** – Animal glue was used in the production of furniture and internal joinery for many years, until the introduction of PVA (polyvinyl acetate) in the mid to late twentieth century. It was created from collagen found in the connective tissue of the skin, bones and tendons etc. of dead animals such as horses. The proteins extracted from the connective tissue in these areas form a molecular bond between themselves and adjoining surfaces of the

timber. Nowadays animal glue is usually supplied in hard granular form, and requires heating in a glue pot initially to blend it together but also whilst it is in use. The glue has very little 'open time' before it begins to cool and eventually harden, although it can be re-activated again if heat is applied, or become brittle and crack if it comes into contact with water. Animal glue is rarely used commercially today, but some cabinet makers still prefer to use it to renovate furniture

FIGURE 6.1 Scotch glue pot

because of its ability to bond to any remaining adhesive on the repaired item.

2. **Polyurethane adhesive** – Polyurethane adhesive is resistant to ultraviolet (UV) light, heat and moisture, allowing it to be used for a vast number of interior and exterior applications. This one-part adhesive is activated by applying a thin, even layer to one surface of the joint and water through a mist spray gun to the other side. The moisture causes a chemical reaction in the polyurethane, allowing it to form a strong elastic bond between the materials. As the glue 'cures' (dries), it expands and foams up to fill any voids in the joint. To prevent the expanding adhesive forcing the materials apart as it cures, firm pressure should be applied with clamps etc. over the joint between the materials. Under normal conditions the adhesive will cure enough to remove the clamps within 1–2 hours, but should ideally be left overnight to harden properly. Polyurethane adhesive is suitable for bonding a wide range of substrates together including wood, metal, stone and glass. It is also very useful for repair work because it will adhere to any adhesive originally used. When it has completely hardened, the excess adhesive can be removed by scraping it from the joint, or with the use of a chisel, before finishing with some sandpaper to reveal a virtually invisible glue line.

3. **Polyvinyl acetate (PVA)** – PVA is the cheapest and probably the most widely used wood adhesive because it is readily available and can be used straight from the bottle without the need for mixing. It is sometimes referred to as 'carpenter's glue' or 'white glue' because of its coloured appearance prior to drying. As the non-toxic adhesive begins to set through evaporation of its water content or absorption into the wood, it changes colour from white to a clear semi-rubbery finish. PVA also has the ability to bridge gaps between adjoining surfaces of up to one and a half millimetres without shrinking or cracking. Standard PVA may be used for general internal joinery use; in areas of high humidity or external positions a water-resistant grade should be used. In the building industry diluted PVA is commonly used as a sealer on porous masonry walls and floors in preparation for plastering or decorating. The sealer prevents the surface sucking the moisture out of the covering, and causing it to dry out too quickly, which could in turn cause surface cracking.

4. **Contact adhesive** – Contact adhesive is commonly used to bond laminates and veneers to timber-based boards and worktops. A thin, even layer should be applied to both surfaces with a plastic or metal spreader and left until semi-dry before bringing the surfaces together. The length of time required between spreading the glue and sticking together will depend on a number of factors including room temperature, and the thickness of the covering. A good indication of whether or not the glue is dry enough to bond is to use the back of your hand; if it is too wet the adhesive will stick to your skin

and lift from the surface. Under ideal conditions, the hairs on the back of your hand should not stick to the adhesive, but release when lifted from the material surface. Once the two surfaces have been pressed together an instant bond is created. Further pressure should be applied over the entire surface from the centre outwards with a hard rubber roller or wooden block; this will ensure that there are no air pockets between the joint. Cramps are rarely necessary whilst bonding because of the instant grab of the contact adhesive, but on occasions they may be used. Some porous materials, such as MDF, may require an initial primer coat of contact adhesive prior to a second covering once completely dry; this will prevent the glue being absorbed into the material and drying out too quickly. Contact adhesive is solvent based and therefore highly toxic. While it is in liquid form the glue produces an extremely flammable vapour, so should only be used in well-ventilated areas and never exposed to a source of ignition or naked flame.

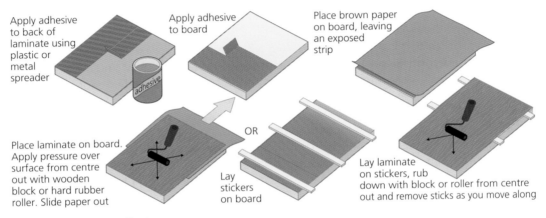

Apply adhesive to back of laminate using plastic or metal spreader

Apply adhesive to board

Place brown paper on board, leaving an exposed strip

Place laminate on board. Apply pressure over surface from centre out with wooden block or hard rubber roller. Slide paper out

OR

Lay stickers on board

Lay laminate on stickers, rub down with block or roller from centre out and remove sticks as you move along

FIGURE 6.2 Contact adhesive

5. **Hot melt glue** – Hot melt glue is commonly used on the rear of wood veneers and melamine edging strips, and is commonly referred to as 'iron-on' edging. The face of the edging is normally heated with either a conventional iron or heat gun until the glue starts to melt, whilst applying light pressure with a wooden block to ensure a good bond to the adjoining surface. Hot melt glue can also be applied through an 'application gun' to join a variety of surfaces together. The gun is usually mains powered to heat a cylindrical glue stick as it is fed through the barrel and out through the nozzle. Within seconds the

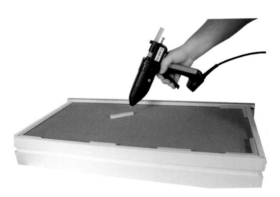

FIGURE 6.3 Hot metal glue gun

glue begins to cool and solidify, forming a strong bond between the adjoining surfaces. A variety of glues are available with increased setting times to suit different materials. Other than the hot melt glue found on the back of iron-on edging it has limited uses in the construction industry, but is commonly used in hobby making and packaging.

6. **Epoxy-resin adhesive** – Epoxy-resin is a synthetic adhesive consisting of two parts: resin and hardener. Equal portions of each must be thoroughly mixed together before applying to the joint; as the glue sets a chemical reaction takes place to create a very strong bond. In

the past, both the resin and hardener were supplied in separate tubes; today the two parts are conveniently dispensed equally at the same time through a plastic syringe. There are a range of different epoxy-resins available to bond a variety of materials together, including:

● wood;
● metal;
● plastic;
● glass;
● stone.

Under normal conditions standard epoxy-resin will cure within 6–16 hours depending on the product, although these times can be reduced with rapid setting versions of the same adhesive. Epoxy-resin adhesive can be used both internally and externally, with excellent resistance to water, solvents and high temperatures.

7. **Urea-formaldehyde resin** – Urea-formaldehyde resin is commonly mixed with wood fibre before undergoing a process of heat and pressure treatments to manufacture man-made sheet materials such as oriented strand board (OSB). This moisture resistant (MR) grade of adhesive has an excellent resistance to moisture as well as heat, and can therefore be used in both internal and external joinery, shopfitting and boat building. In addition it can also be used to laminate and veneer. Urea-formaldehyde is commercially available in powder form and must be mixed with water (ratio two parts resin to one part water), until a smooth consistency is achieved. Once mixed, the adhesive has an 'open time' or 'pot life' of approximately 8–9 hours at a workshop temperature of 10°C, and 1–1.5 hours at 20°C. The resin must be evenly spread over both surfaces before bringing them together and adding pressure to the joint with clamps, or a press until the glue has dried. A suitable barrier cream or gloves should be worn whilst using the resin, to reduce to risk of catching dermatitis if it comes into contact with unprotected skin.

Category	Animal glue	Holt melt glue	PVA adhesive	Urea-formaldehyde adhesive	Poly-urethane adhesive	Contact adhesive	Epox-resin adhesive
Interior/ Exterior	Interior	Interior	Interior and exterior	Interior and exterior	Interior and exterior	Interior	Interior and exterior
Uses	Furniture making and restoration	Jig making, wood veneers and packaging	General purpose wood adhesive	Joinery Shopfitting and boat building	Wood, metal, stone and glass, etc.	Laminates and veneers to timber-based boards	Wood, metal, plastic, glass and stone

FIGURE 6.4 Adhesive categories and uses

TRADE SECRETS

Whenever possible, apply wood adhesive to both surfaces of a joint before assembly; this will ensure a good, even coverage and a strong bond. Rubbing the glued surfaces together before cramping is also good practice, because the pressure applied disperses the waste glue from the joint, allowing the two surfaces to form a tighter bond and reducing the thickness of the glue line.

MARKING OUT JOINERY ITEMS

The process of marking out purpose-made joinery products depends on the quantity of items required at the same size; for example, it may be more productive to mark out a single side-hung panelled door on the actual components rather than a rod. If multiple joinery products at the same overall dimensions are to be marked out, it may be quicker and more accurate to set out a workshop rod and transfer the marking out onto the timber components. A typical working drawing should contain the following basic details to enable production:

- overall (O/A) dimensions;
- rebate or groove dimensions and positions (if applicable);
- positions and proportions of joints;
- additional mouldings, e.g. mortar grooves, anticapillary grooves, weathering, etc.;
- title panel. (Further details are found in Chapter 2 – Information, Quantities and Communicating with Others.)

It is not always practically possible to contain the full lengths and widths of large items onto a workshop rod; in such cases 'break lines' are inserted to remove sections from the drawing. The missing detail must then be reinserted onto the timber components whilst marking out. To prevent the confusion associated with complicated calculations, the sections removed from the rod are usually convenient whole figures such as 500 mm, 1 m, etc.

TRADE SECRETS

Whilst setting out routine joinery products it is advisable to pay particular attention to the positions of the shoulders either side of the mortise and tenon joints. It is good practice to align mouldings and rebates where possible each side of the joints to simplify marking out and cutting (see Figure 6.5).

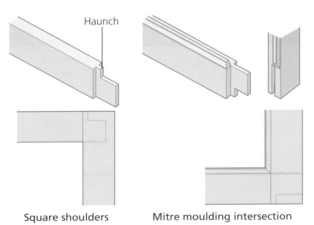
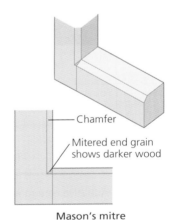

Square shoulders   Mitre moulding intersection   Mason's mitre

FIGURE 6.5 Aligning shoulders either side of a mortise and tenon joint

Before marking out any materials supplied by the machinists they should be compared with the original cutting lists to ensure accuracy and conformity. Machining batches of the same section timber at different times may lead to slight discrepancies in the width and thickness, particularly if the materials have been fed through a 'planer/thicknesser' rather than a 'four-sided planer'.

INSPECTION OF TIMBER

Naturally some species of timber usually contain imperfections such as sap pockets, dead knots and shakes. Although these defects are not always visible when the timber is in a sawn state, they may appear on the surfaces after machining to their finished size. All timber components should be inspected prior to marking out; to identify the best face and adjacent edge, they are then marked for 'face side' and 'face edge' marks. Careful consideration of minor defects may enable them to be removed while they are being rebated and moulded during machining for a second time after marking out. Timber for components such as jambs and stiles would also need to be checked for bows and hollows on the faces and edges. Jambs would need to be paired, hollow sides together, and stiles matched as illustrated in Figure 6.6 to avoid twisting after assembly.

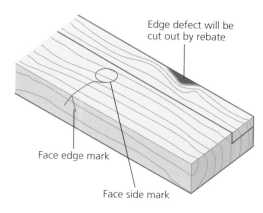

FIGURE 6.6 Bowed jambs paired together

ACTIVITIES

Activity 19 – Marking out efficiently

Read through the following questions and answer them as fully as you can to help you develop your underpinning knowledge of this subject area.

1. Explain the purpose of the 'horns' remaining on a panelled door prior to fixing.
2. What is the most accurate and efficient method of marking out a 90-degree corner on the floor to form a partition wall?
3. List five commercial sawn timber dimensions.
4. Who normally completes a timber cutting list?
5. Why is it important to always check prepared timber prior to indicating the positions of the face marks?

FACE SIDE AND EDGE MARKS

Face marks should be indicated on every component used to construct an item of joinery to assist accurate marking out, machining and assembly. The 'stocks' of marking-out tools should always be in contact with either the face side or face edge during the marking-out process. This enables lines to be squared around all four sides of the timber and still meet on the opposite side; it also ensures that the marking out on one face perfectly aligns through the timber to the marking out on the opposite side. Face marks not only indicate the best face and edge on the timber, but are also used as a reference during the machining process. The face and edge sides should be positioned against the fence and bed of each machine to improve accuracy and reduce that amount of marking out required on each piece of timber. If the timber has been accurately machined, the item of joinery can be assembled with the moulded face side uppermost. Providing the face marks were positioned tightly against the fence and bed of the machines during manufacture, the joints on this side of this assembly should be perfectly flush regardless of whether there are minor differences in the thickness of the timber. Any discrepancies between the components on the reverse side of the assembly are usually removed with a sharp smoothing plane once the assembly has been glued together.

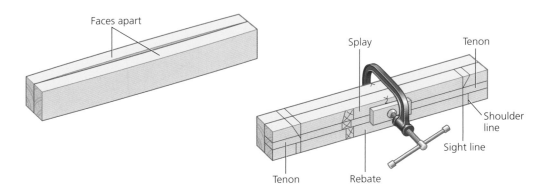

FIGURE 6.7 Face side and edge marks

CALCULATING THE PROPORTION OF JOINTS FROM STOCK SIZE

Timber can be sourced from merchants in a range of standard sawn (also referred to as unwrot) and planed (wrot) sizes. Determining the stock sizes prior to setting out may avoid excessive waste material whilst manufacturing joinery items; it may also enable the joints to be proportioned correctly.

The standard dimensions of sawn joinery grade timber are as follows:

19 mm × 125 mm
25 mm × 125 mm, 150 mm, 175 mm, 200 mm, 225 mm
32 mm × 125 mm, 150 mm, 225 mm
38 mm × 125 mm, 150 mm, 200 mm, 225 mm
50 mm × 100 mm, 125 mm, 150 mm, 175 mm, 200 mm, 225 mm
63 mm × 100 mm, 125 mm, 150 mm, 175 mm, 200 mm, 225 mm
75 mm × 100 mm, 125 mm, 150 mm, 175 mm, 200 mm, 225 mm
100 mm × 100 mm, 200 mm

Woodworking joints are usually calculated using proportions and ratios so that they can be transferred to virtually any section of timber without undermining its strength. Figure 6.8 demonstrates commonly used joints and the proportions used to set out and mark out onto stock material for a variety of joinery applications:

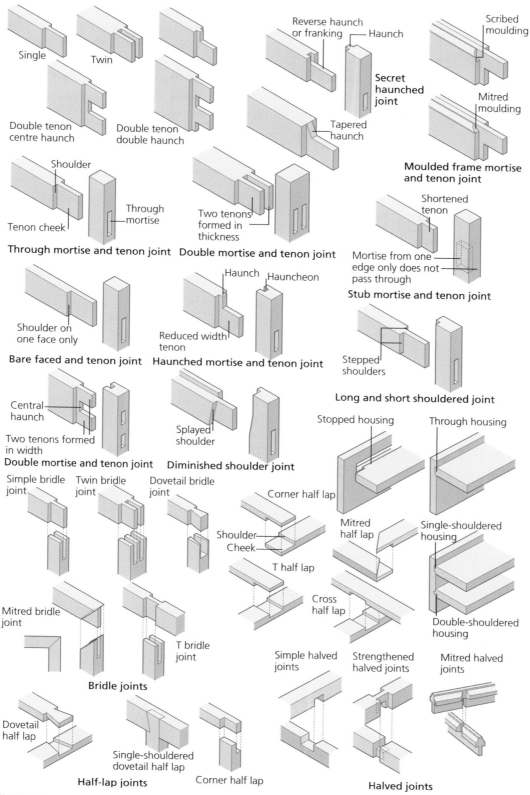

FIGURE 6.8A Commonly used woodworking joints

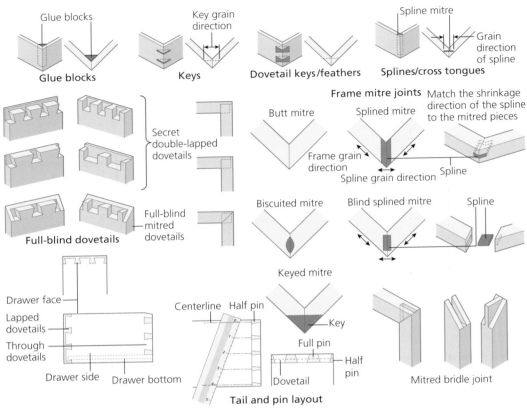

FIGURE 6.8B Commonly used woodworking joints

STAGES OF MARKING OUT FROM A WORKSHOP ROD (EXAMPLE – FRAMED DOOR)

Marking out details can simply and accurately be transferred from a workshop rod onto the timber by following the sequence of stages listed below:

1. It is common practice to begin marking out just one door stile before the rails. It should be placed over the height section on the workshop rod and aligned with the setting-out marks. Care should be taken to ensure that the stiles extend past the lines indicating the top and bottom of the door to allow for a portion of waste material known as the 'horn'.

TRADE SECRETS

The most efficient method of marking lines from one edge to its opposite edge is to draw short, broken lines over the corners of one face side. Marking out using this method prevents drawing unnecessary lines and overcomplicating the marking out; it also avoids having to remove the pencil marks upon completion.

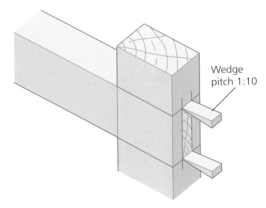

FIGURE 6.9 A horn on the top of a door stile

The horn is used to strengthen the joint on the end of the timber; it remains on the door after manufacture to prevent damage to the top and bottom edges.

2. Align either a set square or combination square with the pencil lines on the rod indicating the positions of the mortises. Mark vertical lines from the joint positions onto the face edge of the timber.

3. Remove the stile from the rod. Transfer the mortise positions from the face edge to the opposite edge.

4. Mark lines 3–4 mm either side of the mortise positions along the length of the door stile, on the edge opposite the face.

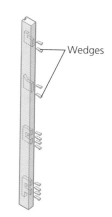

FIGURE 6.10 Wedge room

These lines indicate the increased width of the mortises and the room needed to drive the wedges down each side of the tenons once the joint has been assembled.

5. Refer to the workshop rod to establish the size of the mortise, before adjusting a mortise gauge to the nearest chisel size and marking. Adjust the stock of the mortise gauge to align one pin with the edge of the rebate, moulding or groove to ensure the joint is constructed in the simplest way.

6. The initial stile marked out from the rod should be used as a 'pattern' to mark out its pair, or batches of stiles of the same length. Using a pattern to transfer marking out over multiple components is more productive then repeating the sequence of marking out individual parts. Whilst marking out, it is important that the stiles are clamped together in pairs with the face marks on the outside of the batch. This technique will allow the marking-out lines to be accurately transferred around the individual components. (Note: only the pattern pieces are gauged for mortising and tenoning and the machines are set up to these.)

7. The horizontal and vertical rails should also be laid on the workshop rod to transfer the position of the shoulders from the setting out. The position of any intermediate rails should also be marked onto the horizontal rails at this point. Where a number of doors are being manufactured, intermediate mortises on rails would not be marked until the tenons have been formed. This allows stops to be set up for repetitive runs without tying the machinist down to two shoulder lines. This improves speed, efficiency and accuracy.

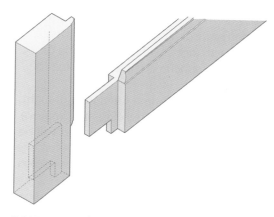

FIGURE 6.11 Alignment of the edge of the tenon with the rebate

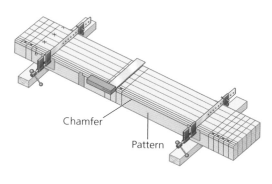

FIGURE 6.12 Cramping door stiles and using a pattern to mark out

It is good practice to complete all the marking out before machining the timber. Whenever possible, start manufacturing joinery items by cutting the joints. This will prevent causing damage to any profiled edges as they pass through the tenoning machine. It is common practice to cut all the mortises initially followed by the tenons; this is because the exact width of the mortise is fixed by the width of the chisel. The thickness of the adjoining tenons can be finely adjusted during the setting up of the 'tenoner' to ensure a perfect 'push fit'. Remember that if you have to knock the joint together with a mallet, it probably does not fit. Each joint should be snug fitting and easily pushed together.

DOORS

DOOR REQUIREMENTS

There is a wide range of different internal and external doors available on the market, each one offering different performance criteria. Doors are capable of regulating the amount of light and ventilation that passes through to other rooms or spaces within a building. Careful consideration should be given to the selection of doors to ensure that they suit their intended positions; for example, a door with a 'vision panel' (glazed section) would not be suitable for a bathroom. Although this seems to be an obvious mistake, it could easily be overlooked if the doors are ordered by referring to the architect's plans alone.

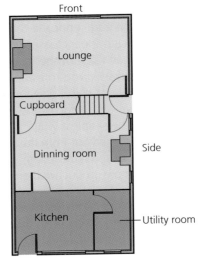

FIGURE 6.13 Door positions shown on an architect's plan

DOOR CHARACTERISTICS

1. **Security** – Doors built of a sound construction and durable materials will offer a good level of security if they are installed correctly. They should also be fitted with good-quality locks and bolts. Some insurance companies insist that mortise deadlocks are fitted to all external doors leading into a domestic property, before insurance cover will be given. Internal doors in domestic buildings are rarely fitted with locks; with the exception of bathrooms, although internal door locks are commonly found in commercial buildings such as schools, colleges and offices.
2. **Weather protection** – An exterior grade door installed into a frame fitted with draught excluders or weather strips will prevent water penetrating into the building, and improve the 'U' value (heat loss). It is important to consider whether any ironmongery that will be fitted to the door can withstand the elements. Ironmongery not suited to an exterior position will tarnish, corrode, rust and potentially over a short period of time break down and fail to function properly.
3. **Privacy** – Privacy is maintained in a room or space by regulating the position of the door. The pivot point or hinged side of a door can usually be established by referring to the architect's plan, or by considering the following factors:

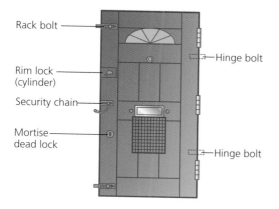

Rack bolt

Hinge bolt

Rim lock
(cylinder)

Security chain

Mortise
dead lock

Hinge bolt

FIGURE 6.14 A typically secured external door

TRADE SECRETS

Fire escapes are considered to be one of the least secure points of a commercial or public building. Although many buildings are entered by intruders through fire escapes, they should not be secured with 'deadlocks' or any other type of fixing that requires the use of a key.

In many situations fire doors are secured with chains and padlocks, and remain in place during periods of time when the building is occupied. This is against factory regulations and may put lives at risk in the event of an emergency evacuation.

- make sure that all light switches are easily accessible as the door is opened;
- privacy is still maintained in the room after opening the door;
- wherever possible, the door should open into the room.

4. **Fire resistance** – There are two types of fire doors; also known as 'fire check' doors, commonly used in the construction industry; these are half an hour and 1 hour resistant. The risk of the spread of flames passing from one room to another can be minimised if a fire door is correctly installed, with a suitable door frame and 'intumescent seals' (fire-retardant strips normally fitted to either the door or frame). Note that fire doors are covered in more detail later in this chapter.

5. **Sound proofing** – Most solid or dense doors will reduce the passage of sound through a door opening. In areas of excessive noise, such as theatres, music rooms or private offices, where privacy must be maintained, acoustic doors must be fitted. The amount of sound that passes through a doorway can be reduced further by installing acoustic seals to both the door and frame.

6. **Access** – Doors provide access in and out of buildings; their width will vary depending on their position. External doors are usually wider than internal doors because they have more traffic passing through them. Consideration should be given to the type of access and performance required by the doors, for instance wheelchair or disabled access.

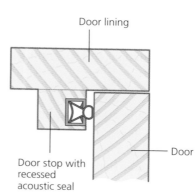

Door lining

Door

Door stop with recessed acoustic seal

FIGURE 6.15 Acoustic seals

? FREQUENTLY ASKED QUESTIONS

▶ What are acoustic seals?

Acoustic seals come in a variety of different shapes and sizes, depending on their position on the door or frame. They work similarly to draught excluders, by sealing the joint between the door edge and the frame.

STANDARD DOOR SIZES

Interior doors (35–44 mm thick)

1981 mm × 457 mm (imperial size – 78" × 18")

1981 mm × 533 mm (imperial size – 78" × 21")

1981 mm × 610 mm (imperial size – 78" × 24")

1981 mm × 686 mm (imperial size – 78" × 27")

1981 mm × 711 mm (imperial size – 78" × 28")

1981 mm × 762 mm (imperial size – 78" × 30")

2032 mm × 813 mm (imperial size – 80" × 32")

1981 mm × 838 mm (imperial size – 78" × 33")

Exterior doors (44 mm thick)

1981 mm × 762 mm (imperial size – 78" × 30")

2032 mm × 813 mm (imperial size – 80" × 32")

1981 mm × 838 mm (imperial size – 78" × 33")

2057 mm × 838 mm (imperial size – 81" × 33")

2083 mm × 863 mm (imperial size – 82" × 34")

2134 mm × 914 mm (imperial size – 84" × 36")

DOOR SCHEDULES AND DRAWINGS

In the construction industry, a 'schedule' is a document that is used to reference all the details needed for a particular component. Schedules are usually supplied by the architect with the construction drawings; they provide repetitive detailed information for individual items such as doors, windows and ironmongery. Details are easily obtained from a schedule by using a referencing system between the architect's drawings. The relevant information is then used throughout the planning, building and completion stages of a project. Schedules are used by the main and subcontractors, to provide the information needed to estimate the total costs of various items before ordering and programming deliveries. The following information could be obtained by referring to a detailed door schedule:

- the overall dimensions (height, width, thickness);
- design/type (flush, panelled, internal/external, etc.);
- glazed/non-glazed (pattern of glass, single/double glazed, safety glass, etc.);
- type of material (oak, beech, ash, redwood, etc.);
- type of ironmongery (stainless steel butt hinges, push plates, mortise latch, etc.);
- finish (colour of paint/stain/varnish, etc.).

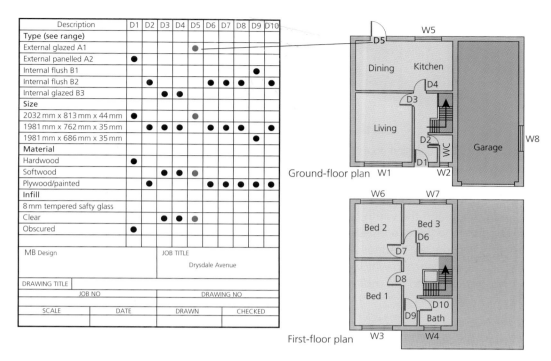

Description	D1	D2	D3	D4	D5	D6	D7	D8	D9	D10
Type (see range)										
External glazed A1					●					
External panelled A2	●									
Internal flush B1								●		
Internal flush B2		●			●	●	●			●
Internal glazed B3			●	●						
Size										
2032 mm x 813 mm x 44 mm	●				●					
1981 mm x 762 mm x 35 mm		●	●	●		●	●	●		●
1981 mm x 686 mm x 35 mm									●	
Material										
Hardwood	●									
Softwood			●	●	●					
Plywood/painted		●				●	●	●	●	●
Infill										
8 mm tempered safty glass										
Clear			●	●	●					
Obscured	●									

MB Design

JOB TITLE
Drysdale Avenue

DRAWING TITLE

JOB NO		DRAWING NO	
SCALE	DATE	DRAWN	CHECKED

Ground-floor plan
W5 · W1 · W2 · W8
D5 · Dining · Kitchen · D4 · D3 · Living · D2 · WC · D1 · Garage

First-floor plan
W6 · W7 · W3 · W4
Bed 2 · Bed 3 · D6 · D7 · D8 · Bed 1 · D10 · D9 · Bath

FIGURE 6.16 A door schedule

DOOR TYPES

Internal and external doors

There are clear distinctions between internal and external doors, as shown in Table 6.1.

TABLE 6.1 Differences between internal and external doors

Internal doors 35–44 mm thickness	External doors 44 mm minimum thickness
Sometimes faced in veneer or laminate	Never faced in veneer or laminate
Lightweight construction (except fire doors)	Mortise and tenon joints in framed doors*
No preservative treatment	Treated to prevent against decay and insect attack
Interior adhesives used	Water-resistant adhesives used
Interior grade timbers	Durable timbers or timber-based materials

*Some cheaper, mass-produced external doors are constructed with dowel joints.

FRAMED/PANELLED DOORS

Panelled doors are available in a variety of different shapes and styles, to suit both modern and older traditional buildings. They are normally constructed with a series of solid timber rails and stiles, formed around either timber or glass panels. Panelled doors have been manufactured for many years with traditional mortise and tenon joints. Alternatively, the rails are 'scribed' over the profile or moulding around the inside of the door stiles and are dowelled together.

FIGURE 6.17 Timber panelled doors

The proportions of the mortise and tenon joints on a panelled door will vary depending on their position and the width of their component parts. The joints are held securely in place between timber wedges. Figure 6.19 highlights the sequence in which the wedges should be knocked into the position.

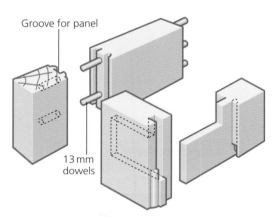

FIGURE 6.18 Dowelled and haunched mortise and tenon joints

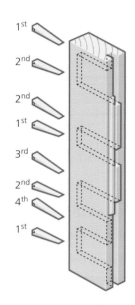

FIGURE 6.19 Joints on a panelled door

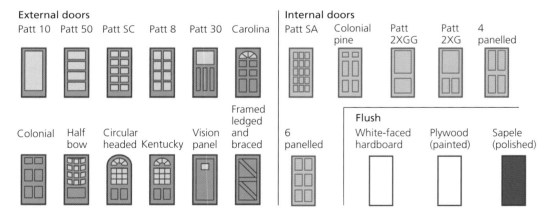

FIGURE 6.20 External and internal doors

? FREQUENTLY ASKED QUESTIONS

▶ Why is it important to install the wedges in this sequence?

Failure to follow these guidelines will result in the rails being wedged out of line. This movement would then cause the joints to 'open up' and reveal unsightly gaps. Gaps between the joints in the frame could result in a weakening in the structure and possibly cause the whole door to twist.

GUNSTOCK STILES

Traditional panelled doors are designed to permit the maximum amount of light through the glazed area without compromising the strength or integrity of the door. This is achieved by reducing the width of the styles on either side of the door along the glazed area, yet still maintaining the full width of the styles where there are panels. Gunstock styles are rarely used these days due to the complexity of the joints between the rails and styles.

PANEL TYPES

The design of panelled doors may vary considerably depending on the materials used, shape of the panels/glazing and the mouldings (also known as 'profiles') used. In most cases the mouldings used on internal doors are purely cosmetic, but consideration should be given to the outward facing mouldings on an external door. These profiles should be designed so that they prevent water from remaining on the large, flat areas for long periods of time, as this may lead to wood decay and water penetration.

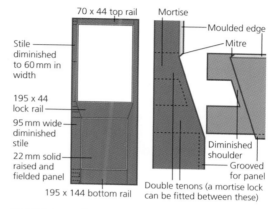

FIGURE 6.21 Gunstock stile

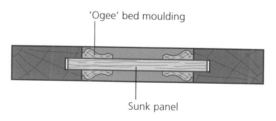

FIGURE 6.23 Panel movement

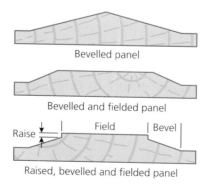

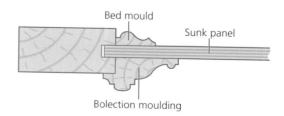

FIGURE 6.22 Panel mouldings

TRADE SECRETS

The panels within a timber framed door will continue to move after they have been assembled, because of the differences in moisture in the atmosphere. This movement in the panels will not affect the operation of the door if the following guidelines are followed:

1. *Never glue the panels in the frame of the door, as this may lead to them splitting;*
2. *Always allow a minimum 3–4 mm gap between the outside edge of the panels and the grooves. This will permit the panels to shrink and expand freely and prevent the joints on the door being forced apart;*
3. *Always prime or stain the edges of the panels with the same finish as the rest of the door before assembly. Shrinkage in the panels after completion may cause any untreated surfaces to be revealed.*

FIRE DOORS

A fire door's primary function is to delay the spread of flames and dangerous smoke and gases onto fire escape routes for a set period of time. This will give the occupants of the building enough time to evacuate in a safe manner to their designated assembly points. Fire doors with increased resistance may be used to protect property or information contained in commercial buildings or offices.

Fire doors have to undergo vigorous testing to make sure that they conform to British Standards before being certified with a fire rating. Ratings and certification of doors will vary depending on their ability to maintain their integrity and stability for a set period of time. The most common types of fire doors are:

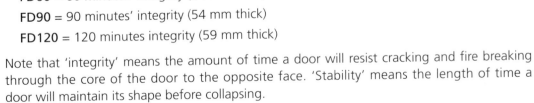

FIGURE 6.24 Fire doors

FD30 = 30 minutes' integrity (44 mm thick)

FD60 = 60 minutes' integrity (54 mm thick)

FD90 = 90 minutes' integrity (54 mm thick)

FD120 = 120 minutes integrity (59 mm thick)

Note that 'integrity' means the amount of time a door will resist cracking and fire breaking through the core of the door to the opposite face. 'Stability' means the length of time a door will maintain its shape before collapsing.

Testing

Fire doors must be tested in simulated conditions as a complete assembly to be approved; this includes the:

- door;
- door frame;
- intumescent seals;
- all of the ironmongery including hinges, locks and latches, and door closers (*Note* – All ironmongery must be made of metal that has a melting point above 850°C; for example steel or brass).

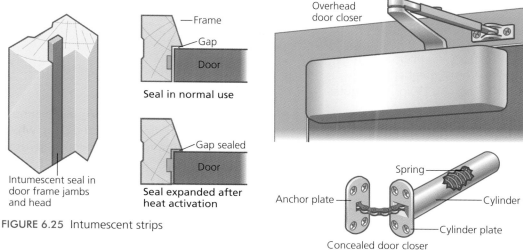

FIGURE 6.25 Intumescent strips

FIGURE 6.26 Door closer

Fire doors that have undergone testing together with their frame etc., are usually sold by suppliers as a 'door set'. If a 'fire door', or 'fire door set' is not installed to the same specifications as the example that underwent the testing, this will invalidate the fire certification and its rating. Any door, or door set that has successfully completed testing to achieve certification must be supplied together with the installation instructions to ensure they are fitted to the same standards. Doors that have been incorrectly installed may have poor workmanship during the hanging or fitting, e.g. large margins between the door edge and the frame (larger than 3 mm), or the incorrect amount of intumescent strips or smoke seals, etc.

 FREQUENTLY ASKED QUESTIONS

▶ **My local builders' merchants stock 'intumescent paint'. How many coats of this do I need to apply to a timber door to achieve a half-hour fire rating?**

All fire doors must conform to British Standards BS 476: Part 22: 1987. Intumescent paint applied to a timber door will not prevent the spread of flame for an acceptable period of time to meet with these minimum requirements.

Fire door identification

It is important to be able to clearly identify fire-resistant doors and frames, to ensure that they meet with specifications and building regulations. Certified fire doors are sometimes difficult to identify through a visual inspection alone, so it may be necessary to request a copy of the test certificate for the exact door performance details. The British Woodworking Federation (BWF) runs a certification system known as 'BWF – CERTIFIRE fire door and doorset scheme'. The purpose of the scheme is for members to have their products rigorously tested to ensure they comply with the minimum requirements to save lives and protect property. Doors and door sets that meet the requirements of the scheme are identified with a unique labelling system. BWF-CERTIFIRE labels are normally attached to the top edge of fire doors, and contain the following information:

- member's name (manufacturer);
- member's phone number;
- certification number;
- unique serial number;
- fire rating (e.g. 30 or 60 minutes).

Alternatively, the Timber Research and Development Association (TRADA) use a simple system of inserting a tree-shaped colour-coded plastic plug into the edge of the door, which identifies the type of fire door/frame and intumescent seals. The following colours are used around the outside of the plugs to identify the rating of the door:

- Yellow – 30 minutes;
- Blue – 60 minutes;
- Brown – 90 minutes;
- Black – 120 minutes.

GLAZED FIRE DOORS

Most fire doors require vision panels or some form of glazed section; this can achieved with the use of wired or fire-rated glass. The fire-retardant glazing must be secured in position with hardwood beads, either screwed or nailed into position, together with an approved intumescent glazing system. This will prevent fire and smoke encroaching through the joint between the glazing and the recess in the door. The exact specification for the installation of glazing in fire doors should be obtained from the fire test data sheet.

HOLLOW CORE DOORS

These are probably the most common type of doors used in the construction industry today because of their relatively low cost and light weight. Although the term 'hollow core' suggests that the door has been constructed without any structure in the middle, this is not entirely true. There are several different methods of building hollow core doors; the most common modern method is with the use of a timber frame infilled with a honeycomb pattern of corrugated cardboard.

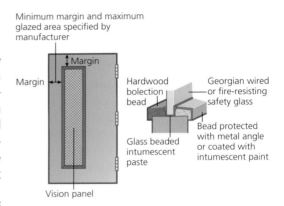

Minimum margin and maximum glazed area specified by manufacturer

Margin

Margin

Hardwood bolection bead

Georgian wired or fire-resisting safety glass

Glass beaded intumescent paste

Bead protected with metal angle or coated with intumescent paint

Vision panel

FIGURE 6.27 Glazed fire door

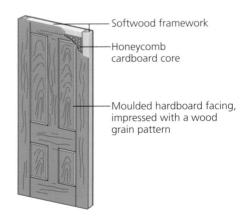

Softwood framework

Honeycomb cardboard core

Moulded hardboard facing, impressed with a wood grain pattern

FIGURE 6.28 Hollow core door

This arrangement is then covered with 3–4 mm plywood on either side, or alternatively hardboard. In most cases hardboard is used because it is cheaper, smoother and can easily be pressed into panel shapes with wood grain effects to give the appearance of a panel-framed door, constructed with solid materials.

LOCK BLOCKS

'Lock blocks' are sections of solid timber of approximately 500 mm × 127 mm sandwiched into the core of hollow doors. They are usually only found on one side of each door to enable locks, latches and handles to be securely fixed, although they can be found on both sides on some better quality doors. It is important that the sides containing the lock blocks are clearly identified to prevent the doors being hinged on the wrong side; this would then result in difficulties in fixing the ironmongery. Manufacturers normally label the top edge of the side containing the lock block with either a key symbol or the lettering 'LOCK'.

MATCHBOARDED DOORS

'Matchboarding' is a term used for a series of timber boards jointed together in their width. The most common way of connecting the boards is with the use of 'tongue and groove' mouldings. Matchboarded doors are probably the simplest method of door construction, and commonly used internally and externally for garden gates, sheds and older buildings such as cottages. Tongue and groove boards are used in the construction of different types of matchboarded doors; these include:

- ledged matchboarded doors;
- ledged and braced matchboarded doors;
- framed ledged and braced matchboarded doors.

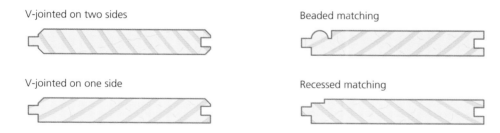

FIGURE 6.29 Board Sections

1. **Ledge** – the horizontal timbers running across the back of matchboarded doors. The ledge is used as a fixing point for the vertical timbers on the face of the door and helps to increase the thickness of the door and its stability.
2. **Brace** – Braces are used diagonally across the back of matchboarded doors to maintain their shape and reduce the risk of 'dropping' under their own weight. 'Dropping' is a term used to describe the side of a door opposite the hinges that has failed to retain its shape due to poor supporting. Bracing should also be positioned so that the side opposite to the hinges is supported; an incorrectly braced door may result in the door failing to function properly. Braces should be fitted at 45 degrees or more to the ledges; if they are fitted below this angle they will not provide adequate support to the door. Commercially produced matchboarded doors usually have the braces left loose so that they can be fitted by the carpenter once the

TRADE SECRETS

To prolong the life expectancy of matchboarded doors installed in exterior positions, all of the top edges of the ledges should be 'weathered'. This will prevent water and moisture holding on the level surfaces for long periods of time, and potentially instigating the onset of rot. The weathering will also direct water away from the joint between the matchboarding and the back of the ledges.

Painting the tongues and grooves, and the back faces of the ledges and braces before assembly will protect the hidden areas from trapped moisture. This will also ensure that any movement in the timber will not reveal any bare or untreated timber.

hanging side of the door has been established. Some suppliers manufacture matchboarded doors, with the bracing suited to both left and right handing. Although this method will provide some support to the door, it is considered to be a compromise and will not offer the same strength as alternative methods.

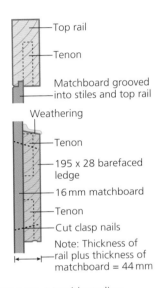

FIGURE 6.30 Matchboarding

Labels in figure 6.30:
- Top rail
- Tenon
- Matchboard grooved into stiles and top rail
- Weathering
- Tenon
- 195 x 28 barefaced ledge
- 16 mm matchboard
- Tenon
- Cut clasp nails
- Note: Thickness of rail plus thickness of matchboard = 44 mm

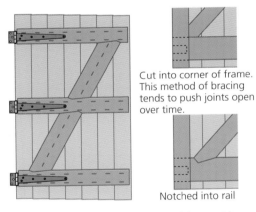

Cut into corner of frame. This method of bracing tends to push joints open over time.

Notched into rail

FIGURE 6.31 Bracing pattern used for a wide door

LEDGED DOORS

Ledged matchboarded doors are probably the simplest form of doors to manufacture, and for this reason they are sometimes manufactured on site by the second-fix carpenters. This eliminates the transport and expensive joinery manufacturing costs; it also prevents delay between ordering, manufacture and delivery. They consist of a set of three ledges screwed at either end to the back of a series of tongue and groove boards; the remaining boards are fixed in

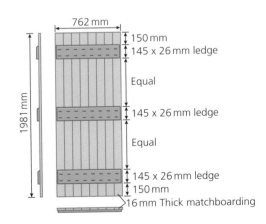

FIGURE 6.32 Ledged door

Labels in figure 6.32:
- 762 mm
- 1981 mm
- 150 mm
- 145 x 26 mm ledge
- Equal
- 145 x 26 mm ledge
- Equal
- 145 x 26 mm ledge
- 150 mm
- 16 mm Thick matchboarding

position using a traditional method known as 'clench nailing' (Figure 6.33). The ledges on hardwood matchboarded doors are usually fixed to the back of the tongue and groove boards with screws, counter bored below the surface of the timber and filled with wooden plugs to conceal the fixing.

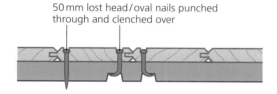

50 mm lost head/oval nails punched through and clenched over

FIGURE 6.33 Clench nailing

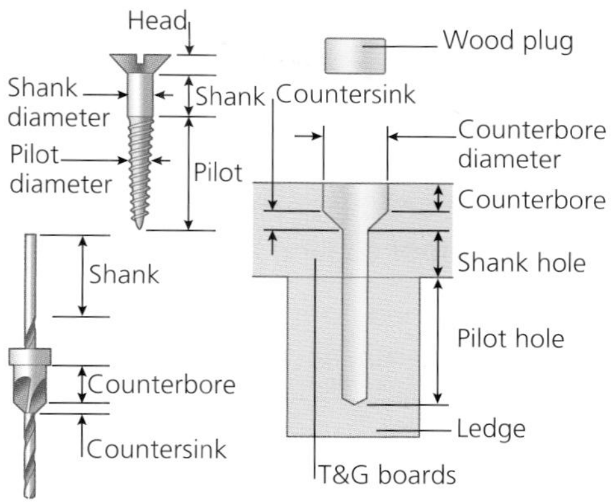

FIGURE 6.34 Screwing and plugging

Ledged matchboarded doors are rarely used these days because they have a tendency to 'drop' on their lock side. The risk of 'dropping' can be reduced if ledged matchboarded doors are only used for narrower doorways. If wider tongue-and-groove boards are used as well this will also help because the number of joints in the width of the door has been reduced.

IRONMONGERY

Ledged doors are relatively thin because unlike many other doors, they do not have a sub-

FIGURE 6.35 Ironmongery positions

stantial frame around their parameter. This means that any ironmongery fitted onto the door should be aligned with the ledges; this will ensure a secure fixing point when screwing or bolting into the timber. 'Black japanned', 'zinc-plated' or galvanised 'T' hinges are normally used to pivot side-hung doors because they are relatively easy to install and they are capable of supporting the light weight of the door.

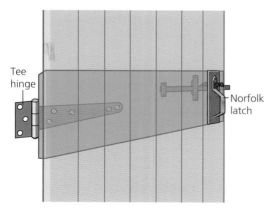

FIGURE 6.36 Ironmongery should be aligned with ledges

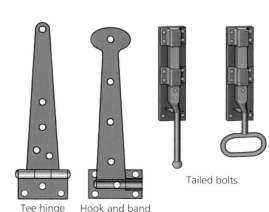

FIGURE 6.37 Black japanned ironmongery

? FREQUENTLY ASKED QUESTIONS

▶ What are 'black japanned' 'T' hinges?

Items that are 'black japanned' have gone through a process of having a black weatherproof coating baked onto them.

Black japanned ironmongery is commonly used for garden gates, sheds and 'rustic' items of internal and external joinery.

LEDGED AND BRACED MATCHBOARDED DOORS

These are constructed in the same way as ledged matchboarded doors but have the addition of diagonal bracing to prevent 'dropping'. The bracing across the back of ledged and braced matchboarded doors increases its rigidity and minimises the potential of twist developing in the door.

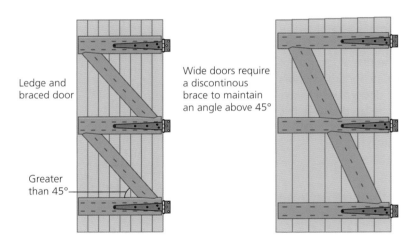

Ledge and braced door

Wide doors require a discontinous brace to maintain an angle above 45°

Greater than 45°

FIGURE 6.38 Alternative bracing methods

FRAMED, LEDGED AND BRACED MATCHBOARDED DOORS

As the name suggests, these types of doors are similar to ledged and braced doors, but unlike these other types they have a framed method of construction to increase their overall strength and performance. The frame, and mortise and tenon joints could be comparable to that of panelled doors. In general, both doors use the same section of timber for the stiles and head, and the same width for the middle and bottom rails. Both the middle and bottom rails should be reduced in their thickness to allow the matchboard covering to pass over their face without increasing the total thickness of the door.

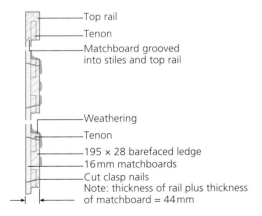

Top rail

Tenon

Matchboard grooved into stiles and top rail

Weathering

Tenon

195 × 28 barefaced ledge

16mm matchboards

Cut clasp nails
Note: thickness of rail plus thickness of matchboard = 44mm

FIGURE 6.39 Framed, ledged and braced door

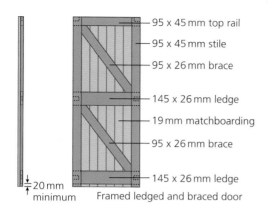

95 x 45 mm top rail
95 x 45 mm stile
95 x 26 mm brace
145 x 26 mm ledge
19 mm matchboarding
95 x 26 mm brace
145 x 26 mm ledge
20 mm minimum
Framed ledged and braced door

FIGURE 6.40 Framed, ledged and braced matchboard door

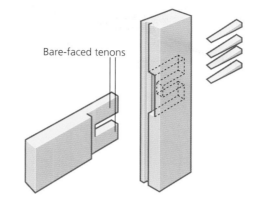

Bare-faced tenons

FIGURE 6.41 Jointing

The reductions in the thickness of the middle and bottom rails mean that standard mortise and tenons with two shoulders can no longer be used. In order to maintain the mortise and tenon position along the length of the stiles, 'bare-faced tenons' should be used; this simply means that there is only one shoulder on one face of the joint.

There are two ways of building the matchboarding into framed, ledged and braced doors:

1. tongue and groove;
2. rebated (inferior).

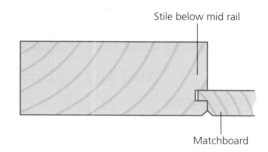

Stile below mid rail

Matchboard

FIGURE 6.42 A section through the stile of a framed, ledged and braced door

TIMBER SELECTION FOR INTERNAL AND EXTERNAL DOORS

Timber is a natural resource that will shrink and expand with changes in humidity and temperatures in the climate. This movement should be considered when calculating the number of boards required for matchboarded doors to avoid distortion. The amount of movement will vary between different timbers or species, and will depend on the initial moisture content of the timber, the sectional size of the timber and the direction of the grain.

The seasoned tongue and groove boards used on internal matchboarded doors are likely to shrink when the doors are fitted. This is likely to continue until the balance is achieved between the timber and the atmosphere; this is known as the 'equilibrium moisture content'. Doors that are hung in exterior positions are also likely to experience movement with the reverse results. The effects of any potential movement damaging or distorting internal doors can be eliminated, if the tongue and groove boards are fitted tightly between the styles or the width of ledged and braced doors. External doors require that the tongue and groove boards have a gap of 2–3 mm between each board to allow for expansion. Poorly spaced matchboarding across the width of a framed door could result in expansion in the timber forcing the stiles apart, and opening the joints along the shoulders. As a result, the structure of the door will be weakened and will probably cause it to 'drop'. It may also lead to an increase in the overall width of the door, causing it to 'bind' in the opening or fail to function properly.

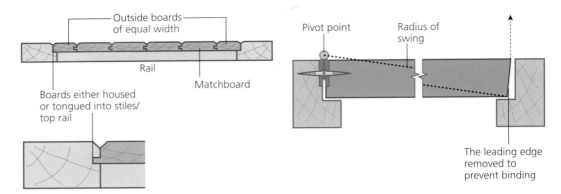

FIGURE 6.43 Ensuring an equal margin on the outer boards

FIGURE 6.44 Determining the angle required for the leading edge

? FREQUENTLY ASKED QUESTIONS

▶ What does the term 'bind' mean?

In relation to doors, the term refers to the leading edge of the door, or the edge opposite the hinges rubbing against the frame as it operates. In the worst cases, doors may fail to close fully within the frame, or the operator may have difficulty opening the door. This can be prevented and overcome by reducing the width of the door, so that a clearance gap of 3 mm is achieved between the edge of the door and the frame on all four sides.

DOOR OPERATIONS

There are many different ways that a single door or combination of doors can be arranged within a frame, to suit different purposes. These purposes may for example include a pair of glazed doors being used to borrow extra light from one room to another, or sliding doors used to minimise the amount of space needed for the doors to function properly. When an opening has more than one operational door, they are then known as 'leaves'. The operation of doors will fall into one of the following categories:

- single-action side hung (single or double);
- double-action side hung (single or double);
- sliding;
- bi-folding;
- revolving.

The term 'action' refers to the operation of a door, for example; a 'single-action' door will only swing in one direction, whilst a 'double-action' door will swing both inwards and outwards through the lining.

SINGLE-ACTION SIDE-HUNG DOORS (SINGLE AND DOUBLE)

This is probably the most common way of hanging any type of internal or external door. In simple terms, a single-action door is hung between the jamb on a door frame or lining and one side of a door, along its edge, and usually with butt hinges. Single-action doors used in conjunction with butt hinges are designed to pivot through a least 90 degrees in one direction.

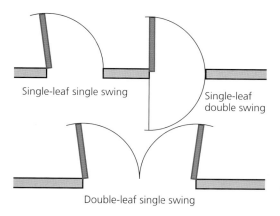

Single-leaf single swing

Single-leaf double swing

Double-leaf single swing

FIGURE 6.45 Single action side-hung doors

FIGURE 6.46 Butt hinges

DOUBLE-ACTION SIDE-HUNG DOORS (SINGLE AND DOUBLE)

Double-action doors swing through at least 180 degrees. They are commonly found in areas of heavy traffic such as schools, offices and hospitals. Double-action doors could potentially become a hazard unless vision panels are positioned at eye level, to avoid the door(s) being used at the same time from both sides. The potentially heavy use that the door(s) could endure should be adequately protected against. This is normally achieved by using rigidly constructed doors and suitable ironmongery, including:

- push plates;
- kick plates;
- bump protectors.

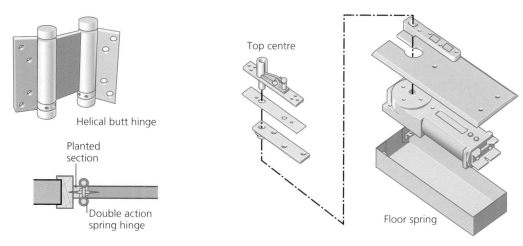

Helical butt hinge

Planted section

Double action spring hinge

Top centre

Floor spring

FIGURE 6.47 Helical butt hinges and floor spring

Double-action doors are hung using either 'helical butt hinges' (commonly referred to as 'bomber' hinges) or 'floor/transom springs'. Both methods provide pivot points for the door to operate in both directions, whilst a spring mechanism concealed in the ironmongery allows the door to return to the closed position after use.

SLIDING DOORS

Sliding doors are commonly used on wardrobes, kitchen units and areas where there is a lack of space. They are beneficial because they do not need the full width of the door(s) to swing or pivot into the room, therefore saving space.

BI-FOLDING DOORS

The term 'bi-folding' refers to doors that are constructed in two parts. They are sometimes preferred to sliding doors, because they retract the full width of the door frame, allowing good access through the opening. There are two methods of pivoting the folding doors:

- side folding;
- centre folding.

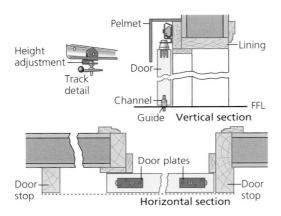

FIGURE 6.48 Sliding doors

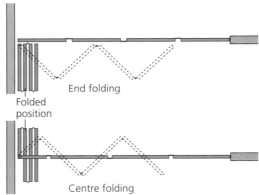

FIGURE 6.49 Folding doors

REVOLVING DOORS

These are usually found in the lobbies of large hotels, shops or offices. They permit a steady flow of traffic both in and out of a building without ever creating a direct draught. Revolving doors are rarely fitted by carpenters because of the complexity of the assembly; they are normally installed by specialist companies.

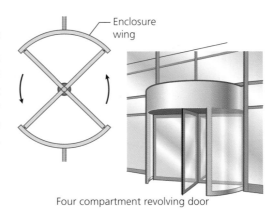

Four compartment revolving door

FIGURE 6.50 Four-compartment revolving doors

DOOR IRONMONGERY

Ironmongery and furniture is readily available for internal and external side-hung doors in a wide range of materials and finishes. Careful consideration should be given to the type of ironmongery selected for doors in damp and exterior positions, to ensure they continue to function correctly without deteriorating prematurely when exposed to moisture.

DOOR HINGES

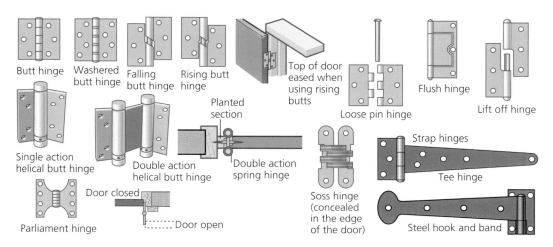

FIGURE 6.51 Types of door hinge

1. **Ball bearing butt hinges** – are generally used for heavier doors such as half-hour and one-hour fire check doors. They consist of a set of small ball bearings encased in the knuckle of the butt hinge. Ball bearing butt hinges will operate almost silently and allow the smooth movement of the door, which should prolong the life of the hinges.
2. **Butt hinges** – are available in sizes ranging from 25–100 mm in length, and a variety of different widths to suit different situations. The leaves on butt hinges are recessed into the door and frame equally with a margin between to allow the door to operate without binding. Standard butt hinges are generally used for lightweight doors. Heavier doors may lead to the hinges grinding and wearing, which may affect the margin along from the hinge side.
3. **Flush hinges** – are generally used for hollow core or lightweight doors. They are simple and quick to install because no recessing is required into the door or frame. They are accurately set out by transferring the centre point of the hinge from the door onto the frame, and aligning the knuckle of the hinge against the face of the door.
4. **Lift-off hinges** – these types of hinges are normally used by shopfitters and partitioning manufacturers, prior to installation. The hinges are split into two

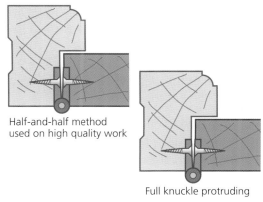

Half-and-half method used on high quality work

Full knuckle protruding

FIGURE 6.52 Hinge positions

parts. The lower section has a fixed pin that is usually fitted to the door frame to allow the upper part of the hinge that is fitted to the door, to be lifted over during the installation stage. 'Lift-off' hinges are 'handed' to suit right and left side-hung doors.

5. **Loose pin hinges** – Removal of the loose pin driven through the 'knuckle' of the hinge allows the disconnection of the two parts of the hinge and the removal of the door without the need to unscrew the fixings. These lightweight hinges are used internally for the quick installation and replacement of doors.

6. **Parliament hinges** – the projection of the pivot point (the 'knuckle') allows doors to swing 180° without binding on large architectural mouldings, such as architraves and plinth blocks. Parliament hinges are available in a range of different sizes offering different projections from the face of the door. Door closers should be avoided with doors hung with this type of hinge, because the large margin created between the door and frame as the door opens could be a potential hazard.

7. **Rising butt hinges** – are used to clear the surface of deep pile carpets and uneven floor surfaces. These hinges are handed to suit both right and left side-hung doors. The rising action of the hinge as it opens will result in the door 'self-closing' under its own weight, which will maintain privacy in the room and prevent draughts. The top corner, on the hinged side of the door will have to be removed to prevent the door binding against the head of the frame, as the door rises as it swings open.

8. **Falling butt hinges** – are used where the door will automatically fall open when not secured. These are commonly used on public toilet doors to inform users that the cubicle is not in use.

9. **Single- and double-action hinges** – These types of hinges are sprung loaded, which means they will return to their original closed position after opening. Double-action hinges are sometimes preferred to other types of door closers, including floor springs and transom door closers. Doors hung with double-action hinges require the leading edge to be removed from both sides of the door, to prevent binding as it swings inwards and outwards. This is achieved with rounded surfaces along the leading edge and the hinged side of the door. Double-action hinges are commonly used in commercial kitchens, restaurants and public houses.

10. **Soss hinges** – are high-quality hinges commonly used by cabinet makers and shopfitters. They are secured into housings located between the edge of the door and frame, to conceal their appearance once the door is in the closed position.

11. **Strap hinges** – there are several different types of hinges that fall into this category; they include 'T' hinges and 'hook and band hinges'. 'T' hinges are generally used for ledged and braced shed doors and garden gates. Hook and band hinges are usually made from thicker gauge metal so they are capable of supporting heavier timber garage doors, framed ledged and braced doors and large gates.

12. **Double washer butt hinges** – are similar to standard butt hinges; the main difference is the use of double washers between each joint in the knuckle of the hinge. The unique design of the washered butt hinges allows the smooth operation of the door and protection of the knuckle wear.

LOCKS AND LATCHES

1. **Cylinder night latches** – are commonly used to secure inward-opening front doors. Some insurance companies insist that the latch alone does not provide a suitable level of security, and require an additional mortise deadlock. Some cylinder night latches incorporate a deadlock to satisfy the standards required by insurance companies and the recommendation of the Police.

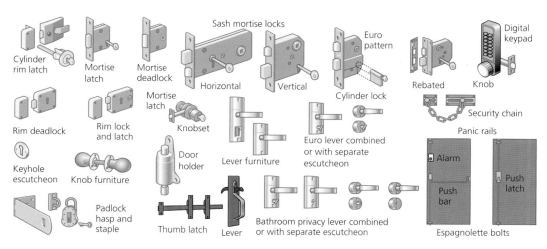

FIGURE 6.53 Locks and latches

2. **Digital key pads** – are used in conjunction with mortise latches to allow keyless entry through doorways. A number combination is required to allow the latch mechanism to release, allowing access by turning either a knob or handle on the body of the pad. The combination of numbers can be reprogrammed into the unit at any time to maintain security.

3. **Escutcheons** – are used to cover key holes cut into the face of timber doors and prevent damage from the key. Some key escutcheons are very discreet with a loose cover that swings either side of the key hole, to give the opening some weather protection and a decorative feature.

4. **Euro locks** – provide high security with hardened anti-drill steel along the length of a cylinder that operates the deadlock within the mortise lock.

5. **Mortise deadlocks** – are available with between two to seven levers, depending on the level of security required. Five levers are normally recommended as the minimum requirement by insurance companies and the Police for exterior doors. Any locks fitted on exterior doors must be certified to meet with British Standard BS3621-2004.

6. **Mortise latches** – are located in the edge of internal doors to hold them in a closed position as they engage with the striking plate; they do not offer any security. Mortise latches are normally operated with a pair of lever handles or a pair of door knobs fitted on either side of the door.

7. **Mortise lock/latch** – is a combination of a mortise deadlock and a mortise latch. They are used to retain side-hung doors in the closed position as well as securing them. The latch part of the lock is shaped with a 'lead' on one side; this allows it to ease into the striking plate as it closes. The location of the lead on the latch will determine the 'handing' of the lock. The handing of the lock can be changed to suit both right- and left-handed doors, although the methods to achieve this will vary between different manufacturers.

8. **Rebated mortise lock/latch** – these are used on pairs of doors, where the meeting stiles/edges are rebated together. Rebated door kits are also available to adapt conventional mortise lock/latches, to enable them to fit over the rebates along the doors edges.

9. **Traditional rim locks** – are available as lock/latches and deadlocks. They are traditionally used to secure matchboard ledged and braced doors, because the thickness of these doors prevents the use of other types of mortised lock/latches.

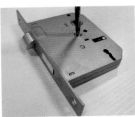

FIGURE 6.54 Changing the 'hand' of a latch

10. **Roller catches** – are commonly used on lightweight internal doors, such as wardrobe doors. The roller ball projecting from the face of the catch can normally be adjusted to suit the margin between the door and frame, and allow the door to glide over the striking plate as it opens and closes.

11. **Thumb latches** (also known as 'Norfolk' or 'Suffolk' latches) – are surface fixed on the faces of ledged and braced matchboarded doors, such as garden gates and also used on internal doors found in traditional style cottages.

BOLTS

1. **Barrel and tower bolts** – are used for external gates and garage doors either as a secondary form of security or to secure one half of a pair of doors. If the bolts are used to secure full-height double doors, they should be used as a pair, one at the top and bottom.

2. **Bow 'D' handle bolts** – are commonly used to secure garage doors. The 'D'-shaped handle allows easy operation of the heavyweight bolts.

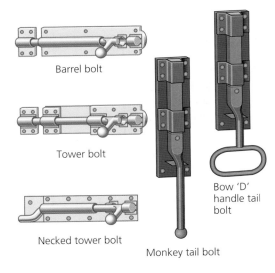

Barrel bolt

Tower bolt

Necked tower bolt

Monkey tail bolt

Bow 'D' handle tail bolt

FIGURE 6.55 Bolts

FIGURE 6.56 Flush bolt

3. **Flush bolts** – are fitted flush to the surface of side-hung doors (on a single door), or on the top and bottom edge of one half of a pair of doors. They provide a discreet appearance that is pleasing to the eye.

4. **Hinge bolts** – are located on the hinged side of the door, in the joint between its edge and the frame. They are installed to improve security and prevent the door being levered and forced away from its hinges.

5. **Monkey-tail bolts** – are very similar to bow 'D' handle bolts except they have a monkey-tail-shaped handle. The extended length of the monkey-tail bolts make them ideal for securing the top half of taller gates and exterior doors.

6. **Necked bolts** – are used to secure one half of a pair of double doors. The end of the bolt has a cranked section to allow it to be fitted on the rear face of doors located in rebated frames.

7. **Panic bolts and latches (espagnolette)** – are used to secure single and double fire escape doors. Panic bolts have a double point locking system, one at the top and bottom of the door; this provides increased security. Once closed, the bolts are released by depressing the panic bar running across the middle of the fire door, which allows an easy exit from the building in the event of an emergency. 'Single-point panic latches' are also available, providing a cheaper, lower level security device, with a reduced installation time. These are operated in exactly the same way as the two-point locking bolts.

8. **Rack bolts** – are used for a number of different applications, including additional security for single side-hung, sliding and double doors. They are either operated with a fluted key, or with the use of a thumb turn mounted on the face of the door. Rack bolts are normally used in pairs at the top and bottom of the door leaves to provide the best results.

DOOR CLOSERS

Door closers are available in a number of different forms ranging from a simple 'gate spring' to 'overhead closers'. Their purpose is to return doors to their original closed position. This is especially important on fire doors, because they are installed to prevent the spread of fire and smoke through doorways. Some door closers are fitted with heat sensors that automatically close the door in the event of a fire. The most commonly used door closers are:

- **Gate springs** – As the name suggests, these are generally used on garden gates to provide minimum security for young children and pets.

- **Overhead door closers** – are usually used for heavier doors to control the speed at which it closes. There are three different types of overhead door closers; each one is designed so the body either fits on the frame, or the top of inward-opening doors. Alternative closers are available to be fixed to the head of the frame, allowing the doors to swing outwards. These are used to prevent the door closer being exposed to the elements and potential damage. Overhead door closers are available in a range of different strength capacities to suit different door sizes, although most of them can be finely adjusted. British Standard BS EN 1154 classifies door closers into seven power sizes and grades them 1–7, 7 being the largest capacity.

- **Concealed spring closer** – is simply a cylinder containing a spring housed into the door edge with a chain attached to an anchor plate, which is then fixed to the frame. These types of closers are particularly useful to conceal the appearance of any door control. The tension on the spring can be adjusted to suit different sized doors, and allow the doors to engage the lock or latch correctly. This can be achieved by sliding the metal holding plate through the chain close to the cylinder and unscrewing the anchor plate from the edge of the door. The tension on the spring can be increased by twisting the anchor plate in a clockwise direction; this will result in the door closing quicker. Turning it in an anticlockwise direction will have the opposite effect.

- **Roller arm closers** – are face fixed to the frame of side-hung interior doors weighing up to approximately 30 kg. They are easily fixed and adjusted, to provide a cheaper alternative to the other door closers mentioned previously. Roller arm closers are normally fitted in the middle of the hinged side of the door; if there is a risk of children using the door it should be positioned at a higher level.

FINGER PLATES (ALSO KNOWN AS 'PUSH PLATES'), AND KICKING PLATES

Finger and kicking plates are fitted to doors in vulnerable locations such as schools, hotels, hospitals, etc. Kicking plates are installed to protect the lower faces of the doors from general wear and tear caused at floor level. Finger plates are usually either positioned directly behind pull handles or adjacent to this height.

DOOR FRAMES AND LININGS

Door frames are often confused with door linings, but there are clear differences between the two:

- door frames are used in mainly an exterior position (the division between the inside and outside of a building);
- they have a thicker section than door linings (approximately 95 mm × 58 mm). This will provide strength to the frame and increased security to the building;
- they have a rebated profile or section rather than 'planted on' door stops;
- they usually have draught proofing or weather strips. Alternatively the door frames will have capillary grooves to prevent water penetrating between the door edge and the inner edge of the door frame.

FIGURE 6.57 A door frame in situ

As mentioned previously, door frames are normally positioned in the openings between the brickwork on the exterior walls of a building, although this is not the only place they could be located. Conventional domestic (residential) buildings will be constructed with cavity walls on the exterior of the building. These are with inner and outer walls with a space between the brickwork; this area is known as the cavity. The cavity prevents the moisture penetration between the two walls and reduces heat loss from the building.

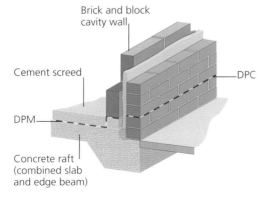

FIGURE 6.58 Cavity wall

FIGURE 6.59 Vertical DPC between a cavity wall and jamb

DOOR FRAMES

A room lit with natural daylight is far better for its occupant's health than with an artificial source, e.g. florescent strip lighting. Some buildings may not have the room or wall space to accommodate extra windows or roof lights. It may also be possible that some rooms may be situated in the centre of a building, therefore with no external walls for windows to be inserted. There are several methods of producing natural light in these areas including:

● **Fanlights** are basically created by extending the length of the jambs past the head of the door lining or frame, to fill the height between the door and ceiling (storey height). The area above the door is known as the 'fanlight'. The fanlight can either be directly glazed into the rebates or against the loose beading; alternatively this area could house an opening in the frame by adding a sash.

DOOR FRAME POSITIONING

Door frames are most commonly used in the openings formed in external cavity walls. These walls are substantially thicker than internal walls due to their double skin of brickwork. The door frames are normally positioned set slightly back from the face of the brickwork. The exact position of the frame will normally be specified on an architect's drawings, although consideration should be given to door frames with thresholds or sills. Thresholds are the section of timber fixed on the bottom of the two vertical sections of the frame; these are known as the 'jambs'. The threshold provides weather protection to the building by deflecting rainwater that runs down the face of the door away from the building. Water

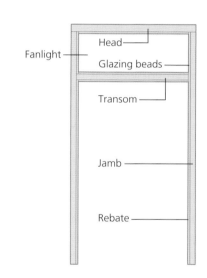

FIGURE 6.60 Parts of a storey height door frame

that travels down the slope or 'weathering' shaped on the front of the threshold may run underneath. To prevent water entering the building under the threshold a drip groove must be formed. The 'drip' on the bottom of a threshold must be situated over the brickwork to work effectively, when it is being positioned during fixing.

DOOR FRAME PROFILES

The exact shape or 'profile' of door frames will vary between manufacturers, but there are several distinct features that should remain the same to enable them to function properly. Each door frame will have a rebated section removed to allow a door, or pair of doors to sit within the

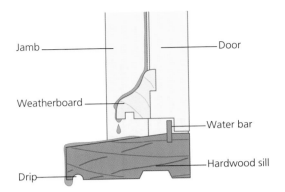

FIGURE 6.61 Threshold

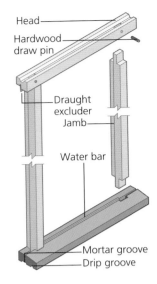

FIGURE 6.62 Door frame profile

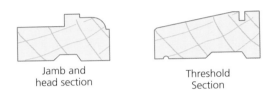

Jamb and head section

Threshold Section

FIGURE 6.63 Traditional door frame profiles

frame. It would *not* be acceptable to 'plant on' (loosely fix) doorstops onto a squared section of timber to form the rebate. It would be difficult to prevent water leaking through the frame using this method, because the joint between the doors stops and the frame would cause capillary action. This type of construction may also lead to a breach of security because of the joint between the frame and planted-on doorstops (see additional information on capillary action in Chapter 4 – Windows).

Door frames may also be used internally in situations that may require additional security, where a heavier door requires supporting. A good example for the use of a door frame in an internal position is a fire-rated door; these are normally substantially heavier than standard lightweight or 'hollow core' doors. In this case the door must withstand the extra load on the hinged side and the weight of the door closing up against the rebates on the locking side.

FREQUENTLY ASKED QUESTIONS

▶ What are hollow core doors?

Hollow core doors are, as the name suggests, doors with a relatively hollow core. Hollow core doors are constructed with two outer faces made of either plywood or hardboard. The 'core' or centre of the door must have some form of support to add stability to the door and prevent the door from collapsing. The cost-effective way of filling the core is to use a web of cardboard on its edge. The web is sandwiched between the two faces of the door and held in position with adhesive. The hollow core door will also contain a section of timber known as a 'lock block'. The lock block is positioned in the middle, on one side of the door to allow the door lock or latch to be mortised into it. The lock block is identified with a symbol on either the top or bottom edges of the door.

FIRE DOOR FRAMES

Frames used in an internal position to hang fire doors will have a slightly different profile. They will not require grooves around the inner face of the rebates for draught excluders or weather strips due to their positioning within the building. Some fire-rated door frames may need to have smoke or fire seals incorporated into the frame; this is normally achieved by having a machined slot around the frame for the seals fit.

DOOR FRAME CONSTRUCTION

It is common practice to connect the jambs to the head and sill with mortise and tenon joints. The head and threshold should run

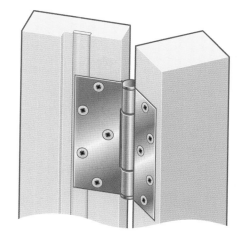

FIGURE 6.64 A door frame suitable for fire protection

past the jambs (these are known as the 'horns'); this allows them to be jointed together whilst the weathering still provides weather protection across the entire front of the frame.

There are several methods of securing the mortise and tenon joints together on door frames. Traditionally the mortise and tenon would include a haunch and wedges to secure the joint. Modern practice would normally include a frame, either pre-assembled in a joinery workshop or factory with through mortise and tenon joints, or all the components supplied in 'flat pack' form. These joints are secured with adhesive and either nails or screws. An alternative method of pulling the joints together on a door frame is to use draw dowels; this will eliminate the need for long cramps.

FREQUENTLY ASKED QUESTIONS

▶ What does the term 'flat pack' mean?

To reduce the transport costs of large joinery items, they are sometimes delivered to site unassembled. Items of joinery that are delivered in this condition are known as 'flat pack'.

WEATHER PROTECTION FOR DOOR FRAMES

Traditionally exterior door frames would have the head, jambs and sill shaped to prevent the rainwater passing from the outside of a building, to the inside, without the use of weather seals. Although the profiles on these types of door frames are functional in restricting some of the elements through the door frames, they do not prevent draughts and heat loss. Modern exterior door frames are complete with draught excluders made from PVC and foam, or rubber around the inner edges of the rebated frames. The exact position and shape of draught excluders will vary between manufacturers. Figure 6.65 shows some alternative draught excluder profiles commonly available and the position in which they should be used.

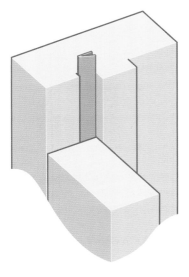
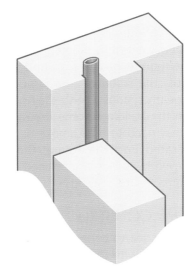

FIGURE 6.65 Draught excluders

Exterior door frames have metal thresholds screwed along the top edges of their sills. Some metal thresholds are supplied with sections that must be secured to either the face of the bottom of the door, or along the bottom edge. These combination thresholds work in conjunction with each other, and should always be fitted following the manufacturers installation guide.

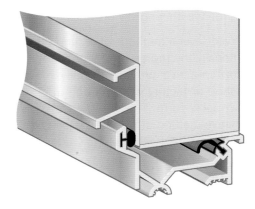

FIGURE 6.66 Metal threshold

DOOR LININGS

Door linings differ to door frames because they can only be used internally, and are smaller in section (26–38 mm thick). The width of door linings is normally determined by the thickness of the internal walls that they are going to be fixed to. A range of standard width door linings is available from building suppliers; the most common widths are:

- 115 mm;
- 138 mm.

FIGURE 6.67 Door lining

'Off the shelf' door linings are produced to accommodate the most commonly used door widths. The head of a standard door lining is manufactured with housing joints on either side of the timber; this reduces the need for suppliers to stock two different width linings and reduces costs. Traditionally the jointing between the jamb and head lining would use a barefaced tongue and trench (housing) and be secured with either screws or wire nails.

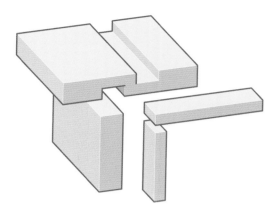

FIGURE 6.68 Head of a standard door lining

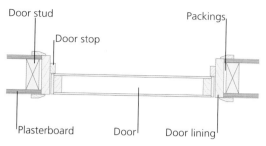

FIGURE 6.69 Door lining construction

DOOR LINING PROFILES

The most commonly used profiles for door linings are squared section material with loose doorstops. The loose doorstops are nailed to the door lining to form a rebate for the door to close against. The doorstop is normally attached to the door lining using 40 mm oval nails, after the door lining has been installed and the door hung and securely fixed.

Door linings that have loose doorstops have the added advantage of allowing the stops to fit to the exact thickness and shape of the door. This will ensure a perfect closing action and the door finishing flush within the face of the lining.

Door linings may also have solid rebates machined in the sections of the lining prior to assembly and installation. This method of constructing door linings is less cost effective, as the lining will require more timber to achieve the rebated profile, and the joints between the components are more complex.

The advantages of using rebated frames are that they are stronger and provide a neater finish on the face of the lining because there are no unsightly joints or redundant rebates (rebates that are not used).

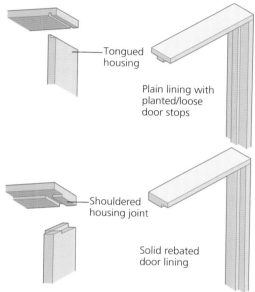

FIGURE 6.70 Door lining fixing

TRADE SECRETS

When installing door linings consider how the fixings can be concealed. This method of fixing will not only reduce the amount of time needed to cover or fill fixing points, it will provide a professional finish. Fixings points can sometimes be hidden behind fire or smoke seals, door stops or even the door hinges.

DOOR LINING CONSTRUCTION

Door linings with loose doorstops have very simple methods of construction; they can either be manufactured with through housing joints or tongued housing joints. Through housing joints are the simplest to construct and are mostly used in the mass production of 'off the shelf' joinery. Through housing joints in the head of a door lining will locate and secure the jambs as the frame is being assembled.

This type of joint may weaken after the horns are removed before installation due to the lack of support on the outer edge of the housing joint. A more secure method of jointing the head of a door lining to the jambs is the tongued housing. This method still offers support to the housing joint after the horns have been removed to allow for fixing.

FIGURE 6.71 A tongued housing joint between the head and jamb of a door lining

DOOR FRAME/LINING MATERIALS

Door frames and linings can be produced in a vast amount of different materials. Most suppliers will carry a limited range of softwood frames and linings; non-standard frames built from hardwood are usually supplied to order. Softwood door frames usually have an optional low-cost hardwood sill; this will provide durability and protection from the traffic that passes over it.

Man-made timber-based sheet materials are widely used in all areas of construction because they are:

- relatively inexpensive;
- easy to cut and shape;
- have no natural defects;
- do not shrink, expand, twist or warp like solid timbers;
- have smooth surfaces ready to apply finishes to such as paint or stain.

Door linings are also manufactured from 30 mm-thick medium-density fibreboard (MDF). They are usually supplied with several coats of primer/undercoat to seal and protect the MDF from moisture.

MDF mouldings and linings are also available with 'foil' or veneers applied to the exposed faces to simulate solid timber. 'Veneers' are thin layers of real wood; they are usually about 1 mm thick and can be sanded and painted just like solid timber. 'Foil' is basically a printed image of wood grains or solid colours that is applied to paper; the foil is extremely flexible and can be wrapped around any shape. Foil-wrapped mouldings, are pre-finished so they do not require any sanding or painting; they are also very durable.

PREPARING DOOR LININGS FOR INSTALLATION

Door linings for low cost work are normally assembled on site, especially if they are purchased 'off the shelf'. It is vitally important that the sequence for preparing a lining for installation is followed; this will benefit the carpenter whilst fitting the lining because the lining will:

- be sanded and prepared for painting;
- have the two jambs parallel to each other;
- be square;
- have strong joints between the head and the jambs.

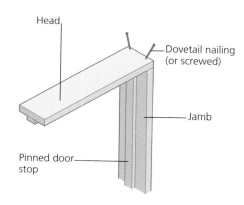

FIGURE 6.72 Securing the head to the joint

Preparing the lining

Door linings and frames should have their inner faces and rebates sanded and the sharp edges (arrises) removed along their longest edges, prior to gluing and assembly. This will prevent difficulty when trying to sand the jointed corners after the linings or frames have been secured together.

SQUARING A DOOR LINING

When preparing a door lining for installation, it is important that the jambs are both parallel to each other and square to the head of the lining.

The best method of aligning and securing these components in position before installation is listed in the following steps:

- **Step 1** – Check the length of the jambs;
- **Step 2** – Secure the housing joints between the head and the jambs with strong wood adhesive and either screws or round-headed nails;
- **Step 3** – Fix a stretcher on either side of the door lining, exactly 150 mm up from the 'feet' of the jambs. This will prevent

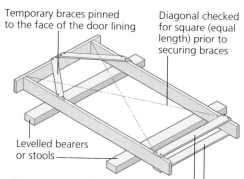

FIGURE 6.73

the jambs of the lining from twisting and keep them parallel to each other.

FREQUENTLY ASKED QUESTIONS

▶ What are the 'feet' of a door lining?

The term 'feet' refers to the bottom of the jambs on a door lining. The term may also be referred to on door frames, architraves and other similar arrangements.

TRADE SECRETS

The length of the stretchers is determined by the overall width of the door lining. The most accurate way of achieving this is to transfer the width onto the stretcher from the head of the lining before fixing.

Use round-headed nails to temporally fix the stretchers to the lining. The heads of the nails should be left above the surface of the stretchers to allow for easy removal after the lining has been installed.

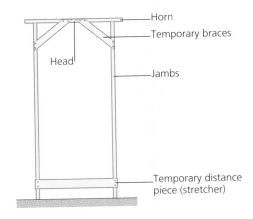

FIGURE 6.74 Stretcher

- **Step 4** – The most accurate method used to check that a frame is square is to measure diagonally across the frame between the stretchers and the head, and repeat the process across the other diagonal. This method is known as squaring from 'corner to corner'. The measurements between the diagonal corners should be equal to each other. If they are not, then pressure will have to be applied between the longest opposite corners to adjust the frame until the diagonal measurements are equal. A brace should be prepared with 45-degree corners cut on both ends. The brace should have a nail started at each end ready to be driven into the face of the lining. When assembled the brace can be positioned and the nail driven into the jamb. When the frame has had the diagonals checked and adjusted to square, the other end of the brace can have its securing nail driven. This will hold the frame square during storage and transportation. The brace should not be removed until the lining has been fixed.

When a door lining is being checked to ensure that it is square, a tape measure can be used to compare the diagonal sizes. This method usually requires two people, one to hold the tape measure tight in one corner and the other to read the measurements from the tape. Using a tape to check whether a frame or lining is square can sometimes be difficult and inaccurate. This is because the end of the tape measure cannot fit completely into the square corners of the lining and it could also sag and twist.

FIGURE 6.75 Using a squaring rod on a door lining

FIGURE 6.76 Adjusting a door lining to square and attaching the brace

TRADE SECRETS

The 'hook end' of a tape measure is securely fixed to the body of the tape with metal rivets through elongated slots. The elongated slots allow slight movement in the hook end to ensure accurate measurements are taken both internally and externally. Excessive use of the tape measure will wear the elongated holes, and the tape will no longer give precise measurements. Accurate measurements can still be taken from a worn tape by holding the end on the 100 mm measurement and extending the tape to the required length. It is essential that the 100 mm measurement has been accounted for when reading the extended tape.

- **Step 5** – Secure the door lining in its square position with diagonal bracing between the head and one of the jambs. The bracing should be nailed in place at an angle of approximately 45 degrees; if the bracing is fixed at a shallower angle than this it becomes ineffective at retaining the frame in its square position.

FIGURE 6.77 Hook end of a tape measure

(*Note* – Bracing and stretchers should be secured in place with two nails at each fixing point. This will help to prevent the frame or lining from twisting or racking on a single fixing point.)

UNITS AND FITMENTS

Handcrafted timber wall and floor units are rarely used in domestic houses because they are usually purpose built by cabinet makers or joiners, which makes them relatively expensive. Modern kitchens and bedroom furniture is mass produced on computer numerical control (CNC) machinery with timber-based sheet materials and simple mechanical joints. Mass-produced units can either be supplied 'flat packed' for assembly on site, or 'rigid' (factory assembled):

- **Flat packed units** – This method of supplying units requires the installer to assemble all the components, following the manufacturer's assembly instructions. Budget ranges of furniture are normally supplied flat packed; this enables the cost of the units to be reduced due to them only being partially completed. Suppliers are able to increase the stock levels of units if they are flat packed because they require less space for storage and delivery. Depending on the quality, carcasses are usually manufactured from 16 mm melamine-faced chipboard (MFC).
- **Rigid units** – These types of units are fully assembled and glued together during their manufacture. They are also higher quality with 19 mm-thick shelves and sides, and 9 mm back panels.

Standard kitchen base units are 600 mm deep and 900 mm high, with widths ranging from 300 mm up to 1200 mm. Wall-hung units range in widths from 300 mm up to 1000 mm and 300 mm deep. This depth prevents people knocking their heads on the wall cupboards, whist still allowing a table plate to be stored; it also allows the full width of the worktop to be viewed whilst standing close to the base units. Corner units are available in a range of different shapes and sizes to make the best use of the difficult space.

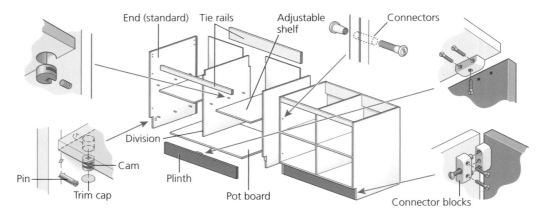

FIGURE 6.78 Standard kitchen base and wall units

TRADITIONAL METHODS OF CONSTRUCTION (FRAMED)

Wall and floor units are traditionally constructed with a series of frames and rails fixed together with mortise and tenons, or dowelled joints. The end frames or 'standards', usually have panels loosely fitted in plough grooves around their inside edges. High-quality units have grooves running down the back of the units to allow the back panels to be fixed. This will reduce the depth of usable space within the units, but allows service pipes such as water, gas and waste to be hidden behind the back panel.

There are two methods of fitting shelves into units, 'fixed' and 'adjustable'. Adjustable shelves are commonly used because they allow more flexibility within the unit. There are several methods used to allow shelves to be adjusted, these include:

- 'tonk' strip and studs;
- shelf studs.

MODERN METHODS OF CONSTRUCTION (BOXED)

The majority of modern units are constructed with melamine-faced chipboard (MFC) in solid neutral colours, or wood grains to match the doors and drawer fronts. Some more expensive units may have solid timber doors and drawers. The carcasses of these units do not require complex carpentry joints, because the man-made boards they are built with are not prone to warping or shrinkage. Each butt joint is located with wooden dowels and pulled tightly together to secure it in position with 'knock-down' (KD) fittings.

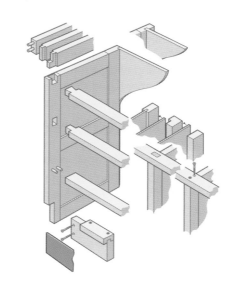

FIGURE 6.79 Traditional framed units

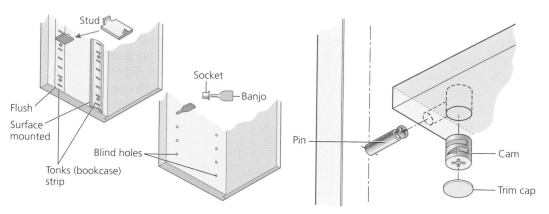

FIGURE 6.80 Tonk strip and shelf studs

FIGURE 6.81 Modern boxed units

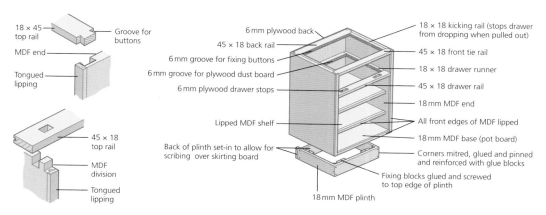

FIGURE 6.82 Constructing a boxed base using MDF

FREQUENTLY ASKED QUESTIONS

▶ Can cupboards be constructed from any other materials?

Yes, cupboard units may also be formed using boxed construction with alternative timber-based materials such as:

▶ Plywood;
▶ MDF;
▶ Blockboard;
▶ Solid timber panels.

These materials are more versatile than MFC because they can be painted, stained, polished, laminated and veneered.

PLINTH CONSTRUCTION

All floor-standing cupboards will require the 'potboard' to be built over the 'plinth', regardless of their method of construction. Raising the potboard off the ground prevents the unit from rocking or becoming unstable as a result of the floor being uneven. Some units may have a separate plinth which may be scribed over an uneven floor surface before installing the unit. This method prevents having to adjust the base of heavy or large units during their installation.

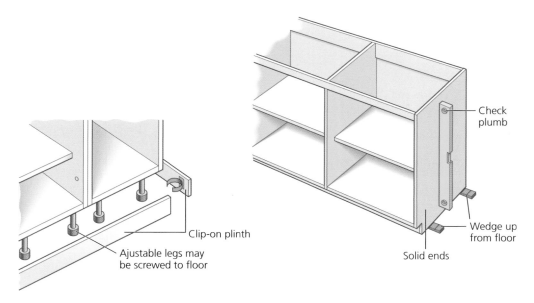

Check plumb

Clip-on plinth

Ajustable legs may
be screwed to floor

Wedge up
from floor

Solid ends

FIGURE 6.83 Plinth construction

WORKTOP SURFACES AND MATERIALS

Kitchen worktops are manufactured from a variety of different materials, these include:

- **Tiles** – usually laid over a minimum thickness of 18 mm plywood. The grain in the ply provides a good surface for the adhesive and tiles to bond. Tiled worktops are rarely used in this country because they are difficult to keep perfectly sterile.
- **Laminates** – post-formed laminated worktops are easily maintained and relatively inexpensive. They are commonly available in a vast range of different colours, surface finishes and materials.
- **Granite, marble and stone** – these materials have grown in popularity in recent years, although they are still relatively expensive. The choice of colours is limited, but the natural beauty and hardness of the material is difficult to replicate with other products. These products are usually cut to shape and size, and installed by specialists.
- **Timber** – worktops are normally made up in their width with narrow strips of wood, laminated together to minimise the amount of movement across the width of the board. The movement in the timber must be accounted for with elongated fixing points in the top rails of the base units. Timber worktops are usually supplied unfinished to allow them to reach their equilibrium moisture content 'in-situ' before sealing with oil.
- **Corian** – is a solid surface material constructed with a blend of natural minerals, pigments and pure acrylic polymer. It is an extremely durable and non-porous material

that can be shaped, moulded, cut and jointed just like timber, although it is usually fitted by specialists. When connected together the joints become seamless and practically invisible. Corian is commonly used in areas where hygiene is of the highest importance, such as dental surgeries and hospitals.

● **Stainless steel** – is normally used in commercial kitchens and canteen areas, because it is extremely durable and hardwearing. The metal surface is not affected by hot items and is easily maintained.

WORKTOP EDGE DETAILS

FIGURE 6.84

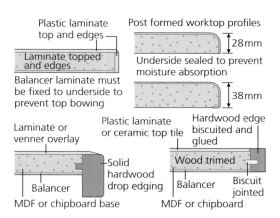

FIGURE 6.85 Worktop edge finishes

Cutting and jointing post-formed worktops

The joints between adjoining sections of worktops can either be connected with 'metal jointing strips' or with 'butt and mitre' joints. Metal jointing strips are simply screwed into position along the joint between two worktop sections.

Butt and mitre joints are formed with an electric router with a plunge facility, and worktop jig. The jig is used as a guide for the router, to remove the moulded front edge of the worktop and square the end of the adjoining piece. Realignment of the jig will allow recesses to be machined across the joint, to allow 'worktop connecting bolts' to be fitted.

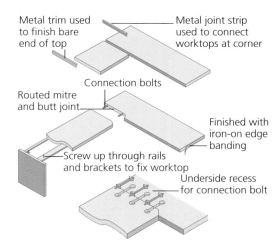

FIGURE 6.86 Jointing post-formed worktops

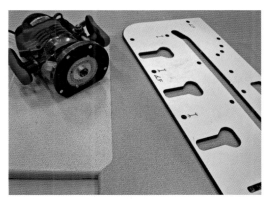

FIGURE 6.87 Worktop jig and plunge router

There are many different styles of worktop jigs, each one requiring a slightly different set up, and capable of additional operations. It is advisable to read the manufacturer's instructions prior to cutting the joint to avoid costly mistakes.

Care must be taken when cutting laminated kitchen worktops, to ensure that no damage occurs to the faces and edges. There are several methods commonly used to overcome these difficulties, including:

● use downward-cutting jigsaw blades to cut out the recesses needed for hobs and sinks. This operation should be done from the face of the worktop.
● use upward-cutting jigsaw blades to cut from the back of the worktops. This method is sometimes preferred by installers, because cut-out guidelines are clearly marked and visible on the chipboard surface. (*Note* – care should always be taken when cutting through thick material with a jigsaw, as they usually have a tendency to cut out of square, resulting in a wider cut on one face than the other);

FIGURE 6.88 Downward and upward cutting jigsaw blades

FIGURE 6.89 Cutting from the back of a worktop

● using a router to make several shallow cuts following a jig, until the full depth of the worktop is achieved. As a general rule, you should always router into the edge of shaped or post-formed edges to prevent breakout.
● portable powered circular saws should be used to cut worktops to length. Straight cuts are simply achieved by clamping a batten to the underside of the worktop, and following this line with the base of the saw.
● apply masking tape over the lines to be cut on the face of the worktop and use a fine upward-cutting jigsaw to remove the waste material.
● 'plastic inserts' in the base of a jigsaw will minimise the amount of breakout on the upward strokes of the blade.

STAIR CONSTRUCTION

Staircases are manufactured in a number of ways, depending on a number of factors. Their shape, size and style will be determined by the size of the stairwell opening and the economical use of space and architectural style, entrance and exit points on and off the stairs, the headroom height and most importantly the finished floor level (FFL) to the FFL. The FFL to FFL; or 'floor to floor', is a measurement taken from the lower floor level to the upper floor level. This measurement *must* take into account finishing of the floors, including floor screeds, under-floor heating, insulation and wooden floor finishes.

? FREQUENTLY ASKED QUESTIONS

▶ What is a stairwell?

A *stairwell* is the opening formed in the upper floor.

Most new-build projects will already have the shape of the staircase determined at the planning stage by the architect, but in some cases such as refurbishment or modernisation the shape of the stairs will be determined by the existing features such as doorways, landings and a suitable headroom height.

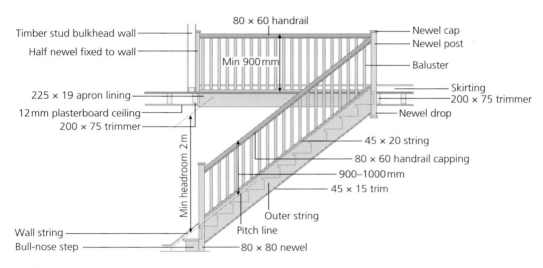

FIGURE 6.90

Before calculating the size and shape of the stairs it is important to be able to understand the components that make up the completed staircase. The names of these components will remain the same, regardless of the shape or size of the stairs; these components can be clearly identified in Figure 6.91.

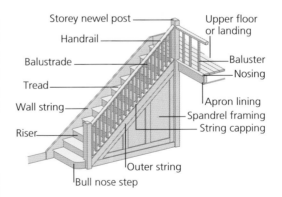

FIGURE 6.91 Components of a staircase

STAIRCASE DEFINITIONS

Apron lining – The component used to cover the rough face of the floor joists and provide a neat finish to the edge of the upper floor;

Baluster – The vertical component between the handrail and string capping used to add strength to the handrail and form a part of the balustrade;

Balustrade – A combination of the handrail, baluster, string capping and string that forms the protection to the open side of a staircase;

Bull-nose step – A step usually found at the bottom of a staircase with a quarter-rounded corner on either one or two ends;

Flight – A continuous series of steps that form a staircase between landings;

Going – The horizontal dimension from the front to back of a tread less the overhang with the next tread above;

Handrail – The component supported by the balusters and usually running at the same pitch as the staircase. It is a requirement of Building Regulations that it is used to support and steady the user;

Newel post – The heavy section vertical component used to support the handrails over long distances or where the stair changes direction;

Nosing – The section of a tread that overhangs the riser. The term is also used to refer to the narrow section of tread positioned at the top of a flight of stairs that sits over the trimmer joist;

Outer string – The structural component of the staircase that is used to support the treads, risers and balustrade on the open side;

Rise – The height between successive treads;

Riser – The component used between treads to form the vertical part of a step;

Spandrel frame – The panelling constructed directly under the outer string to enclose the underside of the staircase, or form a cupboard;

Step – A combination of a tread and riser;

String capping – A length of timber positioned on the top edge of the outer string used to locate the balusters;

Tapered tread – A shaped tread used to change the direction of a staircase, in which the nosing is not parallel to the tread or landing above it;

Tread – The horizontal component of a step;

Wall string – The structural component of a staircase used to support the steps against a wall.

ACTIVITIES

Activity 20 – Produce accurate marking out

Read through the following questions and answer them as fully as you can to help you develop your underpinning knowledge of this subject area:

1. Explain the purpose of face marks when setting out.
2. What information can be obtained from a 'safety data sheet'?
3. Define the terms 'wrot' and 'un-wrot'.
4. Which one of the following adhesives expands as it dries:
   a polyurethane adhesive
   b polyvinyl acetate
   c animal glue?
5. Name one method commonly used to mark out stair strings.

FREQUENTLY ASKED QUESTIONS

▶ **What is the difference between a baluster and a spindle?**

A baluster is the intermediate timber between the handrail and the carriage. A spindle is a baluster that has been shaped (turned) on a lathe.

Staircases can be generally identified by their shape on plan viewed from above: an aerial view. The simplest and cheapest form of staircase is straight between walls also known as 'cottage style'; this means that there is no need for a balustrade (although Building Regulations dictate that there must be a continuous handrail fixed to the wall); if a staircase is not between walls then a balustrade must be instated to guard the space between the handrail, strings and newels on the open sides. The layout of the floors and room positioning will determine the shape of the staircase, and in some cases their shape can become quite complex. In simple terms, generally staircases change direction through 90 degrees (a quarter turn) or 180 degrees (a half turn). A staircase may, however, change direction at any angle depending on the site layout/architectural design. These twists and turns can be produced in a staircase with the use of quarter-space landings, half-space landings or winders (tapered steps); these are known as complex stairs.

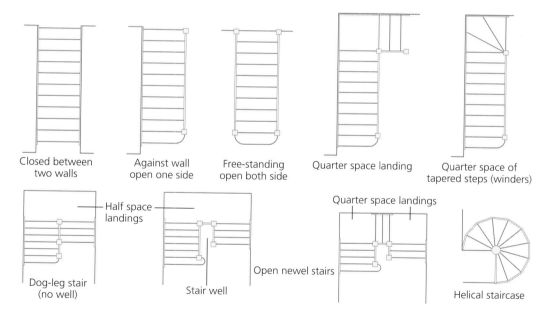

FIGURE 6.92 Staircase layouts

Although staircases come in a variety of styles, their purpose remains the same: to allow pedestrian traffic (people) to move from one level to another with the minimum effort. Staircases can also be further categorised by their construction methods. If a staircase has the strings 'housed out' to accept the treads and possibly the risers then this is known as a 'closed string staircase'; if the strings follow the same profile as the treads and risers then this is known as a 'cut string staircase'. The closed string staircase is commonly used in the construction industry because of a number of factors; these include the fact they are easier to manufacture and assemble and therefore are less labour intensive, which enables costs to be kept down. The cut string staircase, although the more expensive option, offers a grander and more classical appearance, often with embellishments (trims and mouldings).

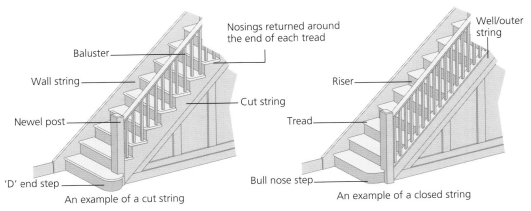

FIGURE 6.93 Examples of cut string and closed string staircases

Not all staircases require strings to support the treads and risers, 'spine beam' being a good example. The stair has a central support that eliminates the need for the strings.

Figure 6.94 clearly demonstrates another example with the use of a central column, which all the steps are jointed into, on the helical staircase. The outer radius of the helical staircase is supported from the balustrade from the next step; this pattern will continue on every step until the upper floor is reached. The balustrade in this case is jointed through the step and bolted into position; this process requires specially manufactured balusters.

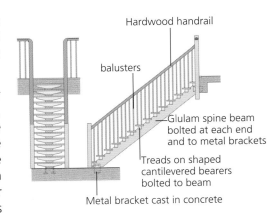

FIGURE 6.94 Spine beam staircase

STEP CONSTRUCTION

The combination of a tread and a riser is known as a step; a series of steps makes up a flight of stairs. A staircase can consist of just one or a number of individual flights. Although every flight of stairs has a series of steps, not all staircases have a riser; this type of staircase is known as 'open riser'. Building Regulations state that the opening between treads on an open riser staircase should not allow a 100 mm sphere to pass through. This can be overcome with the use of an intermediate rail, or a half riser; these can be jointed to the underside of the front of the tread or fixed at the rear of the step. Each of the methods mentioned meets with current Building Regulations, so the choice of guarding will depend upon the style and overall appearance of the staircase required. The use of the half riser will provide additional support to the tread.

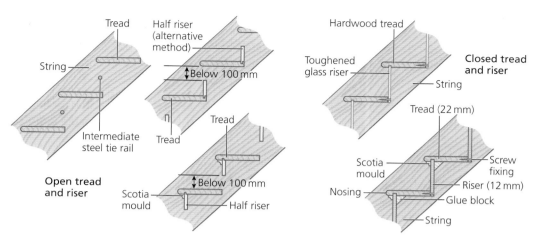

FIGURE 6.95 Step construction

TAKING SITE MEASUREMENTS AND UNDERSTANDING ARCHITECTS' DRAWINGS

Before it is possible to produce, or fit a flight of stairs, it is essential that the following information be established:

- the distance between the finished lower floor and finished upper floor level or 'floor to floor';
- the width of the stairwell;
- the length of the stairwell;
- the length of the balustrade on the landing (if necessary);
- the depth of the upper floor joist;
- the thickness of the upper level flooring (to prepare the nosing so that it is aligned flush with the upper floor level);
- the positioning of any doorways that may interfere with the proposed layout of the staircase;
- the height of the skirting board (to prepare the strings to align with the skirting).

The only accurate way of establishing this information is for the 'setter-out' (a term used for the person who produces working drawings in a joinery workshop) to visit the site. Although the positioning, size and layout of the staircase may have already been designed by the architect or designers, the actual build may have slight differences to the initial design drawings. Although these differences may be minor to the builder, they are the difference between the staircase fitting to Building Regulations or not. In extreme cases the intended layout may not fit, due to unforeseen amendments that have to be made to the build as it progresses. In a situation like this, it is important that the site carpenter or joiner have a strong understanding of both the Building Regulations, and possible solutions of the layout.

 FREQUENTLY ASKED QUESTIONS

▶ What does the term 'off the shelf' mean?

The term 'off the shelf' broadly means that the item is common in shape, size, colour, etc., and is normally carried in stock by suppliers.

A range of staircases are available from suppliers, but the choice of materials, sizes and layouts are limited. If a staircase is required to fit a non-standard opening then it will have to be purpose made. These are normally made by joiners in a workshop, but it is not uncommon for site carpenters to adapt an 'off the shelf' stairs, providing that it meets with Building Regulations.

Although architects work to the same standards, the style of drawing will vary considerably due to the individual's approach. Essentially, the following items are obtainable from the drawings made by the architect:

- layout of the staircase – the 'plan' is the clearest drawing;
- position of shaped treads – e.g. bull-nosed steps;
- newel post positions;
- entrance and exit points on the stairs – this is normally indicated with an arrow pointing in the direction of climb;
- the expected rise, going and handrail heights – this will be drawn to scale on the architect's drawings but also stated in the specification or written in the drawing panel;
- sections of component parts.

In addition to the views displayed on the architect's drawings, a specification supporting the design will be provided. The specification will enhance the architect's drawings and state the materials to be used, references to standard mouldings if applicable (for example – handrail/carriage rail/newel posts), and the applied finishes to the materials used, in other words information unable to be shown on the drawing without cluttering it with wordy explanations.

BUILDING REGULATIONS

In order for a staircase to allow people and materials to move from one floor to another in the safest and most comfortable manner, it must comply with current Building Regulations. It can be assumed that a staircase with an excessively large rise on each step will demand increased effort to reach the desired height and pose a danger, so the Building Regulations will always work to a maximum rise restriction. When a staircase is designed it is not always possible to work with very small rises, because this means that the amount of risers will have to be increased to reach the desired finished floor level. It also means that small rises will make the stair awkward and tiring to use. If the number of risers is increased, then the number of goings is increased, therefore increasing the overall going of the staircase and the space required for it. It is not always possible to accommodate a large staircase into a common dwelling. With these considerations in mind, the design of the staircase must not only comply with the Building Regulations but also the space that it will demand.

FREQUENTLY ASKED QUESTIONS

▶ What is the difference between a 'tread' and a 'going'?

The 'going' is the measurement taken from the face of one riser to the face of the next riser.

A 'tread' is the component used to walk on as you advance on a stairs; the width of the tread is measured from one riser to the next plus the overhang or 'nosing'.

Building Regulations also control the width of the treads on a staircase; these restrictions state the going to be a minimum size of 220 mm. It would be considered that the wider a tread is, the more comfortable the use of the stairs, and ultimately the safer the set of stairs is when in use. Regulations will also control the height of the balustrade, width of the stairs, the pitch and the minimum headroom height (these Regulations are explained in greater detail in Table 6.2).

The restrictions on a staircase depend upon its intended use. Building Regulations split the intended uses of a staircase into three categories: 'private', 'other or common', and institutional and assembly'. An explanation of these categories is as follows:

1. **Private** – intended to be used within one dwelling;
2. **Other or common** – in all other buildings.
3. **Institutional and assembly** – serving a place where a substantial number of people will gather.

Building Regulations 2000: Approved Document Part K

Table 6.2 presents the Building Regulations specifications for each type of stair.

TABLE 6.2 Stair specifications as dictated by Building Regulations 2000: Approved Document Part K

	'Private' stairs	'Other/common' stairs	'Institutional and assembly' stairs
Maximum rise	220 mm	190 mm	180 mm
Minimum going	220 mm	250 mm	280 mm
* Maximum pitch	42 degrees	Must comply with limitations stated below	Must comply with limitations stated below
** Minimum handrail height – flight and landing	Minimum 900 mm	Minimum 900 mm	Minimum 900 mm
	Maximum 1 m	Maximum 1 m	Maximum 1 m
** Minimum headroom height	2 m	2 m	2 m
Minimum width of stairs	1 m if used as a means of escape or used for disabled access; in other situations there is no minimum width	1 m if used as a means of escape or used for disabled access; in other situations there is no minimum width	1 m if used as a means of escape or used for disabled access; in other situations there is no minimum width

*   Regulations state that the relationship between the rise and the going should equate to the following formula: 2 × R + G = between 550 mm and 700 mm (twice the rise plus the going equals between 550 mm and 700 mm). Building Regulations do not state the maximum pitch for a 'common' or 'institutional and assembly' but they must fit with the following limits:

- **Private** with any rise between 155 mm and 220 mm must have a going between 245 mm and 260 mm, or any rise between 165 mm and 200 mm must have a going between 223 mm and 300 mm;
- **Institutional and assembly stair** with any rise between 135 mm and 180 mm must have a going between 280 mm and 340 mm;
- **Other/common stair** with any rise between 150 mm and 190 mm must have a going between 250 mm and 320 mm.

** Stairs should have a handrail on at least one side if the width is 1 m or less; stairs with widths greater than 1 m should have handrails on both sides. There is no requirement for handrails on the bottom two steps of a flight of stairs. Handrail heights should be measured between the nosing line and the top of the handrail;

***The minimum headroom height can be relaxed for situations such as loft conversions; in these situations the headroom should be measured in the centre of the staircase and must be a minimum of 1.9 m. If the ceiling is sloping in the loft conversion then the headroom may reduce further to 1.8 m measured to the sides of the centre line of the stairs.

Part K of the Building Regulations states that if the building is likely to be used by children under the age of five, any gap within the staircase must not allow a 100 mm sphere to pass through it; this is to ensure a child's head does not become trapped.

SETTING OUT STAIRS

Calculating the rise, going and pitch to conform to the Regulations

The angle, or as it is more commonly known the 'pitch' of a staircase is restricted by Building Regulations; these can be found in Table 6.2. Each staircase is designed to suit the environment for which it is intended and considerations for public, private and disabled access are vital to meet with strict regulations. Space-saver staircases usually have an extremely steep pitch; this allows the benefit of less room used on the overall going. Although space-saver stairs serve their purpose, they are less comfortable to access, due to the alternating arrangement of the treads and the severity of the pitch. Building Regulations will only permit space-saver staircases to be used in limited situations, for example for access to one habitable room; these restrictions exist because of the increased risk of injury when these staircases are in use.

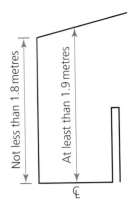

FIGURE 6.96 Headroom height

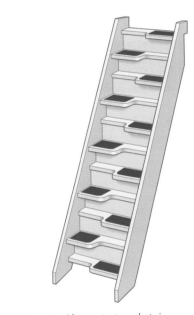

FIGURE 6.97 Alternate tread stair

A suitable rise, going and pitch will be the basis for the layout of a staircase and these can be determined by working within the guidelines of the Building Regulations to calculate suitable measurements and angles. A simpler way to establish these sizes is to refer to one of the following charts; these will provide the user with a simple and easy to use reference.

Transferring information from working drawings

To confirm the calculations of the staircase and to assist in the production of a cutting list, the stairs will need to be set out. It is normal practice for the 'setter-outer' to produce the drawings either by using a drawing board and scaling tools in a small company, or by using a computer-based programme for larger companies. Once the setting out has been completed this will then be transferred into a full-size workshop rod and accompanied by a cutting list. A staircase can be manufactured from a scaled elevation of the stair, from which newel, string and handrail lengths can be obtained. A full-sized section through a step from which the pitch and string width can be obtained and full-sized sections of moulded details will also be required. This is sufficient information for a cutting list to be produced and for the manufacture of the stair.

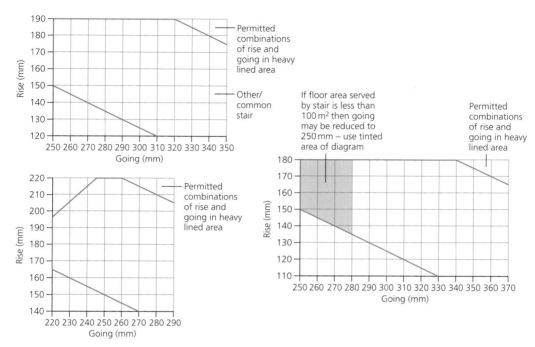

FIGURE 6.98 Tolerances

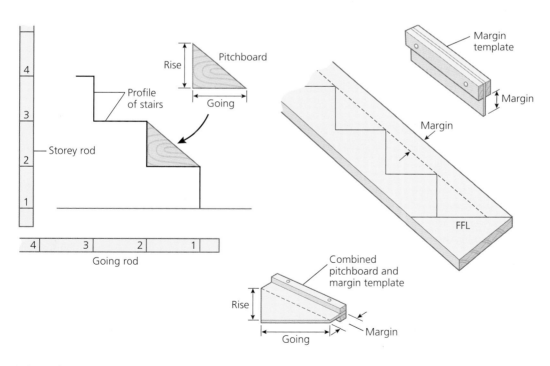

FIGURE 6.99

Marking out

There are two common methods of marking out the strings and newel posts of a staircase:

- pitch board and templates;
- steel square.

In all cases a couple of items will have to be produced to assist with the marking out; first the rise and going will have to be marked out on a 'pitch board'. A pitch board is simply a thin section of timber-based sheet material (normally plywood or MDF); this will have the rise and going marked on two edges.

The pitch board will be used to mark out the staircase in conjunction with a 'margin template'; this is used to position the risers and the treads consistently an equal distance from the front edge on the top of the string. Alternatively the margin template and pitch board can be produced as one item, although it is good practice to use the pitch board for further marking out on the newel post and more complex stairs.

Figure 6.100 demonstrates the first stage of marking out a 'close string' staircase; this method of producing a staircase will require the strings of the stairs to be 'housed' or 'trenched' out 13 mm deep to receive the ends of the steps and for the wedging to secure their position. Each step is generally held in place with adhesive and wedges depending on its method of construction. The process of marking out each step onto the strings is repeated along the length of the string until the correct amount of steps is reached. As mentioned previously, the shape

FIGURE 6.100 Marking out a 'closed string' staircase

and design of the stairs can vary dramatically between jobs, but in most cases the positions of the newel posts should be marked onto the well strings at this stage.

To maintain the integrity (strength) of the newel posts when connecting the strings into them, it is important that the marking out of the hauched mortise and tenon joints are proportioned correctly.

The tenons cut on the string will have either one or two shoulders; this could depend on the thickness of the string (two for additional strength and preventing twisting of the joint) or cost (one is less labour intensive). If using a tenon with one shoulder or 'barefaced tenon', then consideration must be made for the mortise being 'off-set'; this will enable the strings to be lined up with the centre of the newel post and therefore the handrail over the strings, also centralised, will follow the same line. Where possible the housings should not reduce the thickness of the tenons.

FIGURE 6.101 Marking newel post positions

FIGURE 6.102 Bottom newel jointing arrangement and top newel jointing arrangement

FIGURE 6.103 Marking out, drilling and assembling a draw dowel joint

The height of a handrail on a staircase is determined by marking a pencil line along the margin line on the strings, and at the point this line hits the newel post the height can be established to the top edge of the handrail.

The purpose of the handrail is to offer support to people using the stairs and to prevent falling from height, so it is important that a strong joint is formed to the newel post and handrail. This joint can be achieved by one of two ways. The first and best option is to use a mortise and tenon joint, or second by a mechanical fixing through the outer face of the newel post and into the handrail,

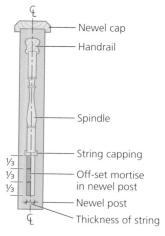

Newel cap
Handrail

Spindle

String capping

⅓
⅓ Off-set mortise
⅓ in newel post

Newel post
Thickness of string

FIGURE 6.104

with a pocket cover to hide the unsightly fixing. This latter method is usually only used for 'off the shelf' stairs.

The mortise and tenon joints on both the handrail and the string are held in place with a 'draw dowel'. The draw dowel is a section of timber driven into the newel post and into a hole in the tenon that is positioned 2–3 mm towards the shoulder of the tenon; this will allow the dowel to pass through the tenon but at the same time pull the joint tight.

Some more complex stairs may have continuous handrails formed over the top of the newel posts, or over geometrical/continuous string stairs (more often than not these stairs do not incorporate newels). In this case specially formed newel posts are required in order for the handrail to 'fly' over. There are also a variety of shaped handrail sections available 'off the shelf'; these short sections of handrail will offer solutions to overcome difficulties encountered when trying to keep a continuous handrail maintained at the correct height up a flight of stairs, on landings and around corners.

To connect these example sections of handrail, or to extend a handrail in its length, a handrail bolt is needed in conjunction with a pair of dowels to prevent joint twisting. The handrail joint will provide a strong and secure fixing that is formed by drilling a series of location holes with the use of a jig; this will provide a consistent, accurate joint.

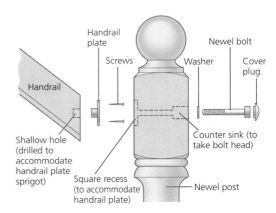

FIGURE 6.105 Joining the newel post and handrail

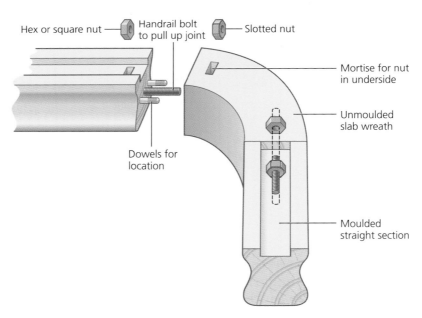

FIGURE 6.106

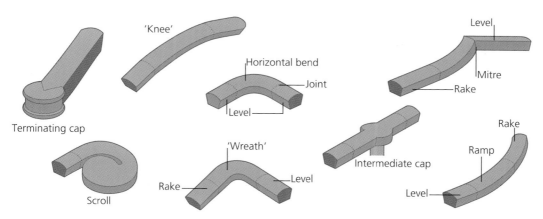

FIGURE 6.107 Handrail terms

STEPS

There are several methods of constructing steps within a staircase (see Figure 6.95). The advantages of the more complex jointing of the riser to the tread are that they provide added strength; this is due to a larger surface area for the glue to adhere. The disadvantages of these methods are that they are time consuming to manufacture and assemble, so this will invariably increase the overall cost of the staircase.

It is normal practice for the whole thickness of the riser to be recessed into a groove on the underside of the tread and the lower

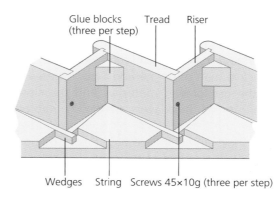

FIGURE 6.108 Methods of housing strings

portion of the riser to be screwed through the back of the tread. This method will provide the minimum standard for a staircase manufactured from timber-based man-made sheet materials. A staircase manufactured from natural timber will be better suited with the complex joints; this will prevent any movement between the treads and risers and therefore eliminate any potential squeaks (noise heard when using the stairs caused by the movement between the treads and the risers or steps and strings). To provide additional strength between the treads and the risers, glue blocks are fitted as demonstrated in Figure 6.108. Generally two to three glue blocks are fitted across the width of the staircase depending on the overall width of the stairs and these are glued and rubbed (gently pushed back and forth until the suction holds them in place). Some joiners nail these into place, but this is counterproductive and when the nail is driven through the block, a gap is formed, where the grain is pushed out on the underside. This creates a gap, which later causes the glue joint to fail more quickly. The thin nature of modern risers also excludes this practice (for more detail consult BS 585). For further details on stairs, see Chapter 7.

MARKING-OUT SITE CARPENTRY ITEMS

Integral parts of the new Level 2 Bench Joinery Diploma are elements of Site Carpentry practice. The relationship between manufacturing routine joinery products and installation by site carpenters is vitally important, to ensure that the correct considerations are made for ease of fitting. The use, construction methods and setting out of studwork and floor joists are covered in detail over the following pages in this chapter.

STUDWORK (PARTITION WALLS)

The term 'partition walls' is the name generally given to the non-load-bearing, internal walls that are commonly used to divide open areas into smaller rooms. They can be constructed using a variety a different materials, including:

● timber (carpenter);
● bricks or block work (bricklayer) (*Note* – these are generally loadbearing partitions and used on the ground floor);
● metal stud (carpenter/shopfitter).

The methods used to build partition walls will usually depend on the location of the walls and their use; e.g. thermal insulating, sound proofing or a barrier to prevent the spread of fire. Generally, partition walls that are constructed using bricks and mortar are less cost effective than other methods; this is because of the use of wet materials and the slow drying times. Bricklayers are also limited by the amount of bricks or blockwork courses that they can lay in one day; this restriction prevents the weight of the newly laid courses distorting the shape of the wall. As a rule, the less material that is used to construct a partition that requires 'drying out', the quicker the partition can be formed and completed.

Partition walls that are built using dense materials usually have good insulation and sound-proofing qualities. The majority of partition walls built on upper floors in new constructions will be built using lightweight materials; this will reduce the amount of weight on the upper floor joists. Timber partition walls are used in many situations because the materials are readily available from suppliers, and are also easy to cut to length and fix. Hollow partition walls can be adapted to create resistance to fire and passage of sound, and restrict the loss of heat through the wall (this is explained in greater detail later in this chapter).

FIGURE 6.109 Timber stud

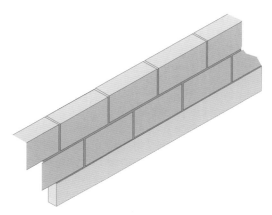

FIGURE 6.110 Lighweight blockwork

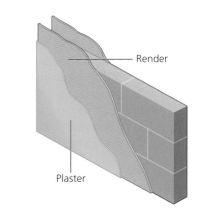

Render

Plaster

FIGURE 6.111 Partition walls

TIMBER PARTITIONS

Timber partition walls are one of the most common and simplest methods of constructing dividing walls. This method of building walls has been used in traditional house building for many years and is still used in new building today. There are two methods commonly used to construct timber partition walls: 'built-in' or 'framed-up'.

Materials

Generally, fast-grown, low-grade carcassing timber is used to build timber partition walls. This type of timber is commonly available in different forms ranging between:

● **Sawn** – All four sides have rough sawn edges from the saw mill. Sawn carcassing timber may vary in width between + or – 4 mm;
● **Regularised** – At least two edges will have machined edges, to provide a uniformed accurate thickness between timbers. The use of sawn timber for partitioning is considered bad practice because of the inconsistency between the sectional sizes;
● **Canadian Lumber Sizes (CLS) or American Lumber Sizes (ALS)** – Commonly used in timber framing, CLS and ALS have all four edges planed, with rounded edges. The use of these timbers originated in North America, but it is now also commonly produced in European countries. Its uniformed section (at the machine sizing stage), rounded edges, and relatively low cost make this partition material the most popular choice for most site carpenters;

FIGURE 6.112 Sawn carcassing timber

FIGURE 6.113 Regularised caracassing timber

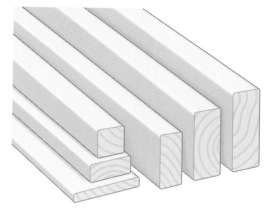

FIGURE 6.114 CLS caracssing timber

FIGURE 6.115 PAR caracassing timber

- ## Planed all round (PAR)
  As the name suggests, this carcassing timber has all four surfaces planed square. This is rarely used in house building, although the square edges give a greater bearing for the facing material.

Joints

Although the basic layout of the timbers within the partitions has not altered over recent years, the method used to join them together has developed. Traditionally the joints between the timbers in the partitions included housings, bridle joints and mortise and tenons. Although these methods perform well to prevent the timbers within the partition wall from moving and twisting, they are complex and time consuming to form.

Alternative fixing methods

'Butt' joints are mostly used to connect the timbers within partition walls, because they are simple to cut and fix, which increases productivity and reduces labour costs. The simplified butt joints rely heavily on the strength of the fixings holding the timbers together. An alternative method of securing the butt joints is with the use of mechanical 'framing anchors'.

Framing anchors are available in sections of folded galvanised mild steel, designed to sit over each butt joint and provide additional support to prevent the timber moving. Framing anchors have a series of 2 mm holes located evenly over each side; these provide easy fixing points for the galvanised round-headed nails used to hold them in place.

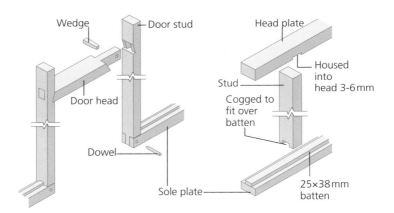

FIGURE 6.116 Traditional jointing methods

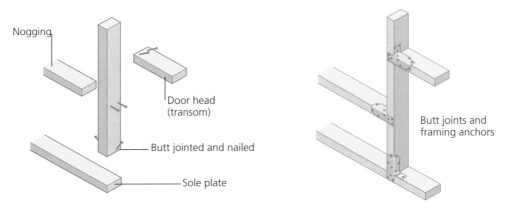

FIGURE 6.117 Nailed butt joints

FIGURE 6.118 Framing anchors

? FREQUENTLY ASKED QUESTIONS

▶ How are the joints in traditional and modern timber walls secured?

The majority of the joints within a timber partition wall are securely fixed in position with round-headed nails. The most common lengths of round-headed nails used to fix the frames together are between 75 mm and 100 mm, depending on the section of the timbers used.

Doorways that are created within timber stud partition walls, particularly in the centre of a stud partition, are subject to the stresses of constant use. The continual opening and closing of doors within an opening may cause the studs to twist over a period of time. This movement in the timbers around the opening may also cause the door lining to twist. This may then reduce the margin between the lining and the door; this will prevent the door from operating properly. Traditionally, any timbers fixed above a door opening would have been connected to the vertical studs using 'housed, shouldered tenon' joints. These joints would provide an extremely strong connection between timbers and reduce the likelihood of movement.

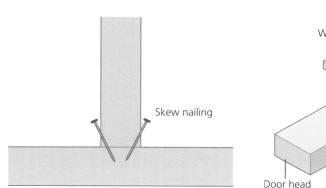

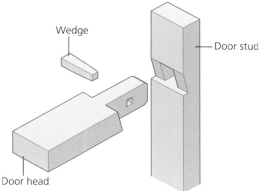

FIGURE 6.119 Round head nails

FIGURE 6.120 Traditional joint used at door head

Timber partition walls are constructed with horizontal timbers along the top known as the 'head plates', and the timbers along the bottom are known as the 'sole plates'. The vertical intermediate timbers fixed at intervals between the head and sole plates are known as the 'common studs'.

The positions of the vertical studs within a hollow wall are determined by the covering materials. The most common material used to cover the internal framework of a partition wall is 2400 mm × 1200 mm plasterboard sheets. It is vital that the edge of each sheet is supported and has sufficient bearing for a sound fixing to the vertical stud to prevent movement between the boards. The most common spacing for the studs is either 400 mm or 600 mm; this usually depends on the thickness of the covering sheet materials (for examples see Figures 6.122 and 6.123).

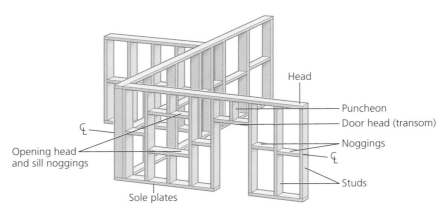

FIGURE 6.121 Timber partition wall

Labels: Head, Puncheon, Door head (transom), Noggings, Studs, Opening head and sill noggings, Sole plates

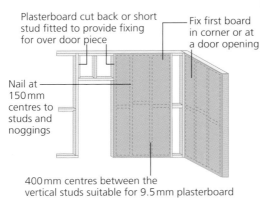

Plasterboard cut back or short stud fitted to provide fixing for over door piece

Fix first board in corner or at a door opening

Nail at 150mm centres to studs and noggings

400mm centres between the vertical studs suitable for 9.5mm plasterboard

FIGURE 6.122 400mm stud spacing

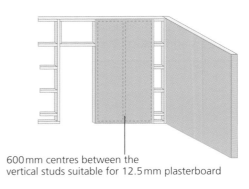

600mm centres between the vertical studs suitable for 12.5mm plasterboard

FIGURE 6.123 600mm stud spacing

It is important to remember *not* to change the predetermined centres for the studs to suit the length of a wall, or to create openings for doorways or hatches. These changes may not suit the covering sheet materials and may fail to provide an adequate fixing point.

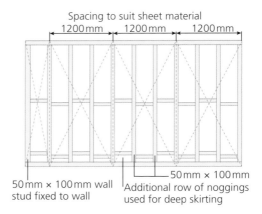

Spacing to suit sheet material

1200mm 1200mm 1200mm

50mm × 100mm wall stud fixed to wall

50mm × 100mm Additional row of noggings used for deep skirting

FIGURE 6.124

Forming corners and 'T' junctions

The arrangement of the vertical studs will have to be altered where a timber partition wall has to be returned at 90 degrees, and also within the intersection of adjoining walls. Additional studs will have to be positioned within the corners and junctions between connecting walls so that a suitable provision is made for a fixing of the covering sheet materials. Failure to build extra studs into the areas will result in a poor joint between the sheets, and possibly lead to cracks appearing along the joints after completion.

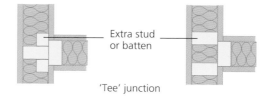

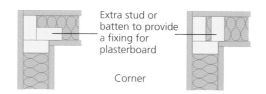

FIGURE 6.125 Forming corners and 'T' junctions

Noggings

The full-length studs between the head and sole plate of a timber frame partition wall will distort and buckle if they are not adequately supported. Intermediate support should be provided with the use of 'noggings' fixed between each stud at approximately 1200 mm centres. This size will be reduced to allow for even spacing of the noggings if the covering sheet material is larger than 2400 mm. Covering sheet materials can be laid either vertically or horizontally, with noggings installed accordingly to provide adequate support. Whichever method is used to lay the boards, the joints should be staggered to minimise the risk of weakness lines. Noggings are also installed between the studs just above the sole plates if deep skirting boards are used along the bottom edge of the wall; this will allow an additional fixing point for the top edge of the wide moulding, preventing the skirting from cupping away from the wall and revealing unsightly gaps.

Additional noggings are usually required within partition walls to provide a fixing point for heavy items to be fitted, for example:

● kitchen and bedroom cupboards;
● fuse boards;
● sanitary ware (e.g. wall-hung sinks and WCs).

There are several different methods of installing these intermediate supports between the vertical studs within a timber stud wall:

● In-line – The 'in-line' method of nogging is rarely used as an intermediate support, because of the difficulty encountered when nailing the timbers into position between the studs. Noggings should be installed in this manner where edge support is required to adjoining boards, if the full height of the covering sheet material requires support along the shortest edge or longest edge where boards are laid horizontally.

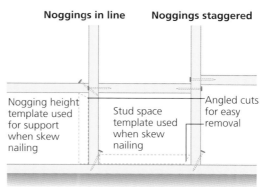

FIGURE 6.126 In line and staggered noggings

TRADE SECRETS

Measuring and marking the positions of the noggings in a timber stud wall can be very time consuming. A more efficient method is to use a packer, cut between the top of the sole plates and the underside of the nogging. During installation, each nogging is simply positioned in between the vertical studs, with the spacer used underneath to govern its position, before it is fixed securely.

Alternatively, the heights of the noggings can be indicated at each end of the partition wall, before a chalk line is used to mark a straight line between these two points.

- Staggered – 'Staggered' noggings are simply cut to length and positioned either side of a central line marked along the face of the wall. The staggered positioning of each nogging between the studs provides enough room to insert fixings square to the face of the timber.
- Herringbone (traditional method of nogging) – The main advantage of using 'herringbone' noggings over staggered or in-line noggings is that they remain tight between the studs, even if the timber dries out after fixing. However, this is rarely used today because it is the least efficient method. Noggings installed square to the studs will have gaps appear between the joints if the timber shrinks; this may lead to the twisting of the studs and 'hairline' cracks being revealed on the finished surface of the wall.

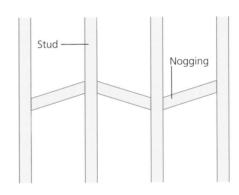

FIGURE 6.127 Herringbone noggings

'Framed-up' timber partitions (pre-constructed)

Timber partition walls are usually either built on site, or manufactured in a factory as part of a timber frame house. There are many benefits of using factory-made partitioning, including:

- accuracy of construction under controlled factory conditions;
- speed of erection of the walls after delivery to site.

Hollow timber partition walls can also be constructed on site, and wherever possible within the area in which they are going to be used; this will prevent unnecessary manual handling of the frames across the building site.

The easiest method of constructing partition walls on site is to assemble them on a flat, level surface on the ground. The following steps should be used as a guide to help produce a framed partition wall on site:

1. Refer to the architect's drawings to establish the correct position and size of the proposed new wall;
2. Measure the actual size of the space from the position that the wall is going to be located. Deduct approximately 25 mm from the overall measured height and width of the proposed new wall sizes to allow a tolerance to manoeuvre the assembled frame into

position. Alternatively, additional sole plates can be fixed at ground level prior to the timber frame being erected. This method creates 'double' sole plates at floor level, which allows the frame to be simply located and fixed in position. It also allows sufficient clearance between the floor and ceiling for framed-up partitions to be easily erected without wedging in their height;

3. Clear a floor space directly in front of the proposed new wall, to ensure a flat, level assembly area;

4. Cut all the components to length for the wall and lay them out in position on the floor;

5. Securely fix all the joints together and check the frame is square. This is normally achieved by measuring diagonally across the frame, to the opposite corners; these measurements should be equal. If these measurements are not equal, then light pressure needs to be applied across the frame between the longest diagonal measurement to correct the discrepancy. This method of squaring a frame is known as measuring from 'corner to corner';

FIGURE 6.128 Measuring a stud wall frame

6. The overall sizes of the frame should be checked one more time against the size of the opening that it is going to be fitted. Any door openings in the frame should also be checked for square and braced; this will ensure that there will be no problems at a later stage when fitting the lining;

7. Carefully lift the frame into position, and begin to insert 'folding wedges' between the top of the timber frame and the underside of the opening, to temporally hold the frame in place. Check the frame is vertical with a spirit level at several points across the wall;

? FREQUENTLY ASKED QUESTIONS

▶ What are folding wedges?

'Folding wedges' are simply a couple of wooden wedges that work together as a pair by sliding against each other. They are particularly useful when timber frames require packing around the outer edges, because they are easily adjusted during installation.

Alternatively, plywood of various thicknesses can be used, or standard purpose-made plastic packers. These are readily available from building suppliers and are commonly used by plastic window fitters. They are available in various sizes ranging from 1 m to 10 mm, and identified by corresponding colours, e.g. yellow = 1 mm; blue = 2 mm.

8. Once the frame has been correctly aligned and further wedges have been inserted to hold the frame firmly in place, secure the partition with the appropriate fixings.

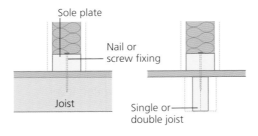

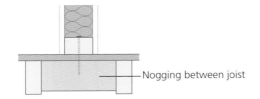

FIGURE 6.129 Fixing

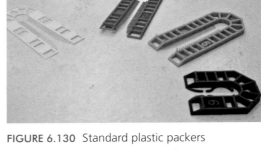

FIGURE 6.130 Standard plastic packers

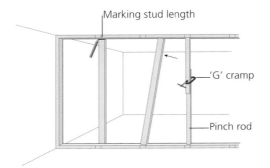

FIGURE 6.131 Built-in timber partitions

TRADE SECRETS

Don't forget – you must always fix either through the packers that you insert around the frame you are fitting or directly underneath. This will prevent the packers slipping out of position if any drying out of the timber or movement occurs between the frames.

'Built-in' timber partitions (constructed in position)

It is not always possible to pre-construct timber partition walls; this could be due to a lack of space, or the complexity of the wall to be built; however, this can be overcome by building the frame in its position. This means that each piece of the frame will have to be cut, installed and fixed independently. Constructing frames in this manner can be time consuming but it ensures a perfectly fitted partition, and unlike the pre-constructed method this process needs no allowance for fitting.

SETTING OUT PARTITION WALLS

Before any partition wall is erected, it is important that it is accurately set out in its intended position. The vast majority of walls in residential house building are either straight, or will have at least one 90-degree bend in them at some point.

Complex partitioning of an entire area is normally marked out on the floor by the site carpenter; this is usually done before lifting the wall sections into position prior to fixing. The position of partition walls may be laid out on the ground with lengths of timber of the same section as the studwork, prior to erecting the walls. As the lengths of timber (sole plates) are laid out on the floor to replicate the layout of the rooms to be created, they are permanently fixed down to the ground. Although this method uses additional sole plates it is easier to fix and build the frames up from the ground once the exact position has been established.

Methods of accurately finding a square line to a wall

FIGURE 6.132 Accurately finding a square line to a wall

Figure 6.132 demonstrates the basic principle of a right angle triangle, and how this can be related to any partition wall with a 90-degree corner. In practice, the bigger the scale used to apply these principles the more accurate the walls. For example, the scale demonstrated in Figure 6.134 is too small to accurately apply it to a large partition wall. This is because it will only check that the wall is square up to 300 mm and 400 mm in each direction.

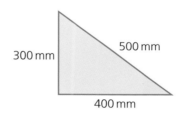

FIGURE 6.133 A folding sight square

FIGURE 6.134

As a rule, 'the bigger the scale the more accurate the corner will be'. This scale works better for a partition wall. It is big enough to be able to set a wall out at 90 degrees, but small enough to be able to measure it without additional labour.

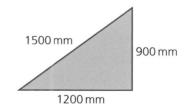

FIGURE 6.135

? FREQUENTLY ASKED QUESTIONS

▶ How do you make sure that the wall you are setting out is straight?

When you are working with carcassing grade timber for partitioning, it will be highly likely that some of the timber will be twisted or bent, especially if the material is sawn. Careful selection and use of this timber will correct the defect, and avoid having bent or poorly constructed walls, for example:

▶ check for bends and twist in the timber before use;

▶ use bent lengths of timber for noggings or short sole plates or heads, and the straightest for the vertical studs;

▶ start fixing sole plates at one end and work along their length, applying pressure to straighten them before inserting the next fixing.

Use a prepared (machined) piece of timber or length of a timber-based sheet material (for example plywood, MDF or blockboard) as a straight edge. This could be used to mark straight lines on the floor for short sections of walls. Longer runs of partition walls should be set out on the floor using a chalk or laser line.

FIGURE 6.136 Checking carcassing timber

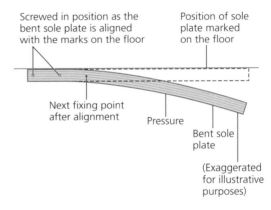

FIGURE 6.137 Aligning timber

Drilling and notching timber studs

Hollow partition walls usually conceal services such as hot and cold water pipes, electrical wires or phone and computer network cabling. In many cases, this will mean that the vertical studs will have to be either drilled or notched to accommodate these services. Too much drilling and notching through the studs in a partition wall could seriously weaken the structure. Building Regulations state that all holes should be drilled through the middle of the timber (the neutral stress line) up to 25 per cent of the stud's width, and positioned

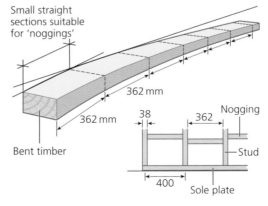

FIGURE 6.138 Using bent timber for noggings, heads and sole plates

between 25 per cent and 40 per cent from either end. Notching of timber studs is also permitted on either side providing it is located no more than 20 per cent away from either end, and no deeper than 15 per cent of the stud's width.

Particular care should be taken to ensure that any holes and notches that are being cut into a partition to accommodate wires, pipes etc. are well away from fixing points. Co-ordinating with service trades such as plumbers and electricians will avoid them fixing in known vulnerable positions in the future. Some of these fixtures could include:

- fixings for dado rails (screws and nails);
- fixings for deep skirting boards;
- adjustable brackets or battens for kitchen wall units;
- fixing for brackets to support shelving, etc.

The most effective method of checking for a buried service is with the use of an electronic wall scanner. These hand-held pocket devices have to be laid flat on the partition wall and repeatedly moved over the area that the fixing may be inserted onto; it will then pinpoint and identify the exact position of the following items:

- vertical studs and noggings (useful if a strong fixing point is required);
- electrical cables;
- water and gas pipes;
- metal objects.

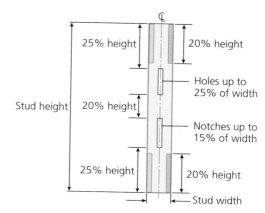

FIGURE 6.139 Notching timber studs

FIGURE 6.140 Wall scanner

FREQUENTLY ASKED QUESTIONS

▶ What is a fixture?

A 'fixture' is a term given to an item that has been secured in position; it is often confused with the term 'fitting'. A fitting is an item that is 'freestanding' and does not require securing or fixing in place. Examples of this are as follows:

- ▶ an exterior door is a **fixture**;
- ▶ a chest of drawers would be considered a **fitting**.

FLOOR JOISTS

Suspended timber hollow – ground floor

These differ in the way they are constructed compared to those on the upper floors, because they have the additional task of stopping moisture penetration from the ground rising into the building. Timber ground floors can also have intermediate support across the span, without disrupting the layout of dividing walls and room layout. Timber joists are normally supported at ground floor level by rows of low-height brick walls; these are known as 'sleeper walls'.

Sleeper walls are normally constructed with bricks or blocks, with gaps equal to half the length of a brick between them on each course (they are also known as 'honeycomb walls'). This will allow air to pass through the air bricks on the external walls and circulate around the timbers, reducing the risk of stale air.

FREQUENTLY ASKED QUESTIONS

▶ What is stale air?

When air becomes stagnant or motionless around timber it will allow moisture to build up in the timber. If the moisture in the timber rises above 20 per cent, dry rot will occur.

The exact spacing of the sleeper walls will depend on the section of the timbers used for the joists, although they are normally either 400 mm or 600 mm centres; the smaller the section the closer the spaces between the sleeper walls.

Ground floor joists are normally smaller in section than those on the upper floors because they benefit from the increased support. The joists are secured in position by 'skew' nailing into the wall plates on top of the sleeper walls. The purpose of the wall plates is to spread the weight of the floor over the entire sleeper walls rather than direct loading. A damp-proof course is positioned between the sleeper walls and the wall plates to prevent moisture being drawn up into the timber.

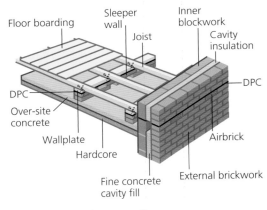

FIGURE 6.141 Sleeper walls

FREQUENTLY ASKED QUESTIONS

▶ What is 'skew' nailing?

Skew nailing is a method of fixing timber with the maximum amount of strength. The nails are used in pairs, and directed towards each other in a dovetail shape.

Solid floor joists – advantages

● Readily available from suppliers;
● Easily cut to size;
● Solid construction.

Solid floor joists – disadvantages

● Drying out will cause the timber to shrink and create gaps between solid strutting;
● Joists are likely to twist or warp before fixing;
● Joists will have to be drilled and notched for services (e.g. electrical cables, water pipes);
● Slower to erect than manufactured joists.

Wood-based panel-web 'I' joists

Floor joists have been developed from conventional solid timber, which has a number of disadvantages compared with manufactured joists and beams. Wood-based panel-web 'I' joists are a surprisingly stronger and cost-effective alternative. They are manufactured under factory conditions to withstand the loads imposed upon them, and are available in the same standard sizes as solid joists.

Each wood-based panel-web 'I' joist is engineered with two parallel stress-graded timbers, usually either 72 mm × 47 mm or 97 mm × 47 mm; these are divided by V-shaped galvanised steel webs. The steel webs are fixed either side of the top and bottom timbers, with nail plates formed in each web and pressed under load into the timber.

Wood-based panel-web 'I' joists are substantially lighter than solid joists so they are easier to transport and handle manually when fixing into position. They also have the benefit of large open areas through the joists, which will allow service pipes and cables to pass through without the need for drilling and notching.

Wood-based panel-web 'I' joists are usually manufactured to order, but some suppliers will keep a limited stock of standard sizes. They are installed similarly to solid joists; they are both returned with joist hangers (although the exact shape of the hanger will differ for wood-based panel-web 'I' joists), and they both will need forms of strutting. It is good practice to infill the cut ends with the same-sized section as the top and bottom timbers of the joists to strengthen the open ends.

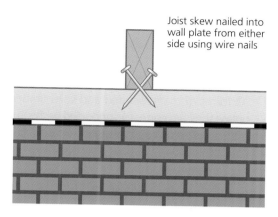

Joist skew nailed into wall plate from either side using wire nails

FIGURE 6.142 Skew nailing

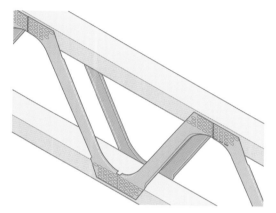

FIGURE 6.143 Wood-based panel-web 'I' joists

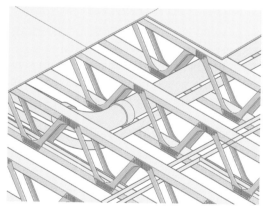

FIGURE 6.144 Services passing through joists between webs

? **FREQUENTLY ASKED QUESTIONS**

▶ What is strutting used for?

All forms of manufactured and solid timber joists will either twist or flex across their length unless they are correctly supported with strutting. Strutting is the bracing fixed between floor joists to prevent any movement occurring. Although the movement of the joists is normally concealed within the floor structure, it will cause damage to the ceiling finish below.

Wood-based panel-web 'I' joists are strutted by allowing a continuous length of timber to run through them and fixing at each intersection. The continuous bridging of all the joists ensures that the load imposed on them is shared evenly across the whole floor.

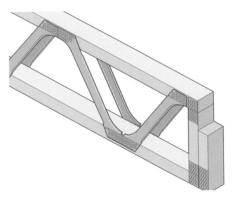

FIGURE 6.145 An infill piece between top and bottom timbers

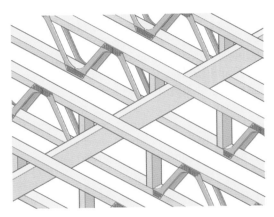

FIGURE 6.146 Strutting

Wood-based panel-web 'I' joists – advantages

- Up to 40 per cent lighter than solid joists;
- Quicker to erect than solid joists;
- No notching and drilling required for services (e.g. electrical cables, water pipes);
- Generally wider than solid joists, which makes fixing the floor and ceiling covering easier;
- Can span up to 6.3 m unsupported.

Wood-based panel-web 'I' joists – disadvantages

- Not readily available;
- Difficult to cut to length.

'I' BEAM JOISTS

Developments in technology have enabled new adhesives, laminated timbers and man-made boards to be used to create 'I' beam joists. 'I' beam joists are factory produced, with an upper and lower section of stress-graded timber known as 'flanges'. These are connected together with either oriented strand board (OSB) or plywood, and bonded together into grooves. 'I' beam joists are available in a range of different depths to suit varying spans and floor loads. They are also manufactured in longer lengths than solid timber joists and have the advantage of a lighter construction together, making them more efficient to install. 'I' beams are a versatile building component that can also be used for walls and structural roofing members.

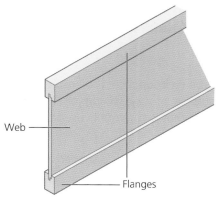

Web

Flanges

FIGURE 6.147 'I' beam joist

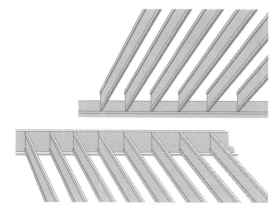

FIGURE 6.148 Using 'I' beam joists for roof construction

'I' beam joists – advantages

- Resists twisting, bowing and shrinking, which could lead to 'squeaky' floors;
- Lightweight;
- Cost effective;
- Easy to install.

'I' beam joists – disadvantages

- 'Backer blocks' must be fitted behind every joist hanger to fill the void. They are produced either from plywood, OSB or solid timber and are secured in place to form a strong fixing point for the adjoining joists. Face-mounted joist hangers must have backer blocks on both sides of the joist at the fixing points. Top-mounted joist hangers only need to have these on the same side as the returned joists. Failure to adequately support 'I' beams with backer blocks may result in the joists twisting and weakening the structure.

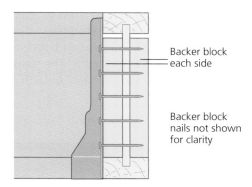

Backer block each side

Backer block nails not shown for clarity

FIGURE 6.149

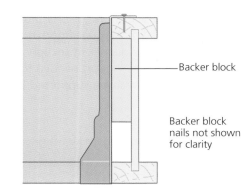

Backer block

Backer block nails not shown for clarity

FIGURE 6.150

- The solid construction of the 'I' beam means that the joists will have to be drilled for service pipes and cables.

? FREQUENTLY ASKED QUESTIONS

▶ What are joist hangers?

All the structural timbers of a building will have to be well supported to ensure a solid and safe construction. This can be achieved in a number of ways. Fixing joist hangers between connecting timbers in a floor is one method that is commonly used to support joists in a floor structure.

Joist hangers are simply galvanised sections of folded steel, each one shaped around the connecting timbers.

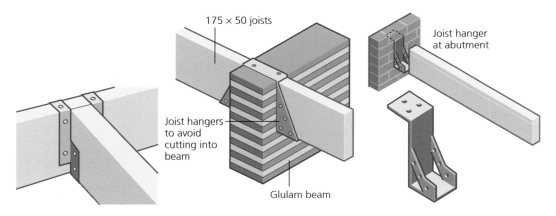

FIGURE 6.151 Joist hangers

UPPER FLOORS

The layout of the upper floor joists is similar to the ground floor layout. The main difference between the two is that upper floors normally span longer unsupported distances. Upper floor joists are usually deeper in section compared to suspended timber ground floors; this provides the additional support needed to bridge the longer unsupported spans. The span of the upper floor joists can be supported by adding load-bearing walls beneath, or with the inclusion of steel joists.

TRADE SECRETS

To prevent repeatedly marking each joist end to be cut around a steel joist, make a template. Templates are normally made from timber-based, man-made sheet materials (MDF/plywood/etc.). Man-made sheet materials are easy to shape with carpentry tools and do not normally misshape, shrink or expand.

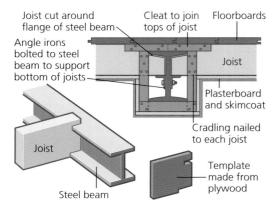

FIGURE 6.152

STAIRWELLS

The positioning of the floor joists will vary between floors; upper floors will normally have openings for stairwells and trimming around chimney breasts/flues. The exact positioning of each stairwell should be detailed on the architect's drawings.

When positioning floor joists to form a stairwell, consideration should be given to the amount of space needed to install the staircase. If the stairwell is constructed to the exact width as the staircase it may become difficult to align, especially if the staircase is manufactured prior to fixing the joists.

FLOOR JOISTS IDENTIFICATION AND LAYOUT

Floor joists should run the shortest distances between supporting walls or steel joists. This method of positioning the joists will keep the maximum depth of the joists to a minimum, and will therefore be the most cost-effective solution. All joists within the same floor should be the same depth.

SINGLE, DOUBLE AND TRIPLE FLOORS

Floor joists that span between supporting walls without an intermediate bearing (clear span) are known as single floors. 'Single' floors are the most common method of constructing upper floors in new buildings, and usually span up to 4.7 m.

The sectional size of the floor joists can be kept to a minimum if the span of the joists is split in two with an intermediate support; this type of construction is known as a 'double' floor. The intermediate support can either be built under the floor joists or within the floor. Traditionally large timbers would have shared the load of the floor from the underside. Although this method was very successful, it had the disadvantage of revealing the full depth of the supporting beam along the ceiling. This beam or 'binder' is usually either covered with plasterboard and a 'skim' (thin) coat of plaster, or left exposed to create a feature.

Triple floors are rarely used in modern construction due to the cost of the heavy sections of timbers needed to span from wall to wall or beam to beam. Modern floors would usually have either an intermediate support from load-bearing walls, steel joists built with the floor, or they would be constructed from concrete beams.

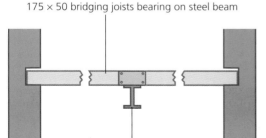

175 × 50 bridging joists bearing on steel beam

Steel beam (halves span of bridging joists)

FIGURE 6.153 Floor joist running over the top of a binder

FIGURE 6.154 Exposed beams

FLOOR COMPONENTS

- **Bridging joists** – run between supporting walls, also known as common joists;
- **Trimming joists** – are parallel to the bridging joists and line the edges of an opening in the floor;
- **Trimmed joists** – are the cut, shortened common joists with the trimmer joists fixed;
- **Trimmer joists** – are fixed at 90 degrees to the trimming joists and are positioned around the opening of a stairwell, chimney breast or flue.

(*Note* – both the trimming joists and the trimmer joists around a stairwell will have increased loads imposed upon them due to the support they give to the staircase. These joists are usually increased in thickness by 25 mm or doubled up and bolted together.)

SOLID FLOOR JOIST SPANS

(*Note* – this table should only be used as guidance; for the exact spans and joist spacing refer to the Building Regulations. Joist sizes may vary depending on the grade of timber used and the loads imposed upon them.)

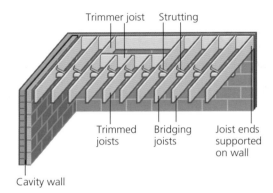

FIGURE 6.155 Floor components

TABLE 6.3 Maximum clear span of joists

MAXIMUM CLEAR SPAN OF JOISTS			
Size of joist	*Spacing of joists (mm)*		
Thickness × depth (mm)	400	450	600
46 × 97	1.93	1.82	1.47
46 × 120	2.52	2.42	2.05
46 × 145	3.04	2.92	2.59
46 × 170	3.55	3.42	3.00
46 × 195	4.07	3.91	3.41
46 × 220	4.58	4.39	3.82
62 × 97	2.20	2.09	1.83
62 × 120	2.78	2.67	2.42
62 × 145	3.35	3.22	2.92
62 × 170	3.91	3.77	3.42
62 × 195	4.48	4.31	3.92
62 × 220	4.94	4.80	4.41
73 × 120	2.94	2.83	2.57
73 × 145	3.54	3.41	3.10
73 × 170	4.14	3.99	3.63
73 × 195	4.72	4.56	4.15
73 × 220	5.15	5.01	4.67

Fixing floor joists

Floor joists are usually fixed in position either with conventional joist hangers, or by building the joists into the brickwork. Each method will provide adequate support to the floor joists, but building the joists into the brickwork is less labour intensive and a cheaper alternative. The disadvantage of building solid timber floor joists into the inner leaf of cavity walls is the potential for the ends to rot, although this risk can be dramatically reduced if the correct precautions are taken during their installation.

Cavity walls are designed to prevent moisture passing from the outer wall to the inner wall of a building. If the gap between two walls is bridged then moisture will travel between and into the building. Moisture that comes into contact with joists will rot the ends of the timber and potentially undermine the integrity of the floor. The following guidelines should be considered when positioning and installing built-in joists:

1. Avoid making the joists overhang the cavity between the two walls. Mortar that falls down the cavity as the build progresses could build up on the joist ends and potentially bridge the gap;
2. Avoid the joists bridging the full width of the cavity. This method could draw moisture through the outer wall and promote the start of rot;
3. Floor joists should bear down on the full width of the inner wall; this is the most effective form of providing maximum support.

TRADE SECRETS

The cut ends of floor joists should have a liberal covering of preservative applied before building-in. The end grain of timber will absorb more moisture than the faces, so it is vital that these areas are protected against decay.

It is good practice to cut the ends of the joists to a splayed angle, making sure that their bottom edges still have a full bearing on the inner wall. Using this method allows the ends of the joists to be encased in mortar, therefore increasing the protection of the ends.

Bricklayers will build up the courses of bricks or blocks to the height of the underside of the floor joists; at this point carpenters will lay each of the floor joists between load-bearing walls.

STRUTTING

The term 'strutting' refers to the support given between the floor joists. Strutting is sometimes confused with noggings, commonly found in timber studwork, although they have similarities. Strutting is positioned between timber floor joists to prevent them from twisting and to tie the joists together to create a solid

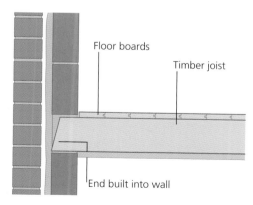

Floor boards

Timber joist

End built into wall

FIGURE 6.156 Cutting the ends of joists to a splayed angle

structure. Any movement between upper floor joists may cause damage such as cracks, and an uneven surface to the finished ceiling. Twisting or bowing of the joists may also distort the finished floor level over the top of the joists.

Strutting is not normally required between joists that span less than 2.5 m and one row will be needed for floors that span up to 4.5 m. All other floors spanning 4.5 m or more will have two rows of strutting, equally spaced along the length of the joists.

Methods of strutting

There are several different kinds of strutting available in common use; each one prevents movement between the joists and has its own advantages and disadvantages. It should be noted that the methods of strutting described are only for solid joists; for all other types of floor joists the manufacturer's recommendations should be followed.

Solid strutting or bridging

Solid timber blocking (strutting) should be at least 38 mm thick and extend at least three-quarters the width of the joist to provide adequate support and prevent the joists from cupping. Full-width strutting should be avoided as it may distort the floor above and ceiling below.

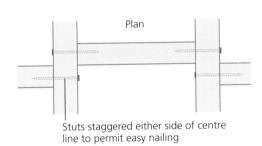

Plan

Stuts staggered either side of centre line to permit easy nailing

Solid strutting

A section through a solid timber floor

FIGURE 6.157 Solid timber strutting

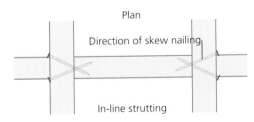

Plan

Direction of skew nailing

In-line strutting

FIGURE 6.158 Staggered and in-line strutting

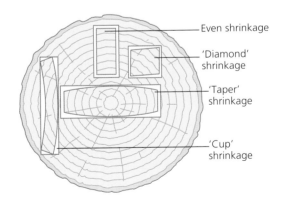

Even shrinkage

'Diamond' shrinkage

'Taper' shrinkage

'Cup' shrinkage

FIGURE 6.159 Cupping

FREQUENTLY ASKED QUESTIONS

▶ What does the term 'cupping' mean?

When a tree has been converted into usable sections, the timber will go through a process of drying out known as 'seasoning'. The amount of seasoning will depend on the type of timber and the position in which it is going to be used. As the sections of timber are dried, ready for use, they may distort or misshape. In most cases the timber sections will 'cup' away from the centre of the tree (the pith).

Herringbone strutting

Although herringbone strutting is time con-suming to cut and install compared with other methods, it does not have to be drilled and notched for services to pass through. The herringbone sections used should be at least 50 mm × 25 mm (although 50 mm × 32 mm is very common) and should not be in contact with each other due to noise transfer through the floor.

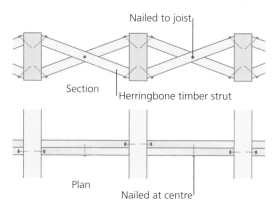

FIGURE 6.160 Herringbone strutting

TRADE SECRETS

Herringbone strutting is normally secured in position with clout nails, fixed directly through the top and bottom edges of each section. If saw cuts are made through the middle of both the top and bottom edges before fixing, the nails can be driven through these slots. This will prevent unnecessary splitting of the timber and a weak fixing.

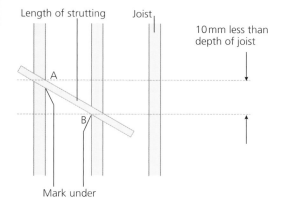

FIGURE 6.161 Marking, cutting and fixing herringbone strutting

Proprietary strutting

Proprietary strutting looks very similar to traditional timber herringbone strutting; the main dif-ference is that the struts are made from galvanised mild steel. Proprietary strutting is approximately 1–1.5 mm in thickness and pressed into shape to provide a very light and strong restraint. There are several manufacturers of proprietary strutting, each one with a slightly dif-ferent method of fixing the strutting into position. In general the strutting can either be bent and fixed over the top and bottom edges of each joist using 30 mm clout nails, or wedged directly into the inner faces of each joist using the pointed ends of each strut to secure them in place.

Proprietary strutting is available in a variety of standard lengths to suit the depth and spacing between the joists. Herringbone strutting should always be fixed in pairs between the floor joists to form a cross, ensuring maximum strength. Care should be taken when fixing the strutting to ensure that they do not touch, as this may lead to noise in the floor when it is under load (in use).

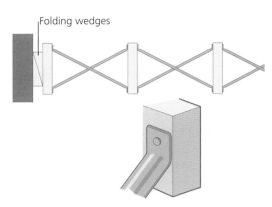

FIGURE 6.162 Proprietary strutting

DRILLING AND NOTCHING JOISTS

Solid timber floor joists may have to be drilled or notched to allow services to pass through. The amount, size and positioning is strictly controlled by Building Regulations to prevent weakening of the structure. Figure 6.163 highlights the areas which are most affected.

The clear span of a joist will be under its own load as well as the weight from the floor covering and ceiling. The area through the centre of the joist is the least affected by loads; this is because the timber above the centre line is under compression whilst below it is under expansion. The centre line across the width of a joist is known as the 'neutral stress line'; this is the point at which all drilling should take place.

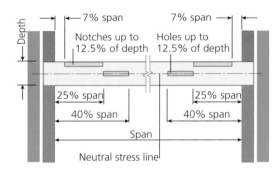

FIGURE 6.163 Positioning for drilling and notching

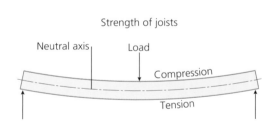

FIGURE 6.164 The neutral stress line

MULTIPLE-CHOICE QUESTIONS

1   Errors made while marking out can be avoided when
   a   using a pen
   b   double checking
   c   copying from the pattern
   d   using well-seasoned timber

2   To avoid errors when marking out, transfer
   a   lines from a scaled drawing
   b   lines using a felt-tipped pen
   c   all the lines possible from the rod
   d   the minimum number of lines required

3   Machines are normally set up from the
   a   pattern piece
   b   working drawing
   c   machine schedule
   d   architect's details

4   Which **one** of the following templates would be used for marking out a stair string?
   a   Pitch
   b   Mitre
   c   Margin
   d   Tangent

5   Which **one** of the following squares is used when marking around moulded and rebated sash stock?
   a   Box
   b   Try
   c   Roofing
   d   Combination

6   The shoulder lengths of muntins are marked from the door
   a   rails
   b   stiles
   c   frame
   d   schedule

7   The straightest timber should be selected for which of the following door components?
   a   Stile
   b   Muntin
   c   Top rail
   d   Bottom rail

8 Which **one** of the following processes would be marked out first?

a Moulding

b Tenoning

c Mortising

d Trenching

9 Floor joists would be marked out at which of the following centres?

a 250mm

b 300mm

c 350mm

d 400mm

10 Which **one** of the following dimensions is **not** required when marking out a common rafter?

a Run

b Rise

c Span

d Storey

MANUFACTURE ROUTINE JOINERY PRODUCTS

LEARNING OUTCOMES

By the end of this chapter you should have developed a knowledge and understanding of:

• Selecting materials;
• Manufacturing joinery.

SELECTING MATERIALS

HAND TOOLS

There is a vast number of woodworking tools and equipment widely available; each one is specifically designed to suit the needs of craftsmen and -women in an evolving industry. Although speed and efficiency have a major bearing on the selection of tools for use, some of the more traditional tools are still used in crafts such as cabinet making and purpose-made joinery.

CHISELS AND GOUGES

Chisels and gouges are identified by the shape and length of the blade, as well as the type of handle used, e.g. wooden, plastic etc. In general, chisels with wooden handles are often used for lighter workshop use when only hand pressure is needed. Striking the handle of a wooden-handled chisel or gouge during heavier operations may cause damage and eventually split the handle along its length. Chisels manufactured with an iron hoop (ferrule) over the end of the handle

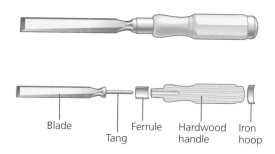

Blade   Tang   Ferrule   Hardwood handle   Iron hoop

FIGURE 7.1 A standard chisel

(termed a 'registered' handled chisel) improve the strength enough to prevent splitting along the grain and therefore allow it to be struck with either a wooden mallet or hammer. Chisels used 'on site' are often subjected to heavy use and are therefore manufactured with thicker 'necks' (the point at which the handle meets the blade). These types of chisels are also constructed from dense synthetic materials such as plastic to avoid shattering when being struck. A 'steel striking cap' moulded into the 'butt end' of the handle improves the performance of the tool by minimising damage, which may later lead to the hammer or mallet head failing to make full contact during use. Poor contact between the tools during use could cause the head of the hammer or mallet to slip off, resulting in damage to the work piece and ineffective chiselling.

Although chisels and gouges have very similar appearances, their uses are very different. Similarly to chisels, gouges differ slightly depending on their use. In general, they may be used for hand carving, shaping on lathes or the scribing of joints etc. The curved blade of a gouge allows it to be easily identified regardless of its use.

The following chisels listed and described as follows are most commonly used by carpenters and joiners in the construction industry today:

- **Firmer chisel** – These chisels are used regularly, generally for workshop and site use. They have a rectangular shaped blade with a slightly thicker shaft to strengthen the joint with the handle. Firmer chisels are available in sizes ranging from 6 mm to 38 mm, with increments of 3 mm up to 18 mm, then 25, 32 and 38 mm.
- **Mortise chisel** – As the name suggests, these chisels are mainly used for cutting mortise joints and are used when increased length and strength are needed. Mortise chisels usually have larger rectangular sections than firmer chisels to prevent their bending or snapping during levering waste material from the mortise.
- **Bevelled edged chisel** – This is one of the most commonly used chisels. The bevelled edges removed from the front of the blade allow this style of chisel to be used to remove waste material from corners less than 90 degrees, such as 'dovetails' etc.
- **Paring chisel** – The increased length and thinner blade of 'paring' chisels allow deep recesses and housing joints to be formed. Paring chisels should only be used with hand pressure applied from the handle towards the cutting edge. Under no circumstances should the wooden handle of a paring chisel be struck with either a mallet or hammer during use, as this may lead to the weakening of the handle.
- **Corner chisel** – The relatively newly designed 'corner chisel' is used in conjunction with an electric powered router. The rounded corners of the router cutter prevent square corners being formed while recessing hinges, locks, door closers, etc. which usually requires removal with a sharp bevel edge chisel. Corner chisels are normally made from robust tungsten metal to withstand the hammer blows incurred to operate the spring-loaded inward cannel chisel. Once the jig is positioned tight against the rounded corner of the recess, a hammer is used to strike the end of the chisel to punch a 90-degree corner into the surface of the timber. Aligning the corner chisel and removing the waste is a simple operation and is usually quicker than using a standard chisel. (*Note* – Some joiners and cabinet makers may use finely made Japanese chisels, for when optimum performance and quality are essential. They differ from conventional chisels as the backs are hollow ground, making the sharpening process easier and quicker.)

? FREQUENTLY ASKED QUESTIONS

▶ What does the term 'paring' mean?

'Paring' is a technique used to chisel across the width of a piece of timber. It is normally carried out by simply holding the handle of the chisel in one hand, while resting the length of the blade flat in the other to 'take the weight' (a term used to describe the balancing of the tool). Careful alignment of the chisel will enable small sections of material to be accurately removed from the joint.

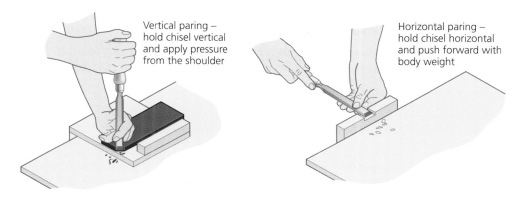

Vertical paring – hold chisel vertical and apply pressure from the shoulder

Horizontal paring – hold chisel horizontal and push forward with body weight

FIGURE 7.2 Horizontal and vertical paring

● **Gouge** – In general, there are two types of gouges commonly used by joiners during the manufacture of routine joinery products:

1. **Internally/incannelled ground** – Inward ground gouges are mainly used for paring and 'scribing' concave joints by hand. They are available in sizes ranging between 6 mm, 12 mm and 20 mm.
2. **Externally/outcannelled ground** – Commonly used for hollowing and carving.

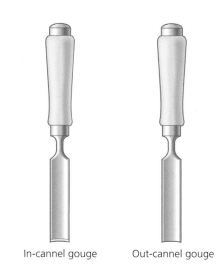

In-cannel gouge   Out-cannel gouge

FIGURE 7.3 Inward and outward ground gouges

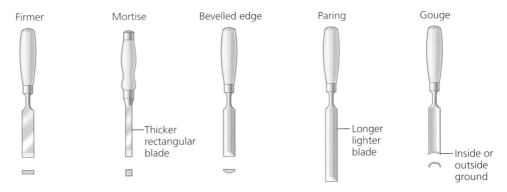

Firmer　Mortise　Bevelled edge　Paring　Gouge

—Thicker rectangular blade

—Longer lighter blade

—Inside or outside ground

FIGURE 7.4 Wood chisels

Maintaining chisels and gouges

Both chisels and gouges will have to be regularly sharpened or 'honed' to maintain their razor-sharp cutting edges. The frequency of the honing will depend on a number of factors including:

1. Density of the timber being 'worked';
2. Amount of use;
3. Damage caused through coming into contact with metal objects such as nails and screws, or masonry.

Difficulty paring across the width or length of timber may require increased force as a result of the cutting edge being blunt. Working with blunt tools usually demands more effort by the user and often results in poor-quality workmanship, as well as increasing the risk of an accident. The cutting edge of chisels and gouges has two angles: the 'grinding angle' and the 'sharpening or honing angle'. The 25-degree grinding angle is used to ease the work required to sharpen the slightly steeper angle of 30 degrees. The sharpening angle will gradually increase the more times it is honed, until eventually the grinding angle is lost. The 25-degree grinding angle must be reinstated on a coarse sharpening oil stone, water stone or a bench grinder. In addition, further grinding of chisels may be needed if they have been honed with a rocking motion, resulting in a 'rounded' cutting edge. Once a uniformed sharpening angle has been achieved evenly across the width of the chisel a 'burr' is usually formed on the reverse edge. The removal of the burr on the flat surface of the blade is just as important a process as the honing; this process is referred to as 'backing off'. During this stage, the blade *must* be kept completely flat on the surface of the oil/water stone as it is moved along its length. Removal of any remaining burr after backing off is completed by sliding the cutting edge sideways through the corner of a section of waste timber several times.

The method used to grind and hone gouges differs slightly to that of standard chisels and plane irons because of the radius cutting edge. The curvature of the blades on gouges requires shaped grinding abrasive wheels to suit the radius of the chisel rather than conventional square stones. Honing gouges is a skilled task that requires the use of a teardrop-shaped 'slip stone' to suit the profile of the cutting edge. Throughout the first stage of sharpening a gouge, the chisel is held firmly in one hand

TRADE SECRETS

Chisels and plane irons can be honed further by 'backing off' on a strap of leather. This process is used regularly by fine woodworkers to improve the quality of the cutting edge for hard timbers and difficult grain.

while resting against a solid surface such the edge of a workbench. Firm pressure should be applied to the slip stone whilst it is rubbed over the cutting edge at an angle of 30 degrees. Both grinding and sharpening gouges are highly skilled processes that require many hours of practice to master the techniques.

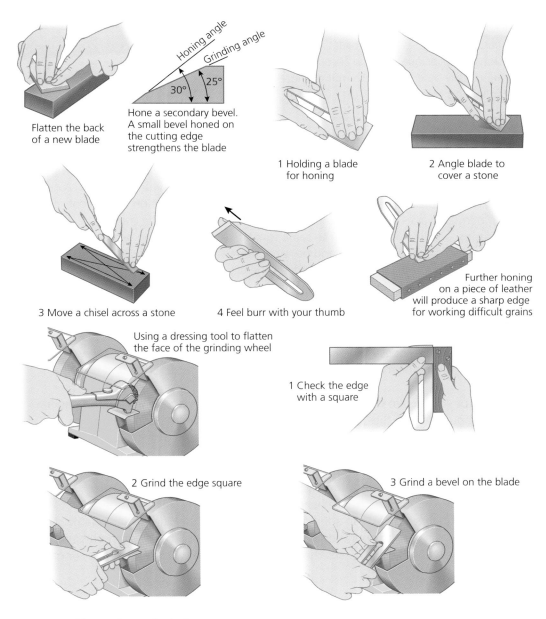

Flatten the back of a new blade

Honing angle
Grinding angle
30° 25°

Hone a secondary bevel. A small bevel honed on the cutting edge strengthens the blade

1 Holding a blade for honing

2 Angle blade to cover a stone

3 Move a chisel across a stone

4 Feel burr with your thumb

Further honing on a piece of leather will produce a sharp edge for working difficult grains

Using a dressing tool to flatten the face of the grinding wheel

1 Check the edge with a square

2 Grind the edge square

3 Grind a bevel on the blade

FIGURE 7.5 Sharpening and grinding

CRAMPING DEVICES

Companies that manufacture standard ranges of joinery items on a large scale usually do so with the aid of industrial cramping devices, such as 'wall cramps'. These machines consist of a large vertical or horizontal rack with several adjustable cramping heads. The heads can simply be moved around the rack and locked in position to suit the item being assembled, before the compressed air 'shoes' are triggered to force the frame together.

This method of assembly is usually only productive when manufacturing large quantities of flat frames with similar dimensions. Smaller quantities or 'bespoke' items are usually assembled with one or more of the following cramping devices:

FIGURE 7.6 Wall cramp

- **'F' cramps** – 'F' cramps have been developed to provide a quick means of securing work together by simply sliding one arm along the length of the cramp to the required position. As the handle of the cramp is twisted, it extends the pivoting 'shoe' against the workpiece; in turn this then causes the arm to twist against the spine of the cramp to hold it firmly in position. The throat of the 'F' cramp normally varies slightly depending on the overall length of the cramp.
- **'G' cramps** – 'G' cramps provide the same function as the 'F' cramp, although they are usually more heavily constructed and have a different method of adjustment. The threaded bar running parallel to the body of the cramp is tightened or 'eased off' (loosened) by rotating the 'tommy bar' through its end. The tommy bar provides increased leverage to increase the pressure between the 'jaw' of the cramp. Overtightening a 'G' cramp, or striking the tommy bar with a hammer to increase the pressure between the jaws will cause it to bend and possibly buckle. If this extent of damage occurs the shoes of the cramp will fail to correctly align, causing the workpiece to slide in opposite directions as the pressure is increased, rather than together as intended.
- **Bar cramps** – There are two different types of bar cramps commonly used for general joinery manufacturing: the 'sash cramp' and the 'T' bar cramp'. Sash cramps are commonly available in a range of different lengths; the most commonly used are 770 mm, 1065 mm and 1220 mm. Smaller sizes are manufactured but rarely purchased because each cramp is fully adjustable from a minimum length of a couple of hundred millimetres to the full extent of the bar.
- **Edge cramps** – Edge cramps have been developed from the standard design of 'G' cramps with the inclusion of an additional third screw on the side. As their name suggests they are normally used to apply edging or lipping to boards. The localised pressure exerted by the edge cramps means they are most effective when used in pairs or groups.

 FREQUENTLY ASKED QUESTIONS

▶ **What does the term 'throat' mean?**

The 'throat' is a term used to describe the distance between the front of a cramp to the back or 'spine'. The additional depth gained on specialised cramps provides a very useful asset whilst 'gluing up' cabinetry.

- **Hand cramps** – Also known as 'spring cramps', the lightweight normally plastic body of these cramps only allows them to be used for light 'gluing-up' applications whilst the glue cures, or jig making. They are simply operated by squeezing the handles together to open the plastic jaws. The heavy-duty spring contained within the cramp forces the cramp shut to hold the work firmly in position.

- **Holdfast** – Traditionally, the end of a holdfast was wedged into the joiner's bench and was fully adjustable with up to 175 mm projection above the surface of the bench. The workpiece was normally fed underneath the single shoe of the holdfast before the screw thread was wound down to cramp the item firmly in position. Holdfasts are especially useful when difficulties are encountered in trying to secure a frame assembly to a bench during the manufacturing process. Developments in recent years have seen the demise of the original design of the holdfast, but the principle generally remains the same.

- **Mitre cramps** – Mitre cramps usually form a jig to place small frame assemblies into whilst gluing up. The cramps are normally fixed at 90 degrees to hold the joint firmly in position whilst the adhesive sets.

- **Speed cramps** – Speed cramps are widely used by carpenters and joiners to hold joints together temporarily. The rubber shoes over the heads of the cramp prevent the need for packing pieces between the workpiece, to avoid bruising. The quality and robustness of speed cramps varies considerably between manufacturers. In general excessive pressure should be avoided when in use, to prevent the relatively lightweight frame of the cramps twisting irreversibly.

- **Toggle cramps** – Toggle cramps are commonly secured to and used in conjunction with jigs to hold pieces of work firmly in position whilst they are being machined. Using toggle cramps to secure components into a jig normally avoids the need for any additional temporary fixings; they are also proven to increase productivity whilst machining batches of similar items. The toggle is operated by a single lever action to spring the lock tightly against the surface of the timber. A rubber cap on the end of the cramp prevents bruising to the workpiece; it also avoids the timber slipping as it is being moulded or shaped. Fine adjustment may be made to the height of the cramp to ensure good contact and pressure across the cramping pad. There are several different examples of toggle cramps, each one differing slightly.

- **Vices** – Bench vices are usually identified by the maximum distance between the jaws, when they are fully open to their maximum capacity, although the thickness of the wooden faces on each face of the jaws should be taken into account. The wooden linings are normally made from beech hardwood to protect the workpiece from bruising, and also to provide a better grip compared to the unfaced metal jaws. Some larger vices are manufactured with a 'quick-release' mechanism. Once the quick-release lever has been depressed, the jaws can easily be slid to the correct position without the need for tiresome winding of the wishbone handle. A metal 'dog' fitted to the handle side of the vice can simply be adjusted in height to project above the surface of the bench, to be used as a bench stop or shallow vice.

- **Web/strap cramps** – Web/strap cramps simply consist of lengths of pre-stretched nylon webbing and quick-release ratchet cramps. They are commonly used during the assembly of picture frames and other difficult cramping tasks that may not allow standard sash cramps etc. to be used. The

TRADE SECRETS

Whenever possible, avoid leaving an unused vice with the jaws tightly squeezed together. If the jaws are left slightly apart and the wishbone handle loose, if anybody 'bumps' into it the risk of bruising will be reduced as the handle moves.

web strap is normally placed around the outer edge of the workpiece before positioning plastic corner pieces over the joints to protect the delicate edges, whist isolating the pressure applied once the ratchet has been engaged.

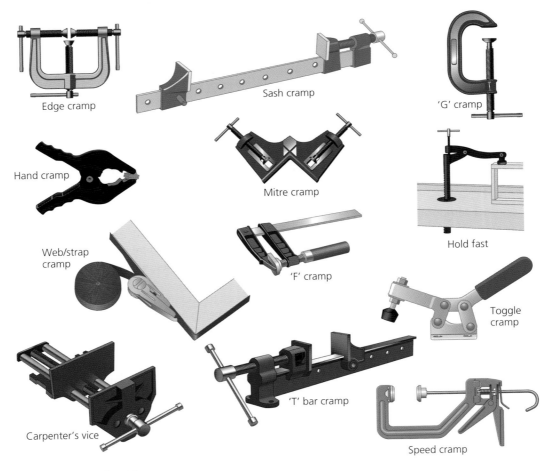

Edge cramp

Sash cramp

'G' cramp

Hand cramp

Mitre cramp

Hold fast

Web/strap cramp

'F' cramp

Toggle cramp

Carpenter's vice

'T' bar cramp

Speed cramp

FIGURE 7.7 Woodworking cramps

GAUGES

Gauges are used to mark parallel lines along and across the grain of the timber, and are considered to be more accurate than pen or pencil. They usually consist of two parts – the 'beam' or 'stem' and the 'stock'. Good-quality gauges are usually manufactured from durable hardwoods such as beech and rosewood, with brass inlays in the face of the stock to prevent wear. When in use, the stock is normally adjusted to a suitable width and temporarily secured in position with a thumb or locking screw. Either a steel pin (or pins) is secured in the end of the beam to scribe along the length of the timber, or alternatively a blade is used to cut across the fibres of the grain when marking laterally. Some combination gauges are manufactured with one pin on one side of the beam (a marking gauge) and two adjustable pins on the other (a mortise gauge); this prevents the need to purchase several different gauges:

- **Marking gauge** – This type of gauge usually has a single pin at one end of the beam and an adjustable stock. Standard marking gauges have a beam length of approximately 245 mm and are commonly used for a variety of applications including marking out the depth of the leaves on door hinges, and various woodworking joints. Once the gauge has been set to the correct position it is normally temporarily secured. Further fine adjustment can be made to the position of the steel pin by lightly tapping the ends on a solid surface, although this can cause some bruising to the stem/beam. This method of adjustment should never be attempted if the stem has brass inlays as it may cause damage to the tool. Marking gauges are usually held with one hand firmly wrapped around the stem, whilst the thumb and forefinger are on the stock for increased control. Several light passes over the area to be marked give the best results for marking out.

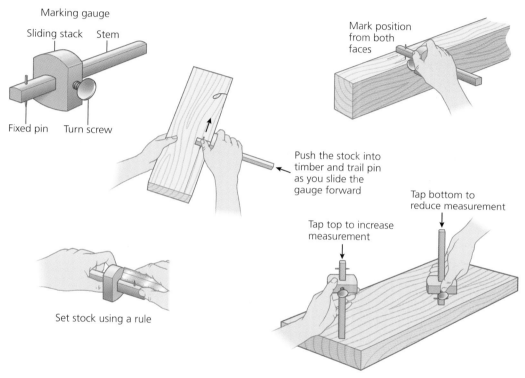

Marking gauge

Sliding stack   Stem

Fixed pin   Turn screw

Push the stock into timber and trail pin as you slide the gauge forward

Set stock using a rule

Mark position from both faces

Tap top to increase measurement

Tap bottom to reduce measurement

FIGURE 7.8 Marking gauge

- Too much weight on the pin while marking out usually results in the scribed lines following the grain direction.
- **Mortise gauge** – Mortise gauges are similar to marking gauges, the main difference being they have two pins positioned along the length of the beam rather than one. This allows two parallel lines to be marked simultaneously approximately 105 mm off the face sides. Mortise gauges are commonly used for

TRADE SECRETS

Marking gauges can be adapted for dual purposes. This can be simply achieved by boring a hole large enough to insert a pencil; the marking gauge can then be used as a 'pencil gauge' while working from the opposite end of the beam.

marking out mortise and tenon, finger and bridle joints. The pin nearest the top of the beam is permanently secured in position with an adjustable pin below. The distance between the pins can be altered to suit the thickness of the mortise joint via a brass screw slide inlaid into the beam. Once the gauge has been set to the width of the mortise the stock is normally adjusted to the position of the joint on the timber and locked into position with a thumb screw. The distance between the pins on a mortise gauge is normally adjusted by raising or lowering the brass slide along a tee slot in the beam. The difficulty encountered with this method of adjustment is trying to prevent the adjustable slide from moving while securing the pressure plates in the stock to the beam. Alternatively, higher quality mortise gauges have a brass screw slide inlaid into the length of the beam. The fine screw thread on the screw slide allows the pins to be precisely adjusted, while preventing the stock from moving unintentionally. Mortise gauges should be maintained regularly to ensure that the tips of the pins are projecting from the beam at the same height, and that they have needle points. Oiling the thread of the slide screw should be avoided as this may attract saw dust and eventually lead to clogging of the thread. It may also cause difficulties when adjusting the distance between the pins.

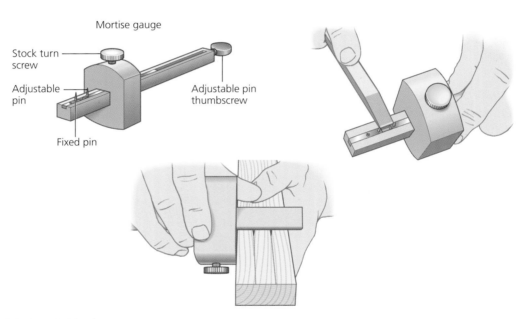

FIGURE 7.9 Mortise gauges

● **Cutting gauge** – Cutting gauges are fine woodworking tools that are rarely used for marking out routine joinery products these days, but are often used by cabinet makers. They have similarities to a marking gauge, with the main difference being a high carbon hardened knife wedged into position through the beam to replace the marking pin. The razor-sharp edge of the knife is used to cut across the fibres of the grain when gauging lines parallel to the end grain.

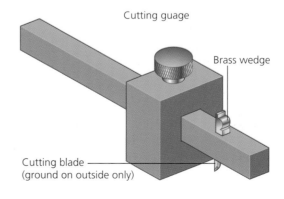

FIGURE 7.10 Cutting gauge

- **Profile gauge** – Profile gauges are frequently used by carpenters and joiners to transfer the contours of a fixed moulding onto another section of timber or drawing. A copy of the profile may be used to create a pattern, a duplicate of the moulding or for marking out scribed joints. Profile gauges are very simple hand tools to use and very accurate if the pins remain undamaged. The maximum depth of the profile the gauge can be used on is approximately 45 mm, providing all the pins are aligned before use. If the pins are much longer than 45 mm, the unsupported ends begin to flex, therefore preventing the taking of accurate detail.

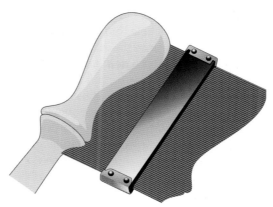

FIGURE 7.11 Profile templet

Profile gauges are available with either plastic or steel pins. Although the steel gauge is vulnerable to irreversible bending if mistreated, it is preferred by many tradesmen and - women because the smaller diameter pins produce a more precise outline.

DRILLS AND BRACES

- **Bradawl** – Bradawls are used to bore shallow holes into the fibres of wood grain to enable starter points for screws. The sharpened tip of a bradawl resembles that of a screwdriver, and works by severing the fibres of the wood as hand pressure is applied through the handle across the grain (rather than wedging the timber apart, which would have a splitting effect), prior to using a twisting action. The tip or cutting edge on a bradawl can be maintained by re-sharpening it on a conversional oil or water stone.
- **Gimlet** – Similarly to bradawls, a gimlet is used to manually bore slightly larger holes deeper into the surface of timber. Unlike a bradawl, the waste material is drawn from the hole to the surface as it is twisted deeper into the timber. The auger bit contained on the front of a gimlet is designed with a tapered lead screw to pull the drill bit into the timber as

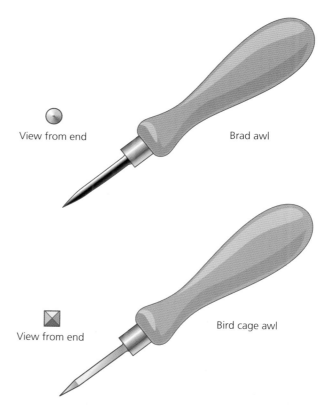

View from end

Brad awl

View from end

Bird cage awl

FIGURE 7.12 Bradawl

it is twisted, therefore reducing the effort needed to bore a hole. Gimlets are rarely used these days since the introduction of quicker methods such as the use of corded and cordless drills.

- **Hand drill** – Rotating the drive handle of a hand drill rotates a system of gears to turn a three-jaw chuck contained on the front of the drill. Steadying the drill and twisting the keyless chuck will loosen or tighten the self-centring jaws of the drill to secure or remove drill bits. This traditional tool requires little maintenance, other than regular cleaning to ensure saw dust does not clog the gearing system.

FIGURE 7.13 Gimlet

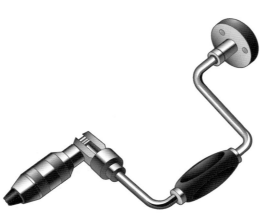

FIGURE 7.14 Swing brace

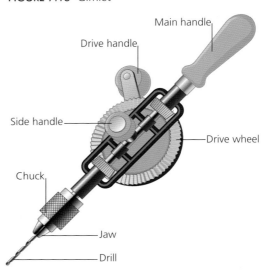

FIGURE 7.15 Double pinion wheel brace

- **Swing brace** – Swing braces have been used for many years to bore holes into timber. The brace is normally rotated in a clockwise direction with pressure applied to the round handle contained on top to bore holes (or tighten screws with the correct attachment). Swing braces usually have a ratchet mechanism to enable them to be used in positions where space will not allow a full sweep of the frame. Twisting the neck of the ratchet above the chuck engages the mechanism to allow the brace to be used in an anti-clockwise direction to remove screws, or the lead screw contained on some auger (drill) bits.

HAMMERS AND MALLETS

The size, shape and weight of hammers and mallets vary considerably depending on the type of work to be undertaken. In general terms both hammers and mallets have two main parts: the 'shaft' (the handle) and the 'head'. The length of the shaft is usually designed to counterbalance the majority of the weight contained by the head, therefore

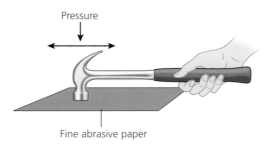

FIGURE 7.16 Cleaning a hammer face

giving good leverage and minimum effort. The laws of physics suggest that the further away a lever is from the pivot point the less effort or force exerted; in practical terms this proves that the most effective and efficient position to hold a hammer is towards the bottom of the shaft. It is good practice to clean the head of hammers regularly to prevent glue and resin buildup etc. and to reduce the risk of bending nails and slipping. Rubbing the face of the hammer head on a piece of very fine abrasive paper while holding it with one hand on the shaft will remove any dirt. Maintaining a hammer regularly using this method will eventually flatten the surface of the head and lead to better contact with the fixing when struck.

It is common practice to only drive small- to medium-sized nails and pins to the surface of the timber to avoid bruising the workpiece. The remaining length is normally buried just below the surface of the timber with a 'nail punch' to allow the fixing to be concealed with wood filler; when it has dried the excess filler should be sanded level with the surface of the timber. The tips of nail punches are slightly cupped to maximise the contact with the nail heads and minimise the risk of slipping. Nail punches vary in size to suit the diameter of the nail head, therefore minimising the appearance of the fixing.

FREQUENTLY ASKED QUESTIONS

▶ **Whenever I nail close to the end of a piece of timber it causes the grain to split. Is there any way this could be avoided?**

There are several methods of preventing splitting. The simplest is to turn the nail over before fixing to flatten the point with a couple of light hammer blows. Removing the point prevents the fibres of the timber being wedged apart, the flattened end cutting through the fibres as it is driven into the timber, and therefore reducing the likelihood of splitting. Dense softwoods and some hardwoods may have to have a pilot hole bored into them prior to fixing to prevent the same defect occurring.

TRADE SECRETS°

Occasionally the head of the hammer may slip or miss the head of a nail and possibly cause bruising to the surface of the timber. If the impact has only caused minor damage it can sometimes be repaired by soaking the affected area with clean water. The water is normally absorbed into the timber, causing the fibres to swell to the surface. This process can be speeded up if a hot iron is placed over the bruising; it will also dry out the damp timber, allowing it to be lightly sanded flat.

Various types of hammers include:

● **Pin hammers** – Commonly 100 g (3.5 oz), the pin hammer is probably the lightest used by a joiner. The relatively small head of the hammer is usually ideally balanced with a longer wooden shaft, for perfect balance. It is commonly used for panel and veneer pins, tacks and small staples. Pin hammers are less frequently used nowadays since the development of electric, gas, battery and air nailers.

FIGURE 7.17 Air nailers

- **Cross-pein hammers** – The most common being a 'Warrington' hammer, they are mainly used in joinery workshops because of their lightweight construction. They usually range in weight between 175 and 400 g (6–14 oz) and are generally considered to be medium weight hammers. The narrow wedge-shaped hammer head section (cross-pein) is used for starting short nails when difficulties are usually encountered while trying to hold a nail, at the same time avoiding hitting your finger and thumb. Good-quality cross-pein hammers normally have shafts made from shock-absorbing hardwoods such as ash and hickory rather than brittle hardwoods such as oak.
- **Claw hammers** – Claw hammers range in weight to suit different purposes; the most common weights are 450 g (16 oz) and 570 g (20 oz). Traditionally made claw hammers are produced with wooden shafts to absorb some of the vibration caused by the impact of the blow while hammering. The wooden shafts are usually produced from hickory or a similar hardwood for comfort; they also enable a good grip and reduce the risk of slipping. A

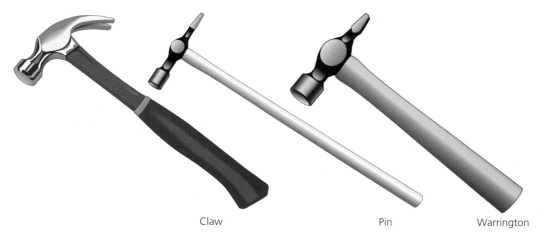

Claw   Pin   Warrington

FIGURE 7.18 Hammers

hammer wedge is usually driven into the top of the shaft to secure it to the head while it is in the socket in the head. The disadvantage of wooden claw hammers is the risk of breaking at the neck when using the claw (also known as the 'split pein') to extract large nails, and for this reason they are rarely used for site work. Alternatively, claw hammers with forged steel heads and fibreglass shafts may be used because these offer reduced weight and improved strength. The risk of the head detaching itself from the shaft can be completely eliminated with the use of one-piece tempered steel hammers. This style of hammer is preferred by many tradesmen and -women because it offers the user a stronger and safer tool that is likely to last for many years. Heavyweight claw hammers with metal shafts usually have moulded rubber, nylon or leather handles for superior grip and cushioning.

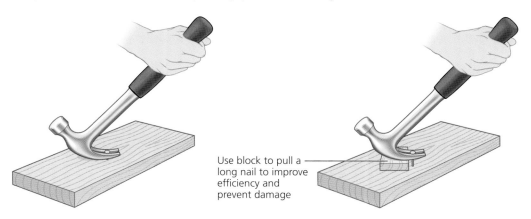

Use block to pull a long nail to improve efficiency and prevent damage

FIGURE 7.19 Using a claw hammer to extract nails

PLANES

Hand planes have been commonly used by woodworkers for hundreds of years, to remove paper-thin shavings to mould and reduce the dimensions of timber of all shapes and sizes. Trimming down or moulding timber to create profiles such as rebates, chamfers and ovolos can be a tedious task, particularly if large 'runs' are required. Nowadays the vast majority of specialist planes have been replaced with respective portable power tools and woodworking machinery to increase productivity with minimal effort, while still maintaining consistency. Although electric planes and routers, etc. are capable of producing outstanding results when set up and used by a competent tradesperson, there is still a need for traditional hand tools.

FREQUENTLY ASKED QUESTIONS

▶ What does the term 'run' mean?

'Run' is a term often referred to by carpenters and joiners when referencing quantities of timber machined at the same time. Profiles produced on timber with either a hand or power tool on another occasion might have sight discrepancies between them. This is normally as a result of inaccuracy when resetting the plane irons, fences or tooling, etc. Whenever possible during the manufacture of joinery items, always use material produced at the same time to avoid difficulties that could possibly occur when jointing.

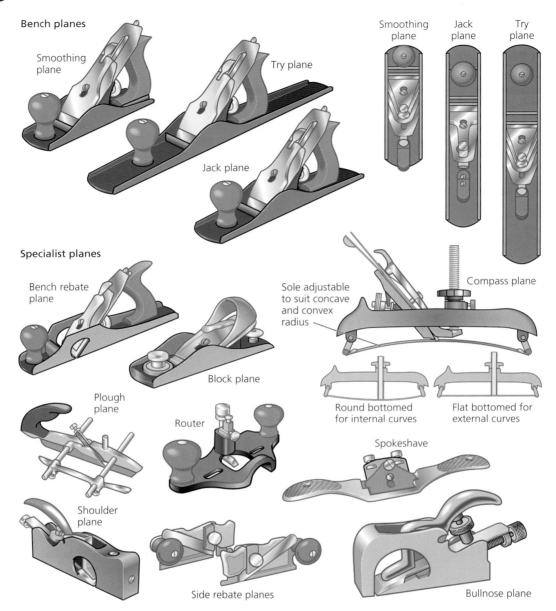

Bench planes

Smoothing plane

Try plane

Jack plane

Smoothing plane

Jack plane

Try plane

Specialist planes

Bench rebate plane

Sole adjustable to suit concave and convex radius

Compass plane

Block plane

Round bottomed for internal curves

Flat bottomed for external curves

Plough plane

Router

Spokeshave

Shoulder plane

Side rebate planes

Bullnose plane

FIGURE 7.20 Bench planes and specialist planes

Planes are divided into two categories:

1. Bench planes (used to true and reduce timber in section);
2. Specialist planes (moulding planes).

- **Smoothing plane** – Smoothing planes are approximately 245 mm in length and often range in width up to a maximum of 60 mm. The selection of plane width will depend on the type of work being undertaken and the amount of use. As the name suggests, smoothing planes are used to remove any pencil marks or pitch marks remaining from

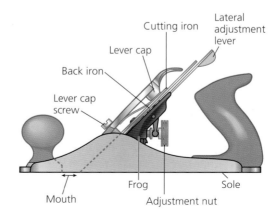

Cutting iron

Lateral adjustment lever

Lever cap

Back iron

Lever cap screw

Frog

Sole

Mouth

Adjustment nut

FIGURE 7.21 Components of a bench plane

FREQUENTLY ASKED QUESTIONS

▶ What are pitch marks?

Timber is normally fed through planers and moulding machines at a constant speed, while the cutting block rotates to remove the waste material (shavings). Cutting blocks usually contain either two or three knives/cutters depending on the type of machine and diameter of the block. The speed at which the timber is fed through the machine (feed-speed) and revolutions per minute (RPM) will determine the surface finish. For example timber fed through a planer at a fast speed and slow RPM will have raised 'pitch' marks. Alternatively, if the feed-speed is reduced and the RPM of the cutter block is increased this will result in lower 'pitch' marks and a smoother surface finish.

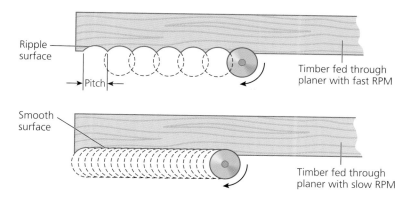

FIGURE 7.22 The effect of machining speeds on timber

machining operations, to leave a smooth finish. A well-maintained and sharpened smoothing plane is capable of producing a finish that is sometimes compared to the surface of a pane of 'glass'.

- **Jack plane** – The extended length of the sole plate on a jack plane makes it most suited for general-purpose planing tasks, such as hanging doors and flushing the surfaces of joints etc. The jack plane was traditionally used for the removal of rough sawn surfaces when hand preparing timber.
- **Try plane** – Also referred to as 'jointer planes', they are the longest in the range of bench planes with a sole measuring approximately 558 mm. In general, the longer the length of the sole on a plane, the more accurately it will produce straight edges. Therefore try planes are commonly used for preparing the edges of timber boards before joining in their width.

TRADE SECRETS

The friction caused between the 'sole' of a bench plane and the surface of a workpiece can often increase the effort required for use. This difficulty can be overcome with the use of specially manufactured planes with anti-friction grooves milled into the sole of the plane (known as a corrugated sole). Alternatively, bench planes with smooth soles can be used with a small quantity of 'silicone' or candle wax to reduce the friction. (Note – Never overlubricate the sole of the plane as this may cause staining on some species of timber.)

Sharpening bench planes

The process of sharpening hand planes is very similar to that used to hone chisels (see 'Maintaining chisels and gouges' for additional detail and techniques). The main difference between honing chisels and plane irons is the resulting shape of the cutting edge. In the majority of cases, chisels have square cutting edges unless of course they have special requirements. Bench planes with square plane irons will remove an even shaving across the width of the workpiece, which may result in parallel plane marks being produced across the surface of wider boards. The presence of plane marks can be reduced to virtually nothing, if both corners of the plane iron (smoothing plane only) are slightly rounded on the oil or water stone during the sharpening process. Jack planes should be honed with a slight radius across their width; this will to allow thicker shavings to be removed more effectively. Try and rebate planes have grinding, and sharpening angles straight across the width of their plane irons with their square corners still maintained.

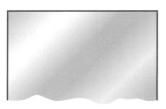

Try plane, rebate plane, plough plane and chisels (straight)

Jack plane (slightly convex)

Smoothing plane (straight corners radiused)

FIGURE 7.23 Smoothing, jack and try plane irons

SAWS

There are many saws commonly available; each one is specifically designed to produce an effective saw cut in the most efficient way. They are normally divided into several categories depending on the shape of their teeth, length of the saw and design:

- backsaw;
- frame saw;
- handsaw;
- narrow-blade saw.

Saw blades

The shape and number of teeth on a saw blade vary considerably between tools to suit the density of the material being cut, while producing a clean cut with minimum effort. The coarseness of a saw blade is usually identified by the number of teeth in a given inch (25 mm); this is known as 'teeth per inch' (TPI). The more teeth per inch on a saw blade the finer the saw cut that will be produced; alternatively the fewer teeth per inch the coarser the cut. The teeth on a saw blade are bent either side of the body of the blade alternately to give a clearance as the saw passes through the timber. The margin of bend on the teeth is referred to as the 'set'. The amount of set on the saw blade will vary between the different types of saws and often determines the width of the saw cut or 'kerf'. Excessive wear on the blade will result in a loss of the set on the blade, often leading to the saw jamming in the saw cut and increased effort required. This problem can usually be rectified on most saws by resetting and sharpening the blade.

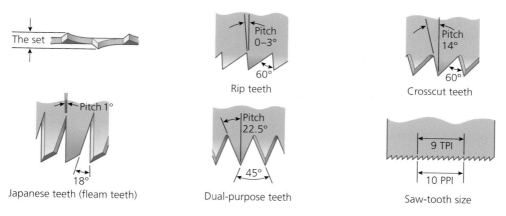

Japanese teeth (fleam teeth)

Dual-purpose teeth

Saw-tooth size

FIGURE 7.24 Measuring teeth

Backsaws

The section of metal, often brass or steel (depending on the quality), folded over the blade along its top edge gives backsaws their strength and rigidity, therefore enabling accurate joint cutting. The following backsaws are commonly used by joiners during the manufacture of routine products:

- **Tenon saw** – These saws range in length from 300 to 400 mm with 14 TPI. They are general use workshop saws for operations such as cutting across the grain to produce the shoulders on joints;
- **Dovetail saw** – These are normally 200 mm in length with 20 TPI. Dovetail saws are a smaller version of a tenon saw with the addition of an increased number of teeth per inch for the accurate cutting of fine dovetail joints. The majority of dovetail saws have D-shaped wooden handles for increased comfort and grip, while some specialist Japanese saws have straight handles for added control;
- **Gents saw** – These are rarely used nowadays during the production of general joinery items. They offer a fine precision cut with approximately 22 TPI along a 150 mm blade.

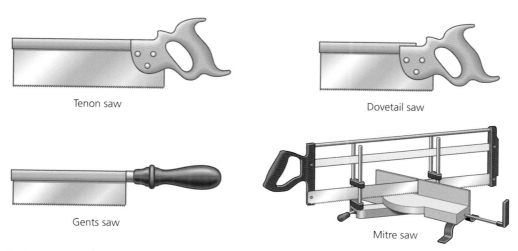

Tenon saw

Dovetail saw

Gents saw

Mitre saw

FIGURE 7.25 Backsaws

Frame saws

Coping saws are regularly used by carpenters and joiners to cut complex curves and shapes in thin timber sections as well as timber-based sheet materials. The direction of the teeth in a coping saw frame should point towards the handle to allow the saw cut to be made on the pull stroke, keeping the frame in tension. Coping saw blades are easily changed by twisting the handle in an anti-clockwise direction to reduce the tension on the blade, before applying some pressure between the end of the coping saw frame and the handle to release the blade. When the saw is no longer in use, the tension should be reduced to avoid stretching the blade, which could result in it snapping during use. During use, the position of the blade may have to be readjusted to avoid the frame snagging on the workpiece. Other saws such as 'Bow saws' fall into the category of 'Frame saws' but are rarely used these days, as their use has been replaced by jig saws.

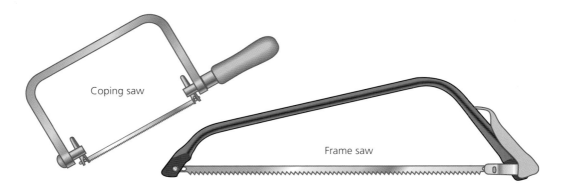

FIGURE 7.26 Frame saws

Handsaws

Joiners for many years have used a variety of different handsaws for different operations, such as:

- **Rip saw** – Approximately 650 mm in length with 5 TPI. The coarseness of the teeth allows the waste material to be effectively removed from the kerf while cutting along the length of the wood fibres. The teeth are designed to act as a series of narrow chisels cutting down the length of the grain;

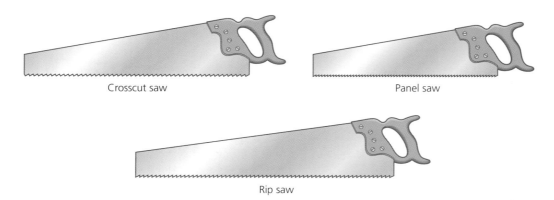

FIGURE 7.27 Cross-cut, panel and rip saws

- **Cross-cut saw** – Ranges from 600 to 650 mm in length with 6–8 TPI. The angle and quantity of teeth make the saw ideally suited for cutting across the width of solid timbers, severing the fibres of the grain and minimising the breakout on the underside of the timber;
- **Panel saw** – Ranges from 500 to 550 mm in length with 10–12 TPI. The relatively fine cut produced by this handsaw minimises the breakout on man-made timber-based materials such as plywood. Panel saws may be used for general cross-cutting operations on solid timber components and manufactured boards.

Narrow-blade saws

In general, wider saw blades are used to produce straight saw cuts across and along the fibres in timber. Pad and keyhole saws have narrow-width blades designed to cut complex shapes without the use of a supportive frame. The absence of a frame allows these saws to be used in positions that may otherwise be restricted by the depth of the throat.

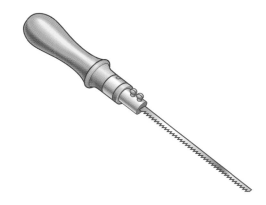

FIGURE 7.28 Narrow-blade saws

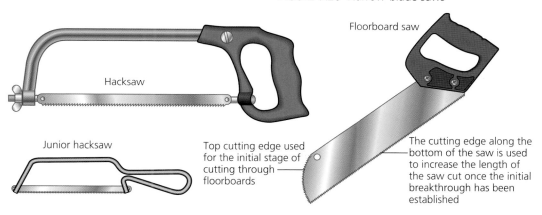

Hacksaw

Junior hacksaw

Floorboard saw

Top cutting edge used for the initial stage of cutting through floorboards

The cutting edge along the bottom of the saw is used to increase the length of the saw cut once the initial breakthrough has been established

FIGURE 7.29 Miscellaneous saws

Hard-point saws

Traditionally, saws were maintained and sharpened by the carpenter or joiner in the workshop. This process is often time consuming and requires patience, skill and specialist equipment such as a saw horse, jigs, files and saw 'sets'. To avoid the loss of production during manufacture to maintain saws, these are often sent to a 'saw doctor', who specialises in the maintenance of such tooling. In recent years lightweight disposable hard-point saws with plastic handles have been developed to take the place of some back- and handsaws. They are often relatively inexpensive and maintain their cutting edge for longer, although once damaged or blunt they cannot be resharpened. Hard-point hand saws are normally designed to cut along and across the grain as well as timber-based sheet materials (universal). Conventional handsaws normally remove the waste material from the saw cut on the 'push stroke', therefore resulting in breakout only on one surface. Some hard-point saws are produced with a cutting angle on the teeth capable of cutting on both the forwards and backwards stroke (known as 'fleam' teeth), resulting in a quicker cut but breakout on both faces of the timber.

Maintaining saws

From time to time saws will either blunt through normal use, or blunt as a result of hitting a nail or screw. The following sequence of sharpening demonstrates **topping, shaping, setting and sharpening** (the order in which sharpening is carried out) to realign, reset, shape and resharpen the teeth.

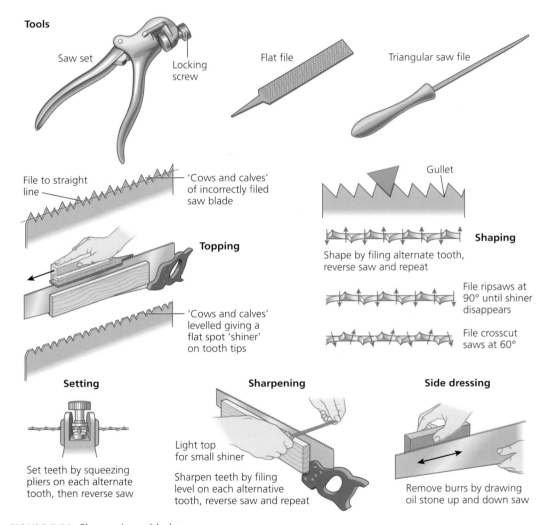

FIGURE 7.30 Sharpening a blade

CABINET SCRAPERS

Some species of timber, particularly hardwoods, have a difficult or 'interlocking' grain that will not allow straightforward planing and moulding operations to be carried out. Very often the grain on such woods is torn up to leave a rough surface finish. With the use of a cabinet scraper, shallow imperfections can be removed with very thin shavings. The sharp edge on cabinet scrapers is produced by forming a burr, rather than the cutting edge of a chisel.

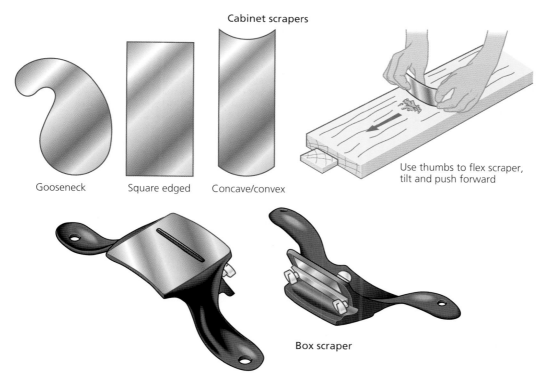

Cabinet scrapers

Gooseneck   Square edged   Concave/convex

Use thumbs to flex scraper, tilt and push forward

Box scraper

FIGURE 7.31 Cabinet scrapers and box scrapers

SQUARES

● **Try square** – The try square is one of the most commonly used marking-out tools. It consists of two parts: the 'stock' (the handle), usually made of rosewood, and a tempered steel 'blade'. The inner edge of the stock usually has a brass face to protect the weaker timber from damage; it also ensures accuracy. Try squares range in length from 75 mm up to 300 mm to suit a variety of different needs. Although the name may suggest the blade is used as a cutting tool, this not entirely true. The blade is usually secured at a right angle (90 degrees) to the stock with four steel rivets to prevent any movement between the two components. It is commonly used to mark out the shoulders etc. on joinery items and other timber products. It may also be used in a joiner's shop to check the accuracy of machined edges on prepared timber. This is normally carried out by holding the item towards the light to check across the full width of the timber for any light travelling underneath the bottom edge of the square. A try square should have its accuracy checked regularly to ensure precision marking out and joint cutting. This can be simply achieved by holding the stock of the square against a straight edge before marking a line across the edge of the blade; once completed the square should be turned over. The initial line marked should align perfectly with the edge of the blade; if there is a discrepancy it is highly likely that the try square is 'out of true' (a term used in the construction industry to describe an inaccuracy). Only if the try square has adjustment screws specifically built into the tool should attempts be made to adjust it; in most cases it should not be used and instead disregarded.

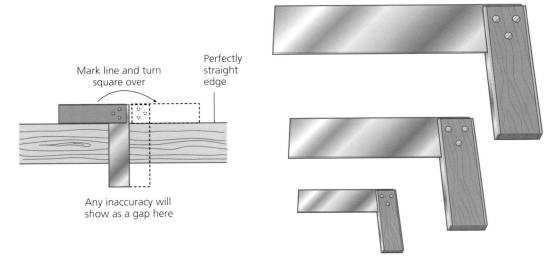

Mark line and turn
square over

Perfectly
straight
edge

Any inaccuracy will
show as a gap here

FIGURE 7.32 How to check a try square for accuracy

? FREQUENTLY ASKED QUESTIONS

▶ What does the term 'tempered' mean?

'Tempering' is a process used on some metals to toughen them. The metal normally goes through a sequence of controlled reheating to a predetermined temperature until the brittle particles are transformed and hardened.

- **Set mitre** – The top edge on the stock of some try squares is sometimes angled at 45 degrees to allow the square to be used for marking out mitres, etc. The reduced width of the stock at this point means a loss of accuracy when marking at this angle. Improved accuracy can be achieved with the use of a set mitre. Set mitres are very similar to try squares, although they are permanently set at 45 degrees rather than 90 degrees. They have a limited range of uses other than marking out mitre joints and checking them for accuracy.
- **Combination square** – Combination squares are preferred by many joiners because they are very versatile hand tools, and very often are capable of doing the tasks of several different tools. The blade is held in place via a thumb screw located in the stock of the square; once loosened the blade is able to be adjusted to different positions, enabling it to be used as a 'depth gauge'. It may also be used as a 'pencil gauge' to mark parallel lines along the edges of timber and sheet materials. The blade has both metric and imperial scales along its length, and is capable of being removed from the stock to enable it to be used independently as a rule. In addition, combination squares usually have a 'scriber' stored in the bottom of the stock to be used if marking across sheet metal while marking out. A small 'spirit level' contained within the stock of the square has been proven to be a useful addition for situations where alternatively a 'boat level' may have been used.

Uses of a combination square

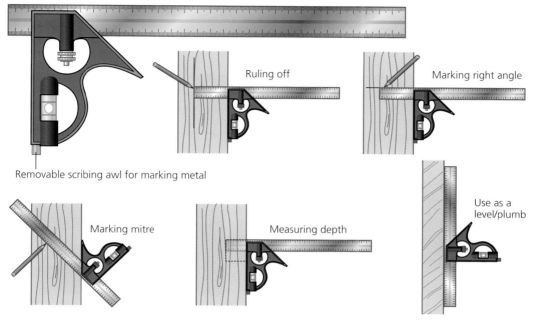

Removable scribing awl for marking metal

Ruling off

Marking right angle

Marking mitre

Measuring depth

Use as a level/plumb

FIGURE 7.33 Uses of a combination square

ACTIVITIES

Activity 1 – Selecting materials

Read through the following questions and answer them as fully as you can to help you develop your underpinning knowledge of this subject area.

1. Draw the shape of the irons in the following bench planes and explain the reason for their shape:
   - Smoothing plane;
   - Jack plane;
   - Try plane.
2. Explain the sequence of grinding and honing a bevel edge chisel.
3. List three uses for a combination square.
4. Explain the advantages and disadvantages of a hard-point saw.
5. Complete the following sentence:

   Gauges are used to mark parallel lines along and across the grain of the timber and are considered to be more accurate than pen or pencil. They usually consist of two parts – the _____ and _____.

MANUFACTURING JOINERY

STAIRS

The most important components of a staircase are the 'strings'. The strings determine whether or not a staircase will reach its intended floor level, and provide the skeleton and strength for the treads (in essence they act as inclined beams), risers and newel posts to be constructed around.

These housings are generally produced with a portable router and a staircase jig; alternatively the strings can be machined on a computer numerical control (CNC) machine.

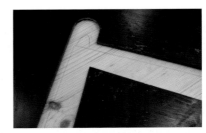

FIGURE 7.34 Methods of housing strings

Staircase jigs are usually made from plastic to withstand everyday use and are commercially available; alternatively a cheaper option is to produce a jig from plywood or medium-density fibreboard (MDF), although these will wear with continued use.

Whichever method is used, it is important that the arrangement of the wedges holding the steps in place is positioned as in Figure 7.35. It is good practice to allow the wedge supporting the tread to run under the riser of the next step; this will prevent any movement between the riser and the tread, and therefore prevent squeaks when it is under load.

Generally, the more work that is done on a staircase in the joinery shop the better; this will cut down on labour during installation and reduce the potential for mistakes by the site carpenters during fitting. The level of assembly will depend on the availability of labour, transport arrangements to the site, clear walkways and the space available when positioning the stairs.

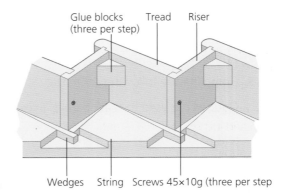

FIGURE 7.35 Correct positioning of wedges

STAIRCASE ASSEMBLY

After dry fitting each step, they are numbered to the string housing and set aside for assembly. All internal faces should be sanded prior to assembly. When assembling the staircase, it is important to ensure that the strings remain parallel to each other and that the overall width is maintained as originally designed; there are a number of ways that this can be achieved.

Where there is a reasonably low beam, the flight can be cramped up by the use of props and pairs of folding wedges. Where this is not possible, flights can be cramped up with the use of balanced pairs of bar cramps.

The newels and handrails may be dry fitted during the flight assembly process, being temporarily secured with the aid of draw dowels/pins. Whichever cramping mechanism is used, the backs of each tread are driven forward until the nosing is tight in the housing. With the wedges and glue ready, each riser wedge is glued and positioned and driven, starting at the bottom, ensuring both wedge ends are driven equally and that the face of the riser is up tight, working your way up the flight. Any part of the riser wedge projecting below the bottom of the riser is trimmed back so as not to affect the tread wedge from driving the underside of the tread home tight. Once the flight is assembled the newels and handrails can be dismantled and set to one side. Each separate component part should be labelled with the contact address, protected and stored safely ready for delivery. In addition to the newels and the handrail, the nosing, top riser, balustrades and any terminating step is also sent loose for assembly on site.

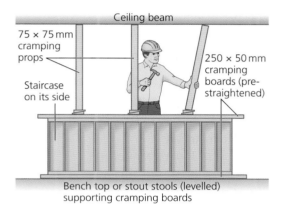

FIGURE 7.36 Staircase assembly

SETTING OUT BALUSTRADE

As well as serving the purpose of guarding the open side or sides of a staircase, the balustrade can add decorative features with ornate newel posts and balusters. It is important that newel posts are securely fixed in position before the balusters (or 'spindles' if turned) are installed. If the newel posts are turned they are normally either in two sections, if the newel cap is formed on the newel turning, or three sections and these include: the newel base, newel turning (mid-section) and newel cap. The newel turning formed from two sections of timber is a cheaper alternative to the three sections, although this option will provide a limited amount of alternative newel top finishes. The connections between each newel post can provide a weak spot in the balustrade if it is not firmly secured. The most effective method of connecting these components is by using a strong wood adhesive, and wedging the bottom of the turned dowel into a blind hole drilled into the opposite section.

The number of balusters required for a flight of stairs is normally calculated by allowing two per step and just one each end of the balustrade where the string joins the newel posts. For example:

A straight staircase with 12 steps would have 10 × 2 = 20 + 1 + 1 = 22 balusters

(*Note* – This is only a guide for costing and material ordering purposes. The exact calculation is normally worked out at the time of installation following the Building Regulations Approved Document K (no openings can allow a 100 mm sphere to pass through).)

The balusters are cut to length and fitted vertically between the bottom of the groove in the underside of the handrail and the string capping (*Note* – An alternative method of fixing the balusters is used if cut strings are used to construct the staircase). In most cases the balusters are secured vertically and equally spaced, with small packers glued between each component along the length of the string capping and the underside of the handrail.

WINDOWS

Generally the main functions of windows are to provide light, ventilation and a means of escape in the event of an emergency. Creative design by the architect at the planning stage can allow the shape, outlook and finish of the windows to enhance the appearance of a dwelling while maintaining their main functions. The size of each window built within a room will be stipulated on the architect's drawings and the accompanying window schedule. Building Regulations contain specific details for the area of light and ventilation needed for a room; this is normally a proportional size of the floor area and in most cases one-twentieth is required to adequately ventilate an area.

Although Building Regulations specify a minimum amount of light and openings needed in a building, only planning permission may restrict the maximum amount of window space used.

The use of large window openings within buildings has become very popular with designers and architects; these large expanses of glazing can allow the loss of heat unless careful consideration for the use of the following are used in construction:

- stable materials;
- double or triple glazing;
- draft excluders.

Windows can be constructed from a number of different materials including softwood and hardwood, uPVC (**p**oly **v**inyl **c**hloride) and aluminium or steel. Metal and uPVC windows are relatively maintenance free and cheap to manufacture due to their simple construction methods; for these reasons they have become very popular in recent years. The use of materials and style of replacement windows will be strictly controlled by the local authority. The restrictions imposed upon developers and builders to control the use of plastic windows etc. will preserve the aesthetic appearance of listed buildings and be 'in keeping' with local historical areas.

The use of any wood-based material in an exterior position will require regular maintenance to preserve its integrity. There are a number of optional methods used to protect exposed woodwork from the elements – generally the use of preservatives, either brushed, dipped or pressure treated will offer the best protection together with a good-quality paint or stain.

Figures 7.37 and 7.38 demonstrate the appearance of each window from a front perspective; as these photographs show, the uPVC windows provide a substantially larger frame section than the timber and metal alternatives. Although metal frames provide a window that is very durable and has slender sections, it remains functional and less decorative in its appearance. Timber windows will provide a compromise between metal and uPVC window frames, and can be designed to suit virtually any shape or design.

FIGURE 7.37 A uPVC window

FIGURE 7.38 A timber window frame

 FREQUENTLY ASKED QUESTIONS

▶ **How long will timber windows last?**

The life expectancy for windows that have been treated with preservative, prior to having a sequence of primer, undercoat and top coat applied for a painted finish or a good-quality base, and top coat of stain, is:

▶ 50 years for softwood;

▶ 75 years for hardwood.

(*Note* – The exact lifespan of a window frame will depend on the type of timber used and regular maintenance.)

WINDOW IDENTIFICATION

All windows are identified by the material they are constructed from and the positioning of the casement (the opening part of a window) within the frame; for example, traditional casements sit flush within the window frame. Windows are further classified by the way that the casements or sashes operate within the window frame:

- **Fixed sash, commonly known as a 'dead light'** – Fixed sashes are constructed in the same way as if they were to open but as the name suggests they are screwed securely into position. Alternatively, a window can be directly glazed into the rebates of the frame, therefore offering a cheaper option.
- **Side-hung casement** – Side-hung sashes can be hinged on the stile of the casement with the use of butt hinges for traditional windows, or cranked hinges for storm-proof windows. Side-hung sashes can also pivot with the use of friction hinges fixed to the top and bottom rails on the casement (see 'Window ironmongery').
- **Fanlight** – Top-hung sashes (fanlights) are hinged using the same methods to the side-hung sashes, only this time they swing from the top portion of the casement to open at the bottom.

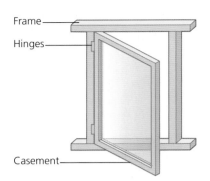

FIGURE 7.39 Side-hung sash

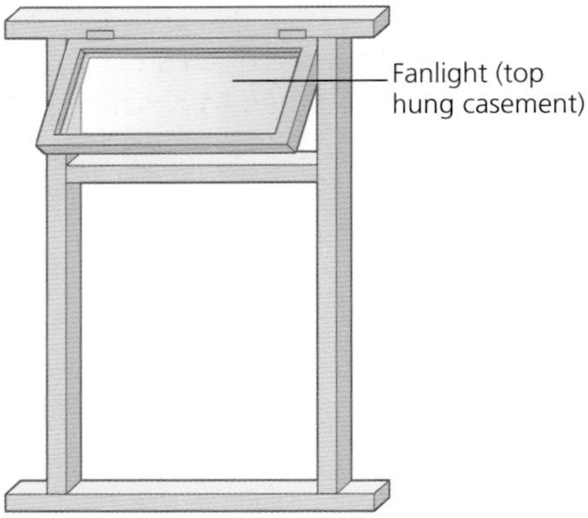

FIGURE 7.40 Top-hung sash (fanlight)

- **Sliding sash/box frame** – These operate by sliding up and down in a groove formed by the construction of the jamb. The sashes are suspended by sash cords and counterbalanced by weights that run in the box formed as shown in the Figure 7.41. An alternative method is to use 'spring balancers'. Sash windows can also be designed to slide horizontally along the window frame, although these are not so common. This style of window frame is known as 'Yorkshire lights'.

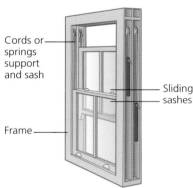

FIGURE 7.41 Vertical sliding sash (box frame)

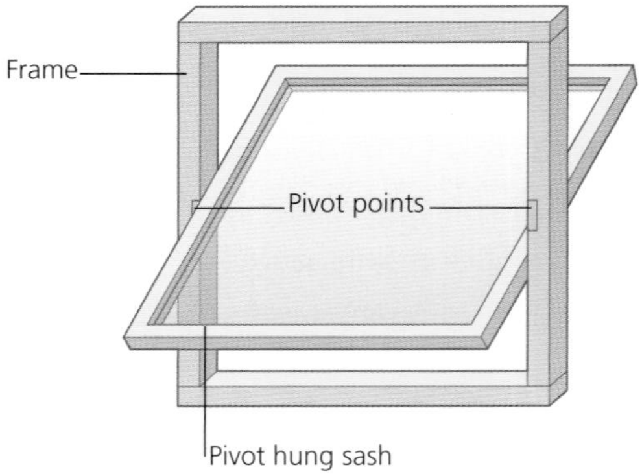

FIGURE 7.42 Pivot-hung sash

- **Pivoted sash** – This style of casement is pivoted in the centre of the sash using either a 'window pivot' for traditional windows or by using 'friction pivots' on storm-proof windows (see 'Window ironmongery').
- **Tilt and turn** – This style of opening can be used on both windows and the top sections of 'stable doors' (stable door – a single door split across the middle to form top and bottom opening sections). This method of opening will allow the frame to hinge in two directions, by bolting one side of the mechanism in the closed position while the other operation takes place.

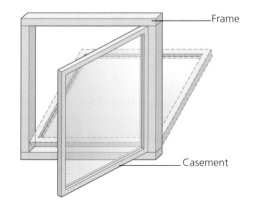

FIGURE 7.43 Tilt and turn

● **Bay window** – These can be constructed from either box frames or casement-type windows, and consist of a combination of several window frames fixed together. The number of frames used to construct a bay and the positioning of each frame will vary from job to job; these can be categorised as follows:
  – square;
  – splayed/cant;
  – segmental.

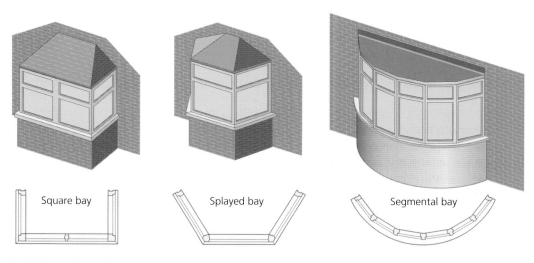

FIGURE 7.44 Bay windows

STORM-PROOF WINDOWS (TRADITIONAL AND HIGH PERFORMANCE)

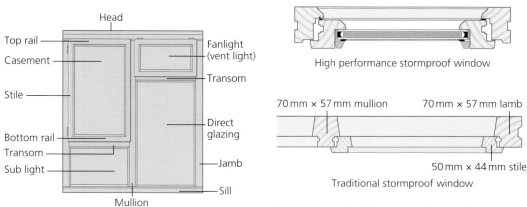

FIGURE 7.45 Storm-proof window

FIGURE 7.46 Traditional and high-performance storm-proof windows

As the name suggests, storm-proof windows are constructed to give superior weather protection compared with traditionally constructed window frames. Storm-proof windows have casements that are rebated over the main frame of the window. The rebates will protect the window opening from direct rain passing through the joint between the sash and the frame. The use of draught excluders between the opening sashes and the window frame will prevent warm air escaping the building in the winter, and cold air entering the property.

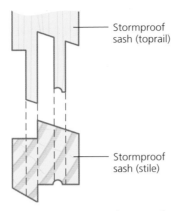

Stormproof sash (toprail)

Stormproof sash (stile)

FIGURE 7.47 Joint connecting the toprail and stile in a storm-proof sash

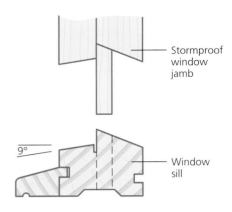

Stormproof window jamb

9°

Window sill

FIGURE 7.48 Joint connecting the jamb and sill in a storm-proof window

For a property to become energy efficient, consideration must be made for the openings within the building, in particular door and window openings. The loss of warm air through the window openings can be almost eliminated with a well-designed window frame, and use of stable and durable timbers combined with double or triple glazing.

In practice a property that is completely sealed from any air flow through the dwelling has proven disadvantages including stale air. Exposure to stale air for long periods of time may affect the occupants and their respiratory organs; this is due to a build up of moisture causing condensation, which in turn causes mould and bacterial growth. To avoid any potential long-term health problems to the occupants, small openings are formed either through the head of the window frame or through the top rails in the sashes, allowing a controlled amount of air to pass through the window.

The small opening in the frame is normally covered with a plastic trickle vent; this will prevent water passing through the window and control the amount or air flow by opening or closing either all or a portion of the vent from the inside of the window frame. The trickle vents are available in a wide range of solid colours to match and suit the window frames.

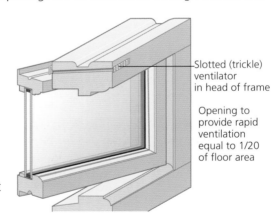

Slotted (trickle) ventilator in head of frame

Opening to provide rapid ventilation equal to 1/20 of floor area

FIGURE 7.49 Ventilation

TRADITIONAL CASEMENTS

Although the component names remain largely the same as with storm-proof windows, the sections vary. In simple terms, the difference between traditional and storm-proof windows is the detailing of the positioning of the casements within the window frame. Traditionally the full thickness of a casement would be positioned flush to the main window frame; this is achieved by rebating the thickness of the casement within the frame section.

Figure 7.50 highlights the use of weathering on the transoms and sill sections. Any water that penetrates between the sash and the window frame would only advance to the 'capillary' groove.

Traditional windows would normally contain sashes (also referred to as casements) in all of the rebated sections of the main window frame regardless of whether the sashes were opening or not. Although a costly alternative, a traditional window frame with this arrangement of the sashes offers a uniform, balanced and aesthetically pleasing appearance. It is common practice for modern-style windows to only contain sashes within the opening sections of the window due to the cost implications of the alternative. This method of glazing a window is known as 'fixed' or 'dead lights'.

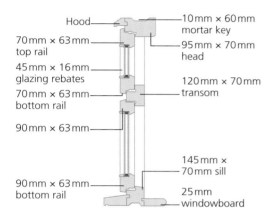

FIGURE 7.50 Use of weathering

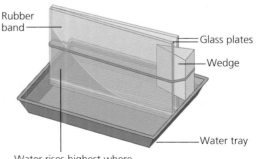

FIGURE 7.51 Box frame window

 FREQUENTLY ASKED QUESTIONS

▶ **What do the terms 'weathering' and 'anti-capillary groove' mean?**

'Weathering' is the slope that is moulded onto the timber during the machining stage of manufacturing. It allows water to run off the window section and prevent the onset of rot. 'Anti-capillary grooves' are the mouldings machined around the edge of the sashes and around the rebate on the frame of the window.

CAPILLARY ACTION

The demonstration in Figure 7.52 shows how water can be drawn upwards between two sections, in this case glass panels. The use of anti-capillary grooves between a sash and window frame will prevent this happening and thus prevent water entering through the window. Water entering this area of the window frame will run down the outer edge

FIGURE 7.52 Capillary action

of the sash, and then be directed out from the window by the weathering on either the transom or sill, depending on the positioning of the casement. The drip moulds formed on the underside of the sill, transom and hood will prevent water travelling over the weathering and back underneath the sections of the window frame.

BAY WINDOWS

As mentioned previously, bay windows are simply made up from a series of window frames fixed together to form one assembly. It is essential that the joints between each window are weather tight. Figures 7.53 and 7.54 suggest some methods of connecting the window frames to corner blocks and infill pieces.

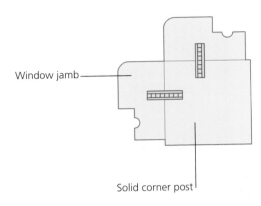

FIGURE 7.53 Connecting window frames to corner blocks

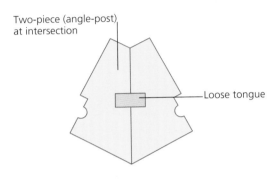

FIGURE 7.54 Connecting window frames to infill pieces

CONNECTING THE SILL

When installed, the bottom section of a window frame will receive the majority of the weather, so it is important that the sill is durable and strongly constructed. This will prevent any unsightly gaps appearing and moisture penetrating through the joints. The best method of connecting the sill at the joints is to use a handrail bolt and hardwood dowels.

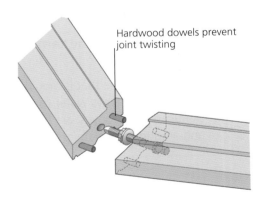

FIGURE 7.55 Connecting the sill

SHOP FRONTS

A shop front is made up from a combination of a window frame and a door frame. Its primary purpose is to house large sections of glass, contain an individual or pair of doors and to attract customers. The majority of replacement commercial shop fronts are produced from aluminium box section frames because they are maintenance free. The disadvantage of using metal frames is the limited range of profiles available and the fact that they are usually limited to a choice of solid colours rather than decorative wood grains.

FIGURE 7.56 A shop front

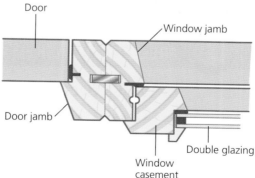

FIGURE 7.57 Box section frame

Wooden shop fronts should be used in conservation areas to preserve areas of historical interest. Timber-moulded sections offer a versatile alternative and natural beauty that other materials cannot.

Careful consideration must be made when designing timber-based shop fronts to ensure the combination of a window frame and door frame section work together. The transition between the two frames can sometimes create difficulties with the methods of jointing; there are two ways in which the two frames can be connected:

● individual frames jointed together;
● one assembly.

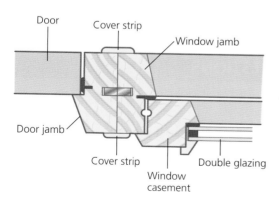

FIGURE 7.58 Individual frames jointed together

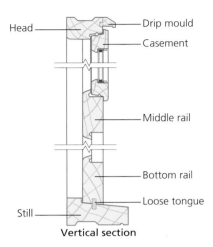

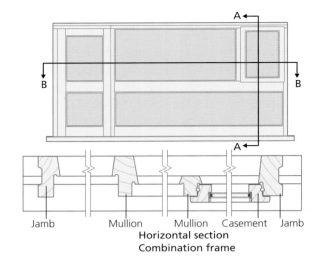

FIGURE 7.59 One assembly

INSTALLING WINDOWS

There are two methods that windows can be installed in position:

- built in during the construction of the brickwork;
- fixed in after the openings are formed.

BUILDING IN

The building in of frames is a process of positioning the window in a plumb and level position when the bricklayers have reached the height of the window sill. The sill should be placed on a bed of mortar with DPC (damp proof course) in between to prevent rot.

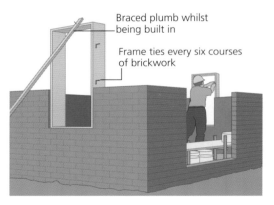

FIGURE 7.60 Building in of frames

  FREQUENTLY ASKED QUESTIONS

▶ What is DPC?

DPC (damp proof course) is a flexible roll of solid polyethylene. It is available in a range of widths from 100 to 900 mm. It is normally used by bricklayers to build into the course of brickwork 150 mm up from ground level. Its purpose is to prevent the moisture travelling up the brickwork.

A temporary brace is then attached to the frame by the carpenter and secured at the other end so the frame will remain in the correct position as the bricklaying progresses. The bricklayer will attach three to four galvanised fishtail frame cramps to the outside of each jamb on the window, in line with the mortar joints in the brickwork. As the bricklayer progresses with the build, the ends of the bricks are buttered with mortar. As these are placed against the jamb the mortar 'keys' into the groove on the outer edge of the window frame. When the mortar dries it will create a

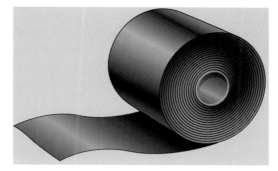

FIGURE 7.61 DPC

secure method of fixing the window along with the frame cramps. Traditionally horns of the head of the frame would also be built into the brickwork for additional support, although this is a method rarely used on new construction work these days.

The disadvantages of building in items of joinery such as window frames are:

- exposed to the elements (water damage etc.);
- increased risk of damage to the frames through work activities;
- possibility the frames may be moved out of level by other operatives or poor weather conditions.

The advantages of building in include:

- no visible fixings;
- the brickwork opening is exactly the same size as the window frame;
- no need for trimming or making good by filling large gaps around the frame;
- reduces the likelihood of mistakes caused by the inaccurate setting out of the window sizes.

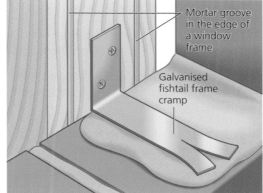

FIGURE 7.62 Galvanised cramps

DUMMY 'BUCK' OR 'PROFILE' FRAMES

These allow brickwork openings to be formed prior to the arrival on site of the windows, therefore preventing damage to the window frames as the build progresses. Dummy profiles are usually made from 100 mm × 50 mm carcassing timber with a diagonal brace to keep the frame square. Timber dummy profiles are relatively inexpensive but can sometimes expand if left uncovered in poor weather conditions. Swollen frames can sometimes become difficult to remove from the window opening without damaging the brickwork, and they rarely survive more than one build. Aluminium dummy profiles are also available to purchase in the most common sizes, and unusual sizes can be purpose built to order.

The disadvantage of aluminium frames is the initial purchase costs. The advantages are:

- they can be easily adjusted so that they can be removed without damaging the brickwork opening;
- they can be easily stored;
- they will not deteriorate;
- they are lightweight and very durable.

FIXED IN

The majority of new window frames installed on building sites are fitted after the roof has been fitted; this will protect the window from any unnecessary damage while the build progresses. As soon as the windows and doors are fitted into a new building it can then become secure and the 'drying out' of the building will begin.

? FREQUENTLY ASKED QUESTIONS

▶ What needs to 'dry out'?

At the early stages of a building project, poor weather conditions can delay progress. When the roof, windows and doors are fitted the weather can no longer affect progress, so the whole building can begin to dry, including the brickwork mortar joints, rendering and plastered walls.

As the bricklayer creates the window opening in a building, architect's drawings will be used as a reference for the window positions and sizes.

Although the bricklayer will sometimes form the openings as accurately as possible without the use of dummy frames, they can sometimes be built ± 3 mm/m under or over the specified sizes.

These tolerances are perfectly normal for bricklayers, but this variation can cause difficulties for window fitters, unless a suitable allowance was used when the frames were produced.

It is vitally important that the window openings are checked before the window frames are produced; this is usually carried out during a site survey by the window manufacturers. The surveyor should check:

- smallest height dimension;
- narrowest width dimension;
- if the opening is square;
- if the sill, lintel and brickwork are level.

Alternatively, an allowance can be made by the bricklayer on the brickwork opening size to allow for easy installation.

When fixing in window frames, unsightly fixing points must be hidden; this will provide a professional finish. There are several ways that this can be achieved:

- Fix through the rebates in the jambs on the window frame. This will conceal any fixings by the closing sash. If possible, pull out any draught excluder in the rebated frame to hide the fixings behind. Draught excluders are normally dry-fixed into a groove in the frame and can simply be removed and replaced.
- Screw galvanised straps to the outer edge of the frame with approximately 400 mm in between. A fixing point can then be concealed by fixing back through the strap when the window frame is positioned. The galvanised straps will then be hidden by the plastered, or dry-lined wall.

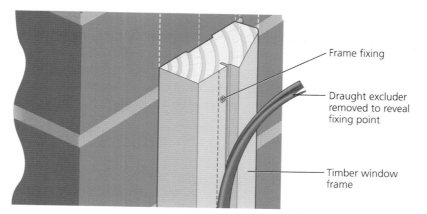

FIGURE 7.63 A window jamb fixed through the rebate into a wall

TRADE SECRETS

Try to avoid fixing through the head and sill of the frame. Fixing a frame using this method is likely to weaken the joints because the fixing is pushing against the joint, forcing it apart. Fixing through the sill may cause water to gather at that point and promote rot.

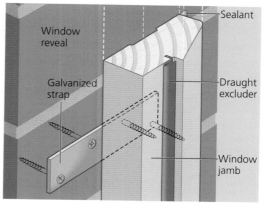

FIGURE 7.64 Galvanised frame straps

- It is not possible to fix boxed frame sliding sash windows using any of the mentioned methods because of their hollow construction. The most effective method to fix this type of frame is to use folding wedges to secure the window from either side.

GLAZING

SINGLE GLAZING

Traditionally windows would have contained one layer of glass (single glazed) within the casement of the window, and would have been either 3–4 mm or 6 mm thick. It was common practice to use the 3–4 mm pane in windows (dependent on the size of the glass) and for increased protection against breakages, 6 mm panes within doors. While single-glazed windows still have to be used in some historical buildings to protect the heritage of the area, there are many disadvantages to using them, including:

- heat loss;
- condensation;
- sound insulation;
- security.

BUILDING REGULATIONS

Approved Document N of the Building Regulations states that any glazing below 800 mm must be made with safety glass to protect against the added risk of accidental human breakage, and any doors containing glazing cannot contain any standard glazing below the height of 1.5 m. Safety glass is produced in a number of different forms; each method offers protection if the glazing is broken. This may be achieved for example by:

- fitting glass that breaks safely;
- small panes of ordinary glass;
- thicker ordinary glass;
- protecting the glass with a permanent robust screen;
- using plastic glazing sheets.

LAMINATED GLASS

Laminated glass is simply two sections of ordinary glass bonded either side of a plastic inner layer. Upon strong impact, the plastic layer provides a barrier to which the broken segments will remain attached, therefore reducing the likelihood of serious personal injury. Laminated glass is a cheaper alternative to toughened glass and is readily available from most glazing companies.

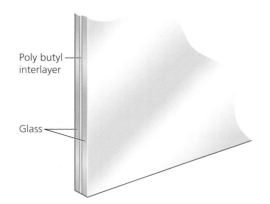

Poly butyl interlayer

Glass

FIGURE 7.65 Section through laminated glass

FIGURE 7.66 Broken laminated glass

TOUGHENED/TEMPERED GLASS

FIGURE 7.67 Broken toughened glass

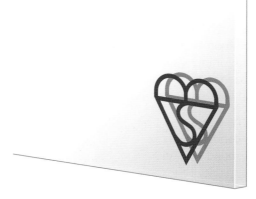

FIGURE 7.68 The British Standards Kitemark

Although toughened glass will give the same appearance as ordinary glass, it has been through an additional special heating process to give it a unique safety feature. The process of reheating the glass under special conditions to just under melting point, and then quickly cooling it down, will allow the glass to disintegrate into very small granular pieces on impact. Each of the granular pieces will have smooth edges, therefore preventing serious injury. Toughened glass is up to *five times stronger* than ordinary glass and cannot be re-cut after being tempered.

WIRED GLASS

Wired glass has a network of visible wires embedded into it; these wires provide the glass with its additional strength. Upon impact the wired glass will break but still remain relatively complete; it is only when the glass comes under an extreme impact that its integrity is compromised. Certain types of wired glass will provide fire protection as well as impact protection.

FIGURE 7.69 Broken wired glass

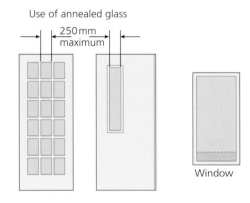

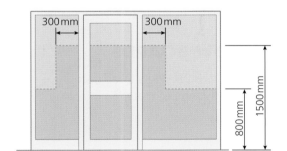

FIGURE 7.70 Critical locations for glazing

Further details of British Standards are contained within BS 6262: Part 4: 1994 Code of Practice for Glazing for Buildings. Specific Regulations relevant to this chapter include:

Doors	Any glazing or part of that glazing in a door that is between the finished floor level and a height of 1500 mm above the floor level is in a 'critical location'.
Side panels to doors	Any glazing or part of that glazing that is within 300 mm of either side of a door edge and which is between the finished floor level and a height of 1500 mm above the floor level, is in a 'critical location'.

Windows, partitions, and walls

Any glazing or part of that glazing that is between the finished floor level and a height of 800 mm above the floor level is in a 'critical location'.

DOUBLE GLAZING

Double glazing is simply a glazing unit made up from two pieces of glass divided by an aluminium spacer, creating an air gap in between. The distance between the two pieces of glass can be increased by using a thicker aluminium spacer around the perimeter of the glazed unit. The increased air space between the two pieces of glass will reduce the amount of heat loss and improve sound transfer through the window. If a window requires the glass to be obscured, then normally only one of the pieces of glass will be patterned to reduce costs.

'U' VALUE

The 'U' value is a measure of heat loss or gain through a material, e.g. windows, door, etc., and is expressed in 'units'. The lower the 'U' value the better the resistance is to heat transfer through that material or object, and therefore the superior insulating value.

TRADE SECRETS

When installing obscured double-glazed units, the patterned side of the unit should be on the inside of the window. This will prevent any dirt in the rainwater holding in the patterned surface and also make them easier to clean. Use plastic packers to give an equal margin around the double-glazed unit when fixing it into the rebated window frame. This will prevent the aluminium spacer between the glass within the glazed unit being visible after installation.

WINDOW BOARDS

Window boards provide a level, decorative trim to complete a window frame. They are available in a range of materials including:

- hardwood;
- softwood;
- uPVC;
- man-made timber-based sheet materials, e.g. MDF, plywood, etc.

All window boards will receive scratches and slight damage through regular use. The advantage that timber-based window boards have over plastic is that they can be sanded and refinished. Window boards have a bullnosed moulding along the front edge and are normally returned along both ends, although this is not possible on plastic window boards. It is natural for timber window boards to have a minimal amount of movement in their width. To conceal this movement, the back edge of the window board will have a rebated edge forming the tongue, which slots into a groove in the back of the window sill.

There are several ways to secure timber window boards into position; this may depend upon the finish on the window board. Screwing or nailing the window board into position through the face is common site practice but can look unsightly. Window boards can be secured by screwing a galvanised window board strap to the under side of the window board and then locating the window board into position. The window board strap will return from the underside of the window board down the face of the inner cavity wall; this is then fixed back to the wall using two or three screws.

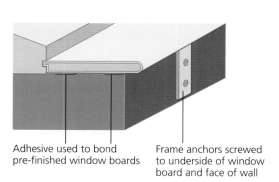

Adhesive used to bond
pre-finished window boards

Frame anchors screwed
to underside of window
board and face of wall

FIGURE 7.71 Securing window boards

Insulation

Distance between
window reveals

Depth of reveal

The bullnose moulding returns
around the ends of the window board

FIGURE 7.72 Securing window boards

WINDOW IRONMONGERY

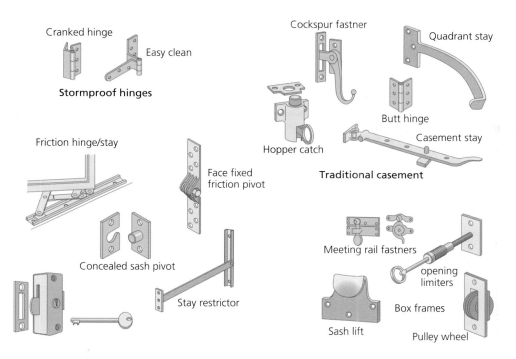

Cranked hinge

Easy clean

Stormproof hinges

Friction hinge/stay

Face fixed
friction pivot

Concealed sash pivot

Stay restrictor

Cockspur fastner

Quadrant stay

Butt hinge

Hopper catch

Casement stay

Traditional casement

Meeting rail fastners

opening
limiters

Sash lift

Box frames

Pulley wheel

FIGURE 7.73 Window ironmongery

Further information relating to the following joinery items can be found in Chapter 6 –
'Mark Out from Setting-out Details for Routine Joinery Products':

● doors;
● door linings and frames;
● stairs;
● units and fitments.

ACTIVITIES

Activity 2 – Manufacturing joinery

Read through the following questions and answer them as fully as you can to help you develop your underpinning knowledge of this subject area:

1. Which one of the following Approved Documents refers to glazing in the Building Regulations?
   - Approved Document K;
   - Approved Document N.

2. A straight staircase has been manufactured with 13 risers and newel posts have been included over the first and last steps. Estimate the correct number of balusters required for the open side of the staircase.

3. Explain the vital checks that should be carried out when assembling a staircase.

4. A bay window can be categorised by its shape. Draw three bay window plans to illustrate each category.

5. Describe the main differences between a traditional and storm-proof casement window.

MULTIPLE-CHOICE QUESTIONS

1   Which **one** of the following manufactured boards tends to sag when unsupported?
    a Ply
    b MDF
    c Blockboard
    d Battenboard

2   Which **one** of the following planes can be used to true a curved bandsawn edge on timber?
    a Badger
    b Bullnose
    c Compass.
    d Rounding

3   Which **one** of the following planes is used to widen grooves?
    a Plough
    b Router
    c Side rebate
    d Bench rebate

4   Which **one** of the following bits is used to bore a shallow flat-bottomed hole?
   a Forstner
   b Jennings
   c Expanding
   d Countersink

5   A Gantt bar chart is used to monitor
   a waste
   b progress
   c deliveries
   d availability

6   A joiner's work is monitored weekly using
   a reports
   b daily diary
   c time sheets
   d day work sheets

7   The correct order of work is:
   a machine, set out, mark out, assemble
   b set out, mark out, machine, assemble
   c machine, mark out, set out, assemble
   d set out, machine, mark out, assemble

8   A frame is checked for square after assembly
   a using a set square
   b using a try square
   c by checking the width
   d by checking the diagonals

9   Prior to gluing up a door the joints should be
   a primed
   b thinned
   c dry fitted
   d pre sanded

10 In door construction, panels are held in position using
   a nails
   b screws
   c grooved framing
   d rebated framing

SWINDON COLLEGE

LEARNING RESOURCE CENTRE

INDEX

Chapter 1 — Safe Working Practices

Q	a	b	c	d
1			/	
2		/		
3			/	
4	/			
5	/			
6				/
7			/	
8				/
9	/			
10			/	

Chapter 2 — Information Quantities and Communication with Others 2

Q	a	b	c	d
1	/			
2	/			
3	/			
4	/			
5	/			
6			/	
7		/		
8		/		
9			/	
10		/		

Chapter 3 — Building Methods and Contruction Technology 2

Q	a	b	c	d
1			/	
2		/		
3		/		
4			/	
5		/		
6	/			
7	/			
8			/	
9		/		
10				/

Chapter 4 — Circular Saws

Q	a	b	c	d
1	/			
2	/			
3			/	
4				/
5				/
6				/
7			/	
8	/			
9	/			
10	/			

Chapter 5 — Produce Setting-Out Details for Routine Joinery Products

Q	a	b	c	d
1	/			
2				/
3			/	
4			/	
5		/		
6	/			
7	/			
8			/	
9			/	
10				/

Chapter 6 — Mark Out from Setting-Out Details for Routine Joinery Products

Q	a	b	c	d
1	/			
2				/
3		/		
4			/	
5		/		
6		/		
7	/			
8		/		
9				/
10				/

Chapter 7 — Manufacture Routine Joinery Products

Q	a	b	c	d
1	/			
2				/
3	/			
4	/			
5	/			
6	/			
7		/		
8		/		
9				/
10	/			